Plural Pasts

Through a study of a variety of Ottoman and modern Turkish accounts of the Ottoman-Habsburg sieges of Nagykanizsa Castle (1600–01) including official documents, correspondence, histories, and more literary genres such as *gazavatnames* [campaign narratives], *Plural Pasts* explores Ottoman literacy practices. By considering the diverse roles that the various accounts served – construction of identities, forging of diplomatic alliances and legitimization of political ideologies and geo-political imaginations – it explores the cultural and socio-political significance the various accounts had for different audiences. In addition, it interweaves theoretical reflection with textual analysis. Using the sieges of Nagykanizsa as a case study, it offers a sophisticated contribution to ongoing historiographical arguments: namely, how historians construct hierarchies of primary sources and judge some to be more truthful, or more valuable, than others; how texts are assigned to particular genres based on perceived epistemological status – as story or history, fact or fiction; and the circular role that historians and their histories play in constructing, reflecting and reinforcing cultural and political imaginaries.

Claire Norton is Reader in History at St Mary's University.

Routledge Research in Early Modern History

For a full list of titles in this series, please visit www.routledge.com

India in the Italian Renaissance
Visions of a Contemporary Pagan World 1300–1600
Meera Juncu

The English Revolution and the Roots of Environmental Change
The Changing Concept of the Land in Early Modern England
George Yerby

Honourable Intentions?
Violence and Virtue in Australian and Cape Colonies, c. 1750 to 1850
Edited by Penny Russell and Nigel Worden

Social Thought in England, 1480–1730
From Body Social to Worldly Wealth
A.L. Beier

Dynastic Colonialism
Gender, Materiality and the early modern House of Orange-Nassau
Susan Broomhall and Jacqueline van Gent

The Business of the Roman Inquisition in the Early Modern Era
Germano Maifreda

Cities and Solidarities
Urban Communities in Pre-Modern Europe
Edited by Justin Colson and Arie van Steensel

James VI and Noble Power in Scotland 1578–1603
Edited by Miles Kerr-Peterson and Steven J. Reid

Conversion and Islam in the Early Modern Mediterranean
The Lure of the Other
Edited by Claire Norton

Plural Pasts
Power, Identity and the Ottoman Sieges of Nagykanizsa Castle
Claire Norton

Plural Pasts
Power, Identity and the Ottoman
Sieges of Nagykanizsa Castle

Claire Norton

LONDON AND NEW YORK

First published 2017
by Routledge
2 Park Square, Milton Park, Abingdon, Oxon OX14 4RN

and by Routledge
711 Third Avenue, New York, NY 10017

Routledge is an imprint of the Taylor & Francis Group, an informa business

© 2017 Claire Norton

The right of Claire Norton to be identified as author of this work has been asserted in accordance with sections 77 and 78 of the Copyright, Designs and Patents Act 1988.

All rights reserved. No part of this book may be reprinted or reproduced or utilised in any form or by any electronic, mechanical, or other means, now known or hereafter invented, including photocopying and recording, or in any information storage or retrieval system, without permission in writing from the publishers.

Trademark notice: Product or corporate names may be trademarks or registered trademarks, and are used only for identification and explanation without intent to infringe.

British Library Cataloguing-in-Publication Data
A catalogue record for this book is available from the British Library

Library of Congress Cataloging-in-Publication Data
Names: Norton, Claire, Dr., author.
Title: Plural pasts : power, identity and the Ottoman sieges of Nagykanizsa Castle / by Claire Norton.
Description: 1st edition. | New York : Routledge, 2017. | Series: Routledge research in early modern history | Includes bibliographical references and index.
Identifiers: LCCN 2016045679 (print) | LCCN 2016056775 (ebook) | ISBN 9781472485342 (hardback : alkaline paper) | ISBN 9781315600918 (ebook)
Subjects: LCSH: Kanizsa, Battle of, Nagykanizsa, Hungary, 1601—Sources. | Kanizsa Castle (Nagykanizsa, Hungary)—History—17th century—Sources. | Nagykanizsa (Hungary)—History—17th century—Sources. | Hungary—History—Turkish occupation, 1526–1699—Sources. | Literacy—Political aspects—Turkey—History. | Historiography—Political aspects—Turkey—History. | Power (Social sciences)—Turkey—History. | Nationalism—Turkey—History. | Turkey—Intellectual life. | Turkey—Politics and government.
Classification: LCC DR521 .N67 2017 (print) | LCC DR521 (ebook) | DDC 943.9/041—dc23
LC record available at https://lccn.loc.gov/2016045679

ISBN: 978-1-472-48534-2 (hbk)
ISBN: 978-1-315-60091-8 (ebk)

Typeset in Sabon
by Apex CoVantage, LLC

For Christine and Nathan with love

Contents

	Note on spellings and transliteration	ix
	Acknowledgements	xi
	Introduction	1
1	The authority of eyewitness accounts reconsidered	19
2	*Fethnames*: not just literary bombast	33
3	The *gazavatnames*: erasing oral residue and correcting scribal error	55
4	The *gazavatnames*: rewriting the exemplar – individual scripta	76
5	Writers reading: reading the *Gazavat-i Tiryaki Hasan Paşa* with Katib Çelebi and Naima	107
6	Nationalism and the reinvention of early modern identities	129
	Conclusion: making the sieges of Nagykanizsa morally defensible	147
	Bibliography	161
	Index	185

Contents

Note on spellings and transliteration

In general, words have been transcribed in accordance with modified modern Turkish conventions with the intention of making the work more accessible to a Turkish-reading, but not necessarily Ottoman-reading, audience. Words such as *vizier, sultan*, and *pasha*, which have a common status in English usage, have been given in their Anglicised form except when part of a Turkish or Ottoman-Turkish quotation.

Names are not just designations of practices; they are complex cultural practices. The naming of a place not only involves a designation, but it incorporates a particular perspective, a historical reference and often an entire narrative expressing the location's historic significance. Whether a place is named as Istolni Belgrad, Székesfehérvár or Stuhlweissenburg reflects a geographical and political viewpoint. Place names in this work are therefore rendered in accordance with the modern spelling of the country they are now located in, except where common English alternatives exist; thus Vienna not Wien. The exception is in direct quotations when a transcribed form of that in the original text is employed. Upon the first occurrence of a place name, common alternatives will be given in parenthesis.

Notes on spellings and transliteration

Acknowledgements

This book has been a long time in the making. It grew out of research that I originally undertook for my PhD thesis many years ago. In the intervening time I have benefitted enormously from the generous support of and thoughtful discussions with colleagues working in a variety of disciplines including Ottoman history, medieval literature and the theory of history – there are too many to name, but my thanks are due to all of them.

The support of a number of institutions was also fundamental to my research. The University of Birmingham awarded me a full grant to cover the costs of undertaking a PhD, without which I would not have been able to complete the research necessary for this book. St Mary's University, Twickenham has not only provided a supportive environment for my work over the past twelve years but generously funded periods of sabbatical leave which enabled me to make progress on this book. Many libraries also allowed me access to their manuscript collections and helped me to locate sources, so my thanks go to the Biblioteca Universitaria in Bologne; the Magyar Tudományos Akademia Konyvtara in Budapest; the Berlin Preussische National-Bibliothek and the Staatsbibliothek; the Universitätsbibliothek in Bratislava; the Dar al-Kutab in Cairo; Cambridge University Library; the British Library and the National Archives in London; the Oxford Bodleian Library; the Hill Monastic Manuscript Library; Millet Kütüphanesi, Arkeoloji Müzesi and Süleymaniye Kütüphanesi in Istanbul; the Bayerische Staatsbibliothek in Munich; the Bibliothèque National in Paris; the Kriegsarchiv and Staatsarchiv in Vienna as well as Bilkent and Istanbul University Libraries. My thanks also go to Dr Waley, Pal Fodor and K. Celanova for providing me with information concerning hard-to-locate manuscripts.

My greatest thanks go to Rhoads Murphey. Without his supervision, continued support and guidance, this book would not have taken the form it has. He has always been very generous with his time and extensive knowledge, but perhaps more importantly, his constant encouragement gave me the confidence to try out new ideas and approach subjects in perhaps unconventional ways. Although the writings of many Ottomanists have been fundamental in the development of my work, the books and articles of Palmira Brummett, Suraiya Faroqhi and Rhoads Murphey in particular transformed how I thought about Ottoman history. Moreover, in the intervening years their support and friendship have meant a great deal to me, and they continue to be an inspiration.

The development of the theoretical arguments concerning the cultural politics of historicisation and the ethical function of history owe a considerable debt to conversations I have had with my colleague Mark Donnelly over the past ten years while co-teaching two historiographically focused undergraduate modules and co-authoring a number of articles and books. To find someone with whom writing and teaching is not a chore, but an intellectual adventure, is a rarity, and I am lucky to have such a perceptive and generous colleague. It would also be remiss of me not to mention the intellectual debt I owe to everyone who attends the Institute of Historical Research (University of London) (IHR) theory of history seminars and the future of history seminars at the Centre for the Philosophy of History (St Mary's University), especially Beverley Southgate, Peter Icke, Kalle Pihlainen, Keith Jenkins, Helena Hammond, Helen Bendon and Alun Munslow. While the cake is a considerable draw, I have also benefitted considerably from the enjoyable conversations, friendship and support.

Drafts of this work were read ad nauseum in different formats by my good friend Cath Nall, whose insightful comments, thoughtful questioning and excellent editing have improved it beyond measure. Discussions with Cath on medieval manuscript culture and reading practices offered me a new way of thinking about texts, while her encouragement kept me going at times when it would have been easier to give up. My thanks go as well to Christine Marriott, who read through a final draft of this work and gave me invaluable feedback on the content as well as meticulously proofreading it. My gratitude is also due to the two readers at Ashgate who provided me with encouragement and thoughtful feedback in equal measure. It goes without saying, however, that I alone am responsible for any errors, infelicities of style or problematic arguments.

The final draft of this book was written over a busy summer season on the campsite and small farm that I call home. As July and August are not the best times to find the solitude needed for writing in what is, otherwise, a very idyllic place, much of it was undertaken in a corner of a local café, where I sat with my very patient dog, Kainaat. Thank you to everyone at *The Fire Station* café not only for the delicious coffee and cake but also for providing me with a space in which to write. Thanks also go to my husband James. Since I have known him, I have been writing this book; I think we are both glad that it is finally finished.

Lastly, the editorial team at Ashgate and Routledge, in particular Max Novick, has been particularly supportive and has made the process as smooth as possible – thank you.

Sections of Chapter 5 were previously published in "Fiction or Non-fiction? Ottoman Accounts of the Siege of Nagykanizsa", in Kuisma Korhonen (ed.), *Tropes for the Past: Hayden White and the History/Literature Debate* (Amsterdam and New York: Rodophi, 2006), 119–130. My thanks go to Brill for allowing me to republish them.

Introduction

Today nothing remains of Nagykanizsa (Kanije) castle. Once a formidable stronghold located in the marshes just south of Lake Balaton, Hungary, it formed part of a series of castles and fortifications that delineated the often-shifting *militärgrenze* dividing the early modern Habsburg and Ottoman Empires. With the expulsion of the Ottomans from Hungary following their defeat at the gates of Vienna in 1683, the castle no longer played a fundamental role in the defence of Christendom or the *dar al-Islam*, and it was destroyed in 1702 by the Habsburgs and the stones used for building material. The site is now largely empty except for a petrol station that stands opposite a newly built section of the old castle gate. The decision taken to partially reconstruct the gate of Nagykanizsa castle in 1996 demonstrates the importance of commemoration and historical narratives for communities. Moreover, the choice to erect a bronze bust of György Thury, Hungarian commander of the castle between 1569 and 1571, rather than an Ottoman commander, demonstrates the role of political and identitary perspectives in remembering and constructing our pasts. Thury signifies the Hungarian nation's long-standing, retrospective claim to the castle, and consequently the surrounding land, and effectively erases Ottoman involvement with the histories of Nagykanizsa castle. There is nothing to remind a casual visitor that following the Ottoman capture of the castle from the Habsburgs in 1600, it remained in Ottoman hands for ninety years.

The triumphant Ottoman capture of Nagykanizsa in 1600 and their equally successful defence of the castle the following year against a Habsburg counter siege are, understandably, not as plentifully documented in western European sources as the 1690 siege, which resulted in the Habsburg reacquisition of the castle and the withdrawal of the Ottomans from Hungary.[1] For Ottoman and modern Turkish audiences, however, the siege was, and still is, deemed culturally and politically important. There exists a range of diverse Ottoman and modern Turkish sources narrating the 1600 siege and the 1601 counter siege, including *fethnames* [victory letters]; *telhis* [summarised reports]; narrative accounts by eyewitnesses; *gazavatnames* [campaign narratives]; later descriptions included in Ottoman histories; nineteenth-century accounts by novelists and historians; various modern

Turkish accounts given away free in newspapers, included in school texts and published by the military; and a Turkish-language film. I am intrigued by these accounts, by their similarities and especially by their differences. As such they form the basis of this book.

Although other scholars have written excellent and informative socio-economic, military and diplomatic histories of the early modern Habsburg-Ottoman marches in general and the Long War (1593–1606) in particular, my study does not situate the sieges of Nagykanizsa explicitly into this broader historical discourse.[2] I have deliberately not chosen to try and reconstruct the events and details of the sieges from the available *evidence*. I have not attempted an analysis of the military, social or economic factors which precipitated the sieges nor evaluated their consequences. Neither have I sought to position the sieges as part of an explanatory teleological process that describes a wider pattern of events.

Theoretically informed by a reading of Davies, I instead explore the cultural significance of the various Ottoman and Turkish-language narratives of the sieges of Nagykanizsa – what they actually *do*.[3] Gabriel Piterberg notes that scholarship on Ottoman historiography generally divides into two distinct approaches. The first seeks to determine the degree to which particular Ottoman historical texts are reliable sources of information for the reconstruction of events, whereas the second takes Ottoman historians and their texts as the object of study.[4] Murphey provides an excellent example of the latter in his article on Ottoman historical writing, where in an appendix he analyses extracts from five Ottoman historians who narrate the key events of the reign of Sultan Ibrahim I. He argues that through an examination of whom the historians blamed for Ibrahim I's failure to assert his sultanic authority, we can gain an insight into their personalities, how they functioned as historians, the effect of perspective and context on their narrative and the role of historians and history writing in society.[5] Fetvacı does something similar in *Picturing History at the Ottoman Court*, where she provides an analysis of how court-sponsored, illustrated Ottoman histories produced in the second half of the sixteenth century articulated various views of sovereignty, promoted the interests of individuals and elite groups, helped contribute to the formation of Ottoman dynastic and courtly identities, and shaped social hierarchies.[6]

I want to argue that there is a third, overlapping approach that one can adopt with regard to historiography, one focused more on Ottoman textualities and literacy practices, one that explores the (re)writing and reception of Ottoman historical texts and the plural uses that these texts often had. This, I would argue, is what Piterberg does in his groundbreaking study of the *Haile-i Osmaniye*, and it is what I aim to do here.[7] In *Plural Pasts* I explore the relationship between acts of textual production and reception: how and why accounts were reinscribed by historians, state officials, soldiers, scribes, intellectuals and storytellers. I focus on elucidating the sociocultural norms and expectations surrounding the transmission and reception of texts within different genres and for different audiences. I explore how genre boundaries were (and are) negotiated and the manner by which texts are authorised: epistemologically, politically, socioculturally and religiously. Accounts of the 1600–1601 sieges of Nagykanizsa therefore act as a fulcrum around which to explore Ottoman textualities, ways of reading, manuscript culture and literacy practices.

It is, of course, fundamentally impossible to re-create or accurately understand Ottoman audiences' reception of texts: how they read; the complex intertextual and cultural matrices they read within; and the meanings they ascribed to texts. However, by exploring how readers annotated their texts through marginalia and how scribes read and reinscribed texts, we can hypothesise about wider literacy practices and textual functions. We know relatively very little about Ottoman manuscript production and circulation, reception practices, textualities and reading strategies. Although some Ottoman scholars have begun to work in these areas recently, in terms of both the range of studies and methodological developments, western European medieval scholarship is currently more advanced. My work in this area therefore owes a considerable debt to various medieval manuscript and literacy scholars.[8]

Moreover, as Piterberg, Kafardar and Fetvacı have argued, Ottoman historiography is deeply ingrained "in the politics and ideological accents" of its time.[9] No acts of reception are neutral; all texts are consumed within and are in dialogue with wider political, cultural and religious contexts. While acknowledging the ultimately textual basis of our assumptions and arguments, this work also seeks to make explicit the diverse and often ignored, legitimising and contesting roles that history-focused narratives may have had in particular social and cultural contexts. However, I do not read Ottoman histories and historians as informants for information about the past; I read them instead as interlocutors, as contributions to a dialogic process by which plural pasts are created or inscribed to serve particular sociopolitical and ontological functions, including the construction of identities, forging of diplomatic alliances and the legitimisation of political ideologies and geopolitical imaginations.[10] I speculate as to how the cartographic spaces of different interpretative communities have impacted upon various narrations of the 1600 and 1601 Ottoman-Habsburg sieges of Nagykanizsa in such a way that divergent, plural pasts were and are constructed or remembered. By foregrounding considerations of textual function, audience and viewpoint and through a deconstructive analysis of the various narratives of these sieges, I demonstrate that none of the accounts reflect or correspond unproblematically to a hypothetically existent, singular past, but rather that these pasts are all constructed, 'literary' remembrances. Every story is narrated from somewhere: accounts are inscribed from particular perspectives for particular audiences and functions, all of which impact upon the shape of the narration.

Theoretical frameworks

Each chapter, using different Ottoman or modern Turkish sources as a starting point, also addresses a number of wider historiographical issues: how and why some sources are judged to be intrinsically more valuable, more accurate or more truthful than others; how and why we assign texts to particular genres based on perceived epistemological status – as story or history, fact or fiction; the role that historians and their histories play in constructing, reflecting and reinforcing cultural and political imaginaries; and whether history can or should have a role in wider ethico-political discussions. As I will outline in more detail, I have chosen not to separate my theoretical discussion from my textual analysis of the sources, but instead I weave the two together. However, it might be useful at this juncture to provide a brief overview of the more general theories of knowledge and meaning that I find most persuasive and which underpin the arguments I make in this book.

The discipline of history is predicated on the supposition that historical narratives constitute a special type of knowledge. Histories have a distinct epistemological status when compared to other types of literature: they are factual and thus accurate; they are true accounts (more or less) of what really happened, not simply subjective, positioned interpretations.[11] As Novick argued many years ago, the assumptions on which historical objectivity (and the historical profession) rests

> include a commitment to the reality of the past, and to truth as correspondence to that reality; a sharp separation between knower and known, between fact and value, and above all, between history and fiction. Historical facts are seen as prior to and independent of interpretation: the value of an interpretation is judged by how well it accounts for the facts; if contradicted by the facts, it must be abandoned. Truth is one, not perspectival.[12]

It is this supposed correspondence (however incomplete or blurred) between historians' accounts and the past itself which provides the foundation to knowledge claims made on behalf of history.[13] This correspondence is achieved, it is argued, through historians' careful analysis of extant remnants from the past (in the form of sources) in accordance with particular, authorised interpretative models. The argument that the authority of history – its status as a factual genre consisting of true or justified belief – lies in its correspondence with a past reality as it is in-itself, free from our interpretation of it, rests on the Kantian metaphysical distinction between phenomenal and noumenal worlds. The phenomenal world is the world of appearances – reality as experienced by us, the observable world, our subjective perception of our environment within the culturally determined interpretative frameworks, classificatory systems and assumptions that we use to apprehend and make sense of it. The noumenal is a hypothetical idea that there is such a thing as the world as it is in-itself, the world independent of us and our interpretations – a mind-independent reality. Within such a metaphysical model, it is argued that the noumenal causes the phenomenal, and thus in some way the phenomenal world of experience *represents* or *corresponds* to the fundamentally inaccessible noumenal world which Kant described as an 'unknowable thing-in-itself'.[14]

In contrast, my approach to understanding historical knowledge is informed both by a Rortian anti-representationalist, pragmatist philosophical model of knowledge justification, and non-correspondence theories of truth and language.[15] Rorty argues that a causal rather than representational model of the world is of greater heuristic benefit when thinking about knowledge claims: we have a causal relationship with a mediated world rather than a representational relationship with an unmediated world (as it is in-itself). He advises us to do away with a metaphysical and epistemological model that includes the conception of a noumenal realm of reality as it is in-itself and instead accept that all we have is our subjective, positioned interaction with the world. But what does this have to do with the claims of history to be a special form of knowledge distinct from other past-focused literary genres? If all we have is our subjective perception of the world framed and made sense of by our culturally given interpretative frameworks, language and experience, then we cannot use reality to provide a neutral foundation to underpin knowledge claims. We cannot claim that a proposition is incontrovertibly true or accurate because it corresponds to the way the world really is or was in-itself separate from our concerns and interests. In the context of history, a mind-independent, neutral (noumenal) past reality can no longer act as a referent or foundation for historians' knowledge claims. Histories do not correspond to the past – even indirectly – they do not provide a neutral account of 'what actually happened'; they simply provide interpretations of other positioned, historical narratives. It is therefore possible for historians to read, analyse and write about the same sources in accordance with the practices and models that constitute the historical method and yet produce qualitatively different narratives. An anti-representationalist model permits the possibility that there are multiple, valid and not necessarily mutually compatible ways of narrating the past, none of which can be adjudicated as the true account outside of institutional or conventional structures or frameworks.[16]

This does not mean however that we no longer have the ability to distinguish between different historical accounts. Justificatory responsibility can be, and in practice is, expressed in terms of relevant community and social practices, norms and expectations. Rather than look to an unobtainable correspondence with the past in-itself to provide a foundation upon which knowledge claims can be based, we could seek it in the protocols of writing history. As I outline in more detail in Chapter 5, it is the practices constituted and legitimised by intersubjective agreement among those who have a stake in the history industry that both guarantee the contingent knowledge claims of particular histories and signal to audiences that a text is trustworthy. What we determine to be *good* history adheres to these practices and *bad* history does not. These rules do not however provide any epistemological foundation for history that is different to, or distinct from, that of other past-focused narratives or literary writings. History is a cultural practice, which has social rather than epistemological significance.

Throughout this book I make reference to what is often called the fact/fiction debate: the idea that history constitutes a distinct type of writing separate from other literary writing by virtue of its special epistemological status. Although audiences can often (but not always) distinguish between histories and other types of literary writing, linguists, theorists, narratologists and philosophers have argued that there is no evidence to argue for a difference based on linguistic, referential or epistemological grounds.[17] Audiences in fact differentiate between these genres of writing on the basis of a cluster of non-essential, contingent, ever-changing criteria, including the contextual framing of the text and other linguistic, stylistic and structural properties.[18] In *Practical Pasts* White provides a useful clarification of terms that help avoid some of the confusions that arise from contrasting history as fact with literature as fiction. Employing the term *literary writing* in the sense in which Marie-Laure Ryan uses it, White contrasts it not with fictional writing but with more utilitarian or communicative writing.[19] However, he notes that within the class of literary writing, there is a subcategory of fiction where fiction is understood not as imaginative writing per se but as writing about the imaginary. Fiction is therefore a very small subset of literary writing restricted to narratives that do not concern themselves with real events or people in any way. There are therefore quite a few genres of literary writing that are not fictional and to some degree take 'the past' as their referent. Such genres might include (auto)biography, journalism, drama, documentaries, historical novels, travel writing and many forms of academic writing, including history. Redescribing history in this way, as a type of past-focused literary writing which adheres to particular contingent generic features, allows us to focus on the role that history plays in cultures and societies and how audiences react to the framing of a text as history. While I therefore try and avoid framing the debate in terms of the fact-fiction distinction, on occasion I use these terms as a shorthand to develop the argument in an economical and coherent manner. In these instances, following on from Andrews and Kalpaklı's use in an Ottoman context of the Derridian concept "under erasure", I acknowledge the anachronistic, inaccurate or unhelpful nature of the terms but accept their necessity and therefore use them as if they have been 'crossed out'.[20]

If one is to think about textualities, reading strategies and literacies in any context, the question of what constitutes meaning and how it is created or found will arise. Is language a set of social practices, or does it describe and thus represent the way things are?[21] I am not convinced by the usefulness nor the coherence of word-object theories of language: the idea that there exists some form of correspondence between the meaning of a word and an object in the world – that the world constructs language rather than vice versa.[22] Instead, I am persuaded by the practical utility of 'meaning as use' explanations of language, particularly as outlined by Wittgenstein and Fish. Both have argued that the meaning of a word or phrase is determined by its use by a community-of-users or an interpretative community.[23] Meaning is thus a product of socially delineated language games and rule following. These rules are not fixed but are fluid and determined through performance by the community-of-users or the relevant interpretative community. Such a model of meaning does not however result in limitless polysemiality: readers are not free to simply impose their own idiosyncratic meanings on texts. Audiences hear or read utterances within a framework of socially agreed-upon interpretative strategies and norms and therefore apprehend what appears to be an inescapable meaning: to hear or read something is already to have assigned it a shape and given it a meaning, to have interpreted it. Interpretation is therefore a "*structure* of constraints", rules and protocols.[24] However, these constraints or practices are contingent and vary among interpretative communities, thereby allowing the possibility that audiences could 'produce' multiple, different, but valid readings from the same 'text'.

One attempt to contain this polysemic potentiality has focused on an appeal to and privileging of authorial meaning. Historians often attempt to provide a foundation for the interpretation of texts by asserting the primacy of authorial intention. However, establishing a definitive authorial meaning is problematic. Even if one could ask authors what they 'meant' by their work, how could it be established that the meaning the author now reads is identical to that intended when the work was first inscribed? How can we be sure that they have not reinterpreted their work against a framing of different experiences, expectations and contexts or remembered the meaning as different? More importantly, for those working with medieval or Ottoman manuscripts, the whole issue of the author is problematic. We often have very authorial scribes and scribal or copying authors. Who is *the* author of the Nagykanizsa *gazavatname* [campaign narrative] corpus? Was there one original author whose views and meaning we should try to reconstruct? Alternatively, should the eminent Ottoman historian Katib Çelebi be understood as an author and thus his 'meaning' be sought, even though he incorporated verbatim large sections of the *gazavatnames* in his narrative of the sieges of Nagykanizsa? Moreover, why privilege authorial meaning? Marginal notes and rewritings in the Nagykanizsa narratives reveal that readers themselves did not construct the same meaning as an elusive, 'original' author. To erase these readings and interpretations is to simplify or ignore not only Ottoman literacy practices but also the diverse functions and audiences of Ottoman works. Lastly, historians sometimes attempt to contain this potential plurality of valid meanings by putting the text 'in context', a practice which is thought to reveal if not a true, then at least an accurate or correct, meaning. However, this too is rather problematic. Contexts are themselves ultimately the product of textual interpretation of one form or another. In short, we cannot tie the meaning of events or texts securely to a foundation constructed from context because this too needs to be fastened down.[25]

In the context of my work on Ottoman textualities, the employment of a reader-response or meaning-as-use model means that it is possible to read the various accounts as polysemic texts that accommodate plural, valid interpretations and which were (and are) read by different audiences in diverse and often contradictory ways. Such an approach also means that rather than read the variations among the Nagykanizsa *gazavatnames* as arising from scribal error or residual orality, they can be understood as providing evidence of the scribes' different interpretations of the narrative, their reading strategies as well as the horizon of cultural, ethical and literary expectations of different Ottoman interpretative communities.[26] It also more coherently explains instances of 'ethical reading' and apparent textual incoherences or peculiarities in the manuscripts.[27] Lastly, a reader-centred model foregrounds considerations of function, reception context, audience and perspective. The 'same' *fethname* [victory missive] may be sent to Queen Elizabeth I, read aloud on the streets in Istanbul, published in an early modern Ottoman history, included in a bureaucratic *inşa* manuscript [a collection of Islamic cultural writing], published in a nineteenth-century printed book or discussed in a twenty-first century academic work. To assume that the potential meanings that readers can plausibly draw from these texts are identical and singular ignores this diversity.

Sources and chapters

Ottoman and modern Turkish sources narrating the 1600 and 1601 sieges of Nagykanizsa date from 1601 to 1986 and cover a wide variety of different literary genres of past-focused writing. In Chapters 1 and 2 I deconstruct a number of eyewitness narratives and accounts of the sieges contained in official reports, diplomatic correspondence and histories. Through this analysis I demonstrate that the authors, rather than just 'telling it like it was', wrote from a positioned perspective and were just as affected by considerations of audience and function in their constructions of the past as later narrators of the Nagykanizsa sieges.

In Chapter 1 I analyse the accounts of the sieges of Nagykanizsa provided by four 'eyewitnesses': three Ottoman historians, Hasan Beyzade, Abdülkadir Topçularkatibi and Ibrahim Peçevi, and that by the grand vizier in his report [*telhis*] of the siege to the sultan.[28] I establish that despite their privileged status as eyewitness observers to many of the events, their narratives are not transparent representations of a singular past but are constructed entities reflecting different viewpoints, literacy practices and considerations of function and audience. In particular, I argue against the tendency to assume that just because the grand vizier was present and recounting events in an official document that his account is more accurate, less constructed or fictional than the *gazavatname* [campaign narrative] accounts. A deconstruction of the tensions inherent in his narrative reveals how his interests permeate his (re)construction and 'fictionalisation' of events.

In Chapter 2 I analyse two versions of the Nagykanizsa *fethname* sent to Queen Elizabeth I in 1600. Rather than simply read and dismiss them as examples of Ottoman bombastic, propagandising literature, I instead approach the two letters as fulfilling distinct diplomatic and political functions. Reading them as examples of imperial, ceremonial protocol and as diplomatic tools, I discuss how these functions have affected the way in which the sieges of Nagykanizsa have been depicted, particularly with regard to the ways in which notions of self and other have been imagined.

The second section of the book primarily explores writers reading: how various early modern Ottoman and modern Turkish writers read and interpreted their exemplars of the siege of Nagykanizsa as evidenced through their rewritings. Simultaneously, I also discuss readers writing and analyse how they created plural subtexts and realised different voices in a single semiotic space through the use of red ink, overlining, scribal interjections and marginalia in the various texts. Such textual interjections not only reify the already present virtual dialogic relationship that exists between audiences and the narrative but also foreground the reading strategies, literacy practices and conceptual worlds of actual, rather than implied, audiences.[29]

In Chapters 3 and 4 I concentrate on the most detailed description of the second siege as contained in a corpus of twenty-five manuscripts collectively referred to as the *Gazavat-i Tiryaki Hasan Paşa* [The Campaign Narrative of Tiryaki Hasan Pasha]. Despite their differences the manuscripts all narrate essentially the same events. The victorious Ottoman siege of Nagykanizsa castle in 1600 commanded by the grand vizier Ibrahim Pasha is related very briefly in a few lines, but most of the narrative is dedicated to a description of the various tricks and stratagems that Tiryaki Hasan Pasha, newly appointed as *beylerbeyi* [governor] of the new province of Nagykanizsa and commander of the castle, employs to defeat the numerically superior, besieging Habsburg forces in 1601.

Reading such manuscripts within a typographic model would necessitate a search for the ur text, an authorial original, of which the other manuscripts are simply degenerative copies.[30] Such a model, while predominant in twenty- and twenty-first century Western academic culture, is not relevant to all types of writing in early modern Ottoman manuscript culture. In addition, not only is there a degree of variation among the manuscripts, but many of the texts include repetition, varied orthographic and grammar practices, episodic narration, digressions and textual incoherency, all of which in the context of Ottoman studies tend to be explicated by utilising models of orality and/or scribal error. Such an approach is rather problematic and can, I argue, lead to a distorted picture of Ottoman and medieval literacy practices and reading strategies. Therefore, in Chapter 3, building on the work of a number of medievalists, I outline three models or interpretative tools with which to read these Ottoman manuscripts. Firstly, I read these scripta within a performative rather than a typographic model. In this manner the individual manuscripts and their differences are viewed as unique instances of creation or performances, and not as derivative or degenerative copies. Applying such a model foregrounds the different literacy strategies, interpretative frameworks and perspectives within which Ottoman readers read the narrative. The diverse ways in which scribes read and made sense of the Nagykanizsa *gazavatnames* is evidenced in their rubrication practices, textual framings and re-inscriptions: while some scribes position the narrative in a framework of orthodoxy, others have read it from a more heterodox perspective; for some the emphasis is on blind obedience to authority, whereas for others it is justice. Secondly, I use the concept of ethical reading as a tool to explicate sections of apparent incoherence in the text without recourse to accusations of scribal illiteracy. Lastly, I posit the idea of an ocularity-vocality spectrum with regard to the reception of manuscript texts to again avoid an overly simplistic ascription of various textual features to scribal illiteracy or an inadequately interiorised literacy in Ottoman textual cultures. In this case I explain the presence of redundancy, repetition, digressions and the absence of titles as indicative of the possible reception of the work, that it was heard rather than read.

Chapter 4 begins with a discussion of the framing of a text and how rubrication and introductions (as well as conclusions) contribute to a reader's horizon of expectation. It then provides a close textual analysis of three manuscripts in the corpus utilising the aforementioned models. I demonstrate how the narrative was variously read, appropriated and reinscribed to reflect more or less politically or religiously heterodox perspectives. The analysis also exemplifies how readers participating in different interpretative communities can construct very different meanings from ostensibly the 'same' text.

Chapter 5 examines the Ottoman historians Katib Çelebi and Naima's readings of a Nagykanizsa *gazavatname* as evidenced through their re-inscriptions of the text in their respective histories.[31] Both are significant in that their accounts have been frequently read as offering *the* state-sanctioned early modern narrative of Ottoman history. Through Katib Çelebi's re-inscription in his *Fezleke-i Tevarih* [*The Summary of History*] of an unidentified *gazavatname* manuscript, I explore his reading and interpretation of the Nagykanizsa sieges. Specifically, I discuss the ways in which he 'orthodoxed' the text, therefore meeting the expectations of a different implied audience and subsequently positioning the narrative to be read as history by both contemporary Ottoman and modern readers. In this way I explain the categorisation of particular texts as fictional or factual – story or history – not in terms of epistemological difference but genre protocols.

In the second half of the chapter I explore Naima's reading and incorporation of Katib Çelebi's text in his *Tarih-i Naima* [*The History of Naima*], a process which essentially establishes *the* version of events for future

Introduction 11

audiences. Lastly, I argue that a series of marginal comments in a manuscript copy of Katib Çelebi's *Fezleke*, because they are also included in Naima's re-inscription of the Nagykanizsa sieges, provides evidence not only of the reception strategy of an Ottoman reader but also the literary practices of a key Ottoman historian. I argue that it is highly likely that Naima owned and annotated this copy of Katib Çelebi's *Fezleke*.

Chapter 6, through a reading of nineteenth- and twentieth-century texts explores how 'present' concerns have impacted on more modern reinterpretations and rewritings of the sieges. In particular, I consider the affect that the nation-state, as a paradigmatic means of conceptualising geopolitical space and as an ideological basis for identity, had on late Ottoman and modern Turkish rewritings of the sieges. I employ a modernist or constructivist understanding of national identity as contingent, invented, flexible and constantly being renegotiated and performed to explicate particular re-inscriptions of the Nagykanizsa narratives. Lastly, by examining the case of Fa'izi's *Hasenat-i Hasan*, I return to the question of how we negotiate between types of literary writing and in particular how 'fiction' is made into 'fact'. In keeping with my comments concerning the epistemological status of history as no different to other genres of literary writings, I determine that such classifications are more usefully explicated in terms of adherence to genre protocols than a putative correspondence to a past reality.

In a work that emphasises the role that audience expectations, genre conventions and intended function have on the construction of historical narratives, it would be remiss to not also reflect on my own writing. This book has developed from my doctoral dissertation and as a result of institutional and publishing norms has been written to conform more or less to the genre constraints and expectations associated with an academic monograph. However, acknowledging the inherent perspectival and ontological nature of all narratives of the 'before now' and therefore the disingenuity of claiming to study the past 'for its own sake' exerts a pressure, I believe, on the historian to reflect on and clearly explicate the motivations and reasons behind their writing. In the conclusion to this book, I address this issue and, drawing on Pihlainen's notion of a post-problematic history and White's notion of a practical past, I briefly sketch out a possible means by which historical praxis can be reorientated so that it usefully contributes to a wider discourse of political and ethical engagement.[32]

By situating my writing about the Nagykanizsa narratives in a frame of ethical relevance, I hope to demonstrate one possible way that non-representationalist, postmodern history might have contemporary relevance. While a postmodern or non-representationalist history cannot provide us with an account of the 'true' nature of the world or human society, there is no reason why, as a subgenre of literary writing, it could not offer a 'historical' lens through which sociopolitical problems and issues could be examined, discussed and defended. In particular, I use my reading of the Nagykanizsa narratives to explore and problematise what is often termed

12 Introduction

the *clash of civilisations* metanarrative. Histories of war are especially prone to normalising conflict and the dichotomous relations of antagonism that underlie such hostilities.[33] In the context of Christian-Muslim histories, there is a tendency for interactions, be they military or other, to be narrated within an interpretative frame that foregrounds the trope of inter-religious or inter-civilisational conflict. The history of the past thousand years or so is thus read in terms of an intrinsic and inevitable pugnacity and enmity between two ostensibly different communities. However, I argue that a close reading of Ottoman and modern Turkish accounts of the sieges of Nagykanizsa demonstrates that while such an explanatory narrative is superficially reinforced in certain historical sources, it is also often simultaneously undermined by a more nuanced consideration of textual function, implied audience and genre norms. I have therefore in this work paid special attention to how descriptions of the siege depict, contest and complicate notions of self and other, thereby hopefully moving the discussion beyond the rather unreflective, simplistic and, from my opinion, morally unhelpful, binary distinction of Muslim-Christian hostility.

Notes

1 The English ambassador mentioned the Ottoman capture of the castle in a letter he sent from Constantinople dated November 30, 1600, London: National Archives (henceforth abbreviated as NA), SP 97/4 fols 111–112. See also NA: SP 97/4 fols 113–114, in which the ambassador notes the dispatch of an army in the "winter [for] the recovre of canisia." The following year there is a further reference in the ambassadorial correspondence to the subsequent Ottoman defence of the castle, NA: SP 97/4 fol.148. John Smith, while narrating his adventures fighting for the Habsburgs in the Long War (1593–1606) between the Habsburgs and the Ottomans, gives a brief description of the failed Habsburg siege of Nagykanizsa in 1601: John Smith, *The True Travels, Adventures and Observations of Captain John Smith, in Europe, Asia, Affrica, and America, from Anno Domini 1593 to 1629* [. . .] (London, 1630), ch. VII "The unhappy Siege of Caniza [. . .]," 379–381. Available online https://ia800802.us.archive.org/22/items/truetravelsadven00smit/truetravelsadven00smit.pdf (accessed 28/6/16).
2 Some excellent studies of this border area which have had a significant influence on my work include: Mark L. Stein, *Guarding the Frontier: Ottoman Border Forts and Garrisons in Europe* (London: Tauris Academic Studies, 2007); Peter Sugar, "The Ottoman 'Professional Prisoner' on the Western Borders of the Empire in the Sixteenth and Seventeenth Centuries," *Études Balkaniques* 7 (1971); M. R. Hickok, *Ottoman Military Administration in Eighteenth Century Bosnia* (Leiden: Brill, 1997); Géza Dávid and Pal Fodor, eds, *Ottomans, Hungarians, and Habsburgs in Central Europe: The Military Confines in the Era of Ottoman Conquest* (Leiden, Boston and Köln: Brill, 2000); Caroline Finkel, *The Administration of Warfare: The Ottoman Military Campaigns in Hungary, 1593–1606* (Wien: VWGO, 1988) and Finkel, "French Mercenaries in the Habsburg-Ottoman War of 1583–1606: The Desertion of the Papa Garrison to the Ottomans in 1600," *Bulletin of the School of Oriental and African Studies* 55/3 (1992); Gustav Bayerle, *Ottoman Diplomacy in Hungary* (Bloomington: Indiana University, 1972) and Bayerle, *Ottoman Tributes in Hungary: According to Sixteenth Century Tapu Registers* (The Hague, Paris: Mouton, 1973); Géza Dávid

Introduction 13

and Pal Fodor, eds, *Hungarian-Ottoman Military and Diplomatic Relations in the Age of Süleyman the Magnificent* (Budapest: Loránd Eötvös University, 1994); and Frederick F. Anscombe, ed., *The Ottoman Balkans 1750–1830* (Princeton: Markus Wiener Publishers, 2006); Gábor Ágoston, *Guns for the Sultan: Military Power and the Weapons Industry in the Ottoman Empire* (Cambridge: Cambridge University Press, 2005). There is considerable fluidity in dating this war. Some scholars, mainly working in a Hungarian institutional context date it from 1591: see Ferenc Szakály, "The Early Ottoman Period, Including Royal Hungary, 1526–1606," in *A History of Hungary*, ed. Peter Sugar (Bloomingdale: Indiana University Press, 1990), 96. In contrast, Markus Köhbach, "Der osmanische Historiker Topçılar Katibi 'Abdü'l-qadir Efendi. Leben und Werk," *Osmanlı Araştırmaları* 2 (1981): 88, dates it from 1592. The majority of scholars working in an Ottoman institutional context however date it from 1593, and it is this dating practice that I will use.

3 Martin L. Davies, *Historics: Why History Dominates Contemporary Society* (London: Routledge, 2006), especially the introduction.

4 Gabriel Piterberg, *An Ottoman Tragedy: History and Historiography at Play* (Berkeley: University of California Press, 2003), 31. Examples of the first approach include Dimitris Kastritsis, *The Sons of Bayezid: Empire Building and Representation in the Ottoman Civil War of 1402–1413* (Leiden: Brill, 2007). Examples of the second approach include Cornell Fleischer, *Bureaucrat and Intellectual in the Ottoman Empire: The Historian Mustafa Ali (1541–1600)* (Princeton: Princeton University Press, 1986); Lewis Victor Thomas, *A Study of Naima*, ed. Norman Itzkowitz (New York: New York University Press, 1972); Christine Woodhead, *Talikizade's şehname-i Hümayun: A History of the Ottoman Campaign into Hungary, 1593–1594* (Berlin: Klaus Schwarz Verlag, 1983); Douglas A. Howard, "The Ottoman Advice for Kings Literature," in *The Early Modern Ottomans: Remapping the Empire*, ed. Virginia H. Aksan and Daniel Goffman (Cambridge: Cambridge University Press, 2007).

5 Rhoads Murphey, "Ottoman Historical Writing in the Seventeenth Century: A Survey of the General Development of the Genre after the Reign of Sultan Ahmed (1603–1617)," *Archivum Ottomanicum* 13 (1993–1994): 290–295. See also Murphey, *Essays on Ottoman Historians and Historiography* (Istanbul: Eren, 2009).

6 Emine Fetvacı, *Picturing History at the Ottoman Court* (Bloomington: Indiana University Press, 2013). See also Cemal Kafadar, *Between Two Worlds: The Construction of the Ottoman State* (Berkeley: University of California Press, 1996), who reads Ottoman historical narratives as articulations of particular ideological positions and not simply as accretions of oral tradition or literary fancy, and the articles in H. Erdem Çıpa and Emine Fetvacı, eds, *Writing History at the Ottoman Court: Editing the Past, Fashioning the Future* (Bloomington: Indiana University Press, 2013); and Baki Tezcan, "The Politics of Early Modern Ottoman Historiography," in *The Early Modern Ottomans: Remapping the Empire*, ed. Virginia H. Aksan and Daniel Goffman (Cambridge: Cambridge University Press, 2007).

7 Piterberg, *An Ottoman Tragedy*. The *Haile-i Osmaniye* refers to the events surrounding the deposition and execution of Ottoman Sultan Osman II in 1622. Piterberg's analysis of how various Ottoman historians narrated the event and particularly how they read and reinscribed Tuği's account was fundamental in the initial stages of my research in shaping my approach to the sources that narrate the sieges of Nagykanizsa. Within the wider context of Arabic textualities, in particular the literacy-orality debate, authoritative versus performative texts, recitational practices and transmission, as well as the physical layout of manuscripts, including spiral texts Brinkley Messick, *The Calligraphic State: Textual*

14 *Introduction*

Domination and History in a Muslim State (Berkeley: University of California Press, 2003) was also especially helpful.
8   In particular the work by Derek Pearsall has greatly influenced me, as have the articles by various authors in the numerous collections he has edited, including Pearsall, ed., *Manuscripts and Texts: Editorial Problems in Later Middle English Literature* (Woodbridge: D. S. Brewer, 1987); Pearsall, ed., *Manuscripts and Readers in Fifteenth Century England* (Woodbridge: D. S. Brewer, 1981); Pearsall, ed., *New Directions in Later Medieval Manuscript Studies* (York: York Medieval Press, 2000). Virtually all of the articles in Alger N. Doane and Carol Braun Pasternack, eds, *Vox Intexta: Orality and Textuality in the Middle Ages* (Madison: The University of Wisconsin Press, 1991); John Dagenais, *The Ethics of Reading in Manuscript Culture: Glossing the Libro de Buen Amor* (Princeton, NJ: Princeton University Press, 1994); and Cath Nall, *Reading and War in Fifteenth Century England: From Lydgate to Malory* (Woodbridge: D. S. Brewer, 2012) were also extremely influential on my thoughts. For the work of Ottoman scholars in this area, see those noted previously and discussed throughout this book.
9   Piterberg, *An Ottoman Tragedy*, 30.
10 The idea of Ottoman historians as interlocutors rather than informants is from Piterberg, *An Ottoman Tragedy*, 60.
11 There are numerous theoretical discussions concerning the epistemological status of history. The journals *Rethinking History* and *History and Theory* are good places to start for articles by historians who profess different epistemological understandings of historical knowledge. Keith Jenkins, ed., *The Postmodern History Reader* (London: Routledge, 1997) and Keith Jenkins and Alun Munslow, eds, *The Nature of History Reader* (London: Routledge, 2004) both provide extracts of texts from different 'sides' of the debate. Works that had a foundational role in developing my thoughts on the philosophy of history include Keith Jenkins, *Rethinking History*, 3rd ed. (London: Routledge, 2003); Jenkins, *On 'What Is History?': From Carr and Elton to Rorty and White* (London: Routledge, 1995); Alun Munslow, *Deconstructing History* (London: Routledge, 1997); Beverley Southgate, *What Is History For?* (London: Routledge, 2005); Frank Ankersmit and Hans Kellner, eds, *A New Philosophy of History* (London: Reaktion Books, 1995); Richard Rorty, *Truth and Progress: Philosophical Papers*, vol. 3 (Cambridge: Cambridge University Press, 1998), and Rorty, *Objectivity, Relativism and Truth: Philosophical Papers*, vol. 1 (Cambridge: Cambridge University Press, 1991).
12 Peter Novick, *That Noble Dream: The 'Objectivity Question' and the American Historical Profession* (Cambridge: Cambridge University Press, 1988), 1–2. There is little to suggest that in the minds of many historians, anything has changed over the past few decades.
13 Many historians do not argue anymore for a complete mimesis between their historical constructs and an external mind-independent reality – often on the basis of incompleteness of evidence rather than the fact that a correspondence theory of knowledge is ultimately scepticism-inducing. Rather they claim only a high degree of probability when measured against the standard of absolute correspondence. For example, Joyce Appleby, Lynn Hunt and Margaret Jacob, *Telling the Truth about History* (New York: W. W. Norton and Co., 1994), particularly in Chapter Seven "Truth and Objectivity", outline their notion of *practical realism* and have concluded that "the past only dimly corresponds to what the historians say about it," 248; the past is thus imagined as only partially knowable and history acknowledged to provide only non-absolute truths. However, they infer that this partial knowledge and dim correspondence is sufficient for historians to reconstruct or re-create the past and to guarantee the non-fictional and

epistemologically distinct status of history. But of course it isn't. See the essays in Elizabeth Fox-Genovese and Elisabeth Lasch-Quinn, eds, *Reconstructing History: The Emergence of a New Historical Society* (London: Routledge, 1999) especially the article by Gertrude Himmelfarb, "Postmodern History", in which she decries the postmodernists denial "of any kind of correspondence between language and reality" as well as their "denial of the fixity of the past", 72. She instead argues for the possibility of "partial, contingent, incremental truths" that importantly do "not deny the reality of the past", 72. While C. Behan McCullagh, *The Truth of History* (London: Routledge, 1997) offers a more nuanced argument, he still argues that although historical narratives do not mirror the past, they can correlate with it and that although they "reflect the interests and ideas of historians, they are not entirely subjective", 1–2. He defines "a 'correlation' theory of truth" as "a close cousin to the correspondence theory", 17.

14 For more on Kant's transcendental idealism, see Michael Rohlf, "Immanuel Kant," in *The Stanford Encyclopedia of Philosophy*, ed. Edward N. Zalta (Spring, 2016 Edition). http://plato.stanford.edu/archives/spr2016/entries/kant/ (accessed 24/8/16).

15 Rorty favours the terms *representationalism* and *anti-representationalism* rather than *realism* and *anti-realism* to explain his approach to knowledge and truth. Anti-representationalists reject attempts to distinguish between what is made and what is found, what is subjective and what is objective, what is mere appearance and what is real. Rorty argues that it "is not that these conceptual contrasts never have application, but that such application is always context and interest bound and that there is, as in the case of the related notion of truth, nothing to be said about them in general." Bjørn Ramberg, "Richard Rorty," in *The Stanford Encyclopedia of Philosophy*, ed. Edward N. Zalta (Spring, 2009 Edition). http://plato.stanford.edu/archives/spr2009/entries/rorty/ (accessed 24/8/16). Representationalists typically adhere to correspondence theories of truth and meaning and conceive of knowledge as representation: they hold the belief that propositions or knowledge claims are justified because in some way they correspond to an unmediated reality.

16 Although of course, one can make judgements about the usefulness or even 'accuracy' of such narratives from within such institutional or conventional frameworks. See Mark Donnelly and Claire Norton, *Doing History* (London: Routledge, 2011), especially Chapters 5 and 6, for a discussion of the epistemic genre choices historians make when researching and writing their histories.

17 Hayden White, "The Historical Text as Literary Artifact," in *The Writing of History: Literary Form and Historical Understanding*, ed. R. H. Canary and H. Kozicki (Madison: University of Wisconsin Press, 1978) is possibly the most well-known historian to point out the "fictions of factual representation" – the argument that history, in keeping with other forms of literary writing, employs both figurative language and the interpretation or, at times, imagination of the author. Quote from White, "The Fictions of Factual Representation," in *Tropics of Discourse: Essays in Cultural Criticism*, ed. Hayden White (Baltimore: The John Hopkins University Press, 1978), 121. See also Claire Norton and Mark Donnelly, "The Siege, the Book and the Film: *Welcome to Sarajevo* (1997)," in *The Fiction of History*, ed. A. L. MacFie (London: Routledge, 2014); Stacie Friend, "Fiction as a Genre," *Proceedings of the Aristotelian Society* 12/2 (2012); Friend, "Fictive Utterance and Imagining II," *Aristotelian Society Supplementary Volume* 85/1 (2011). R. A. Zwaan, "Effect of Genre Expectations on Text Comprehension," *Journal of Experimental Psychology: Learning, Memory, and Cognition* 20/4 (1994) has demonstrated that audiences cannot differentiate between news reports and novels purely on textual grounds without any external contextual clues to the genre of the work.

16 *Introduction*

18 Friend, "Fiction as a Genre," and "Fictive Utterance and Imagining II," provides many examples of such features of categorisation and also discusses how these features have changed over time. While these features do not point to an epistemological difference, as Zwaan, "Effect of Genre Expectations," has argued, they do condition us to employ different comprehension strategies when reading because we expect to do different things with the texts.
19 Hayden White, *The Practical Past* (Evanstone: Northwestern University Press, 2014), xi, citing Marie-Laure Ryan, "Truth without Scare Quotes: Post-Sokalian Genre Theory," *New Literary History* 29/4 (1998). Ryan uses the term to refer to the genres of writing that are often classified as 'fiction', for example, in bookstores.
20 Walter G. Andrews and Mehmed Kalpaklı, *The Age of Beloveds: Love and Beloved in Early-Modern Ottoman and European Culture and Society* (Durham: Duke University Press, 2005), 24, citing Gayatri Chakravorty Spivak's translation of Derrida's concept of *sous rature* as "under erasure" in the translator's preface to her translation of Jacques Derrida, *Of Grammatology*, trans. Gayatri Chakravorty Spivak (Baltimore: Johns Hopkins University Press, 1976), xiv.
21 Robert Brandom, "Truth and Assertibility," *Journal of Philosophy* 73 (1976): 137, quoted in Richard Rorty, "Representation, Social Practise, and Truth," in *Objectivity, Relativism and Truth: Philosophical Papers vol. 1*, ed. Richard Rorty (Cambridge: Cambridge University Press, 1991), 151.
22 Appleby, et al., *Telling the Truth*, appear to hold a version of the word-object theory in that they argue that "some words and conventions, however socially constructed, reach out to the world and give a reasonably true description of its contents", 250.
23 "For a *large* class of cases – though not for all – in which we employ the word 'meaning' it can be defined thus: the meaning of a word is its use in the language." Ludwig Wittgenstein, *Philosophical Investigations*, trans. G.E.M. Anscombe and ed. G.E.M. Anscombe, R. Rhees and G. H. von Wright (Oxford: Basil Blackwell, 1958), § 43. Stanley Fish, "Introduction, or How I Stopped Worrying and Learned to Love Interpretation," in *Is There a Text in This Class? The Authority of Interpretive Communities*, ed. Stanley Fish (Cambridge, MA: Harvard University Press, 1980), 14; and Fish "*Interpreting the* Variorum" in *Is There a Text in This Class? The Authority of Interpretive Communities*, ed. Stanley Fish (Cambridge, MA: Harvard University Press, 1980), 171, defines interpretative communities as "made up of those who share interpretive strategies [. . .] these strategies exist prior to the act of reading and therefore determine the shape of what is read". He adds that "[a]n interpretive community is [. . .] a bundle of interests, of particular purposes and goals." This approach is also often described under the rubric of reader-response or reception theories. Among the many works on reader response or reception theory, I found the edited collection by Susan Suleiman and Inge Crosman, eds, *The Reader in the Text: Essays on Audience and Interpretation* (Princeton: Princeton University Press, 1980), particularly useful.
24 Stanley Fish, "Demonstration vs. Persuasion: Two Models of Critical Activity," in *Is There a Text in This Class? The Authority of Interpretive Communities*, ed. Stanley Fish (Cambridge MA and London: Harvard University Press, 1980), 356.
25 Jonathan Culler, *Framing the Sign: Criticism and Its Institutions* (Oxford: Basil Blackwell, 1988), ix.
26 The term 'horizon of expectations' is from the reception theory of Hans Robert Jauss and is used to refer to the cultural assumptions or norms, frameworks of analysis and interpretative models that audiences bring to their reception of a text.

Introduction 17

27 'Ethical reading' is a term coined by Dagenais. It describes an attitude that certain audiences have towards a text whereby they do not expect to reduce texts to a single 'coherent' reading but instead seek to engage with a text rhetorically and to elicit or construct a system or network of values or ethical models from it; see Dagenais, *The Ethics of Reading*, 62. I discuss this more in Chapter 3, "Erasing Oral Residue and Correcting Scribal Error."
28 Hasan Beyzade, *Telhis-i Tacü't-tevarih* Istanbul: Arkeoloji Müzesi: no.234; Abdülkadir Topçularkatibi, *Tevarih-i âl-i Osman* Vienna: National-bibliothek, Mxt.130; Ibrahim Peçevi, *Tarih-i Peçevi* (Istanbul: 1283/1866–1867); *Telhîs-i Vezir-i Azam Yemişçi Hasan Paşa* Istanbul: Topkapı Sarayı Müzesi: Revan.1303, fols 2b–5a (henceforth referred to as ITSM: Revan.1303). The *telhis* used is also available in print in Cengiz Orhonlu, *Osmanlı Tarihine âid Belgeler: Telhisler (1597–1607)* (Istanbul: Edebiyat Fakültesi Basımevi, 1970), 44–46, no.52. All references are to the manuscripts or printed editions cited unless otherwise stated. See the bibliography for other extant manuscripts of these works.
29 I have found the article by Paul Strohm, "Chaucer's Audiences: Fictional, Implied, Intended, Actual," *The Chaucer Review* 18/2 (1983) to be helpful in thinking about audiences of texts. The *actual* audience is the audience we know actually read it; for example, inscribers of marginalia are *actual* readers. Similarly, Katib Çelebi was an *actual* reader of one of the *gazavatname* manuscripts as he incorporates it into his work. Naima was also an *actual* reader of Katib Çelebi's account as he inscribes it almost verbatim into his history. The *intended* audience refers to the audience we think the text was initially directed towards. The *intended* audience of the grand vizier's *telhis*, for example, was the sultan. Similarly, the *intended* audience of the *fethname* sent to England was Queen Elizabeth I. The *implied* audience is a hypothetical construct on the part of the reader: it is the audience that a reader believes that the author is addressing. The implied audience of a text can of course differ among readers. When I discuss the *implied* audience in this book I am referring to the audience that I think the inscriber of the text had in mind – this is, of course a speculative enterprise.
30 The typographic model takes as its archetype of a literary work the printed book. That is, it conceives of a work as a fixed, original entity written by a single author. Any inscriptions of the work that deviate from the original are seen as degenerations or errors. As the term suggests it arises from a period in which the printing of texts was dominant and thus is not necessarily appropriate for describing manuscript (or digital) culture. For a more detailed discussion of the model see Chapter 3.
31 This work is available in a printed edition: Katib Çelebi, *Fezleke-Katib Çelebi*, vols. 1–2 (Istanbul: Ceride-i Havadis Matbaası, 1286–1287/1869–1870); I also looked at two manuscript copies Oxford: Bodlein Library, Rawl.or.20 and Sale 60 which are both titled *Fezleke-i Tevarih* (henceforth referred to as OBL: Rawl. or.20 and OBL: Sale 60). Naima, *Ravzatü'l-Hüseyn fî hulâsati ahbâri'l-hâfikayn* (Istanbul: Matbaa-i Âmire, 1281–1283/1864–1866) (henceforth referred to as *Tarih-i Naima*).
32 Kalle Pihlainen, "Towards a Post-Problematic History," paper given at the Philosophy of History Seminar at the Institute of Historical Research, University of London, November 22, 2012. I thank the author for generously providing me with a copy of his paper. Pihlainen argues for historians to stop posing problems that need to be investigated and instead to construct narratives that have a present relevance. In *The Practical Past* Hayden White, following Oakeshott, distinguishes between the *historical* past and the *practical* past. The historical past is a rhetorical construction of the past conceived of and authorised by historians as a supposed disinterested study of the past on its

own terms and for its own sake, 9–10 and 15. The *practical* past, in contrast, addresses what Kant called the practical (or ethical) question of 'what should we do?' and is the use of the past made by non-historians to make judgements and decisions 8, 10 and 15. Notwithstanding these claims, the historical past, is of course, as I have argued, not disinterested or neutral and, as White notes, often has very practical uses including serving the interests of the nation-state by providing a genealogical account of group identities and legitimising claims to geopolitical space, 15 and 98.

33 Davies, *Historics*, 7, argues that history tends to affirm violence as historically normal.

1 The authority of eyewitness accounts reconsidered

For political or military historians wishing to provide a definitive, accurate description of particular early modern Ottoman events, be they political incidents, revolutions or military campaigns, the accounts of eyewitness administrator-historians in combination with documentary sources, that is official state-produced texts, such as tax registers, daybooks, reports, treaties, official rescripts and correspondence, play a fundamental role. Representationalist or reconstructionist historians such as Marwick often implicitly suggest that there is a qualitative and maybe even an epistemological distinction between documents of record or state-produced documents and other texts or sources.[1] The latter, they argue, are largely free from interpretation, are far less subjective and thus are more appropriate historical sources. While the discussions surrounding postmodernist approaches to history writing have caused many historians to acknowledge that all texts have a degree of subjectivity, some historians continue to implicitly operate with a hierarchy of sources where documents of record are still given a privileged status and are seen as more reliable, less subjective and thus more likely to 'get the story straight' by providing a more accurate picture of the past.[2]

As I noted in the introduction, Piterberg has identified two main ways in which scholars approach the work of Ottoman historians: they either take the historian and his (and it is generally *his* in the context of Ottoman history) work as the object of their investigation, or they seek to evaluate the degree of reliability of the history with a view to subsequently extracting all useful documentary information should the history be deemed sufficiently accurate and free from an unacceptable degree of contaminating bias or partisanship.[3] Such an approach is evidenced in a comment in the *Encyclopaedia of Islam*'s entry on Ottoman historian Hasan Beyzade. In discussing Hasan Beyzade's history of the Ottoman Empire, the authors comment that, "it remains to be investigated whether a complete edition of the work is required or whether its essential information is in fact already available through these published texts."[4] For these historians the value of early modern Ottoman histories lies exclusively in the information they can provide about events. The interpretative framing of these events, the way in which the historians used their sources, the intricacies of Ottoman historical intertextuality, the evidence

20 *The authority of eyewitness accounts reconsidered*

these accounts provide of Ottoman sociocultural, political and ideological perspectives and what they tell us about Ottoman literacy strategies are not considered as important. However, I am not interested in establishing which of the accounts of the sieges is the most accurate or which corresponds most closely to what really happened, largely because, as I argued in the introduction, I do not think this is epistemologically an achievable goal. Instead I want to foreground the rhetorical: how and why particular participants in events surrounding the sieges may have chosen to narrate events in the ways they did. In doing so, I intend to demonstrate the positioned nature of all sources and argue that eyewitness accounts and state documents are no less subjective by virtue of their genre nor as a result of the predisposition or location of the author.

Three Ottoman historian-administrators were present on the Nagykanizsa campaigns, and they subsequently wrote some of the earliest narratives of the 1600 and 1601 Nagykanizsa sieges included in their more general histories of the Ottoman Empire. They were Hasan Beyzade (d. 1636–1637), Abdülkadir Topçularkatibi and Ibrahim Peçevi (1572–1650). For different reasons, the histories of all three have been held in high regard by modern historians and judged as particularly useful primary sources. Through an analysis of their accounts I will make explicit "the fictions of factual representation" and illustrate the manner in which 'factual' documents such as histories, decrees and correspondence share the same narrative and rhetorical strategies common to all literary writing.[5] By so doing I will demonstrate how the interests of the historian-administrator authors, the politico-cultural contexts in which they wrote and their concerns about the intended and implied audiences of their texts all worked to influence the perspectives from which they narrated the sieges.

Hasan Beyzade worked for most of his career in the service of the imperial council as a civil servant. He was the secretary for a number of high-ranking officials, gradually rising through the scribal-administrative ranks. He participated in a number of campaigns during the Long War (1593–1606) between the Habsburgs and Ottomans in his capacity as secretary to various grand viziers and commanders. In 1599 he was appointed *baş-tezkereci* [chief secretary] and then temporary *re'is ül-küttab* [minister of foreign affairs] during the 1600 siege of Nagykanizsa.[6] Following the siege of Nagykanizsa he held a number of positions in the financial administration, including deputy of the director of the main registry of revenues, director of the registry of landed property and director of financial administration [*defterdar*] in various provinces and regions of the empire, such as Anatolia.[7] He wrote a two-volume history of the Ottoman Empire, considered to be the earliest seventeenth-century example of the *Tarih-i Al-i Osman* [history of the house of Osman] genre and a key reference for many later histories, including those by Katib Çelebi and Naima, which are considered to be authoritative histories in Ottoman studies.[8] His other works include a political treatise, a *mecmu'a* [compendium of writings] and the

Nagykanizsa *fethnames* sent to Queen Elizabeth and the doge of Venice that will be analysed in Chapter 2.[9] His history is divided into two volumes: the first is titled the *Telhis-i Tacü't-tevarih* [*Summary of the Crown of History*] and is an abbreviated version of Hoca Sadüddin Efendi's (d. 1008/1599) *Tacü't-tevarih* [*The Crown of History*]; the second volume is titled *Zeyl-i tacü't-tevarih* [*Addendum to the Crown of History*] and is often described as a more original work encompassing the period from the reign of Süleyman I (1520–1566) to that of Murad IV (1623–1640). Although the first part of the second volume is a synthesis of information provided by other Ottoman historians and an account written by Hasan Beyzade's father who was also *re'is ül-küttab* [minister of foreign affairs], the second section, concerning events dating from the reign of Mehmed III (1595–1603), is largely based on the author's personal observations, particularly his accounts of the military campaigns that he participated in.[10]

Abdülkadir Topçularkatibi was a secretary to the imperial army, and was present at the first siege of Nagykanizsa but was not involved with the subsequent defence as he was accompanying the grand vizier and the imperial army at the siege of Szekesfehérvár (İstolni Belgrad/Stuhlweissenburg). The only source we have for biographical information about Topçularkatibi is his work.[11] He was born in the last third of the sixteenth century and died sometime after March 1644.[12] He was a muster master of the artillery and was present on numerous campaigns including the Erevan campaign against the Persians and the Ottoman-Habsburg Long War, including the 1600 siege and capture of Nagykanizsa castle.[13] As part of his various duties, he describes procuring provisions, delivering payrolls, supervising the production of munitions and the evacuation of weapons stock. Following the capture of Nagykanizsa castle, he says he registered the munitions and cannons that were found in the castle.[14] Topçularkatibi's experience and expertise is evident throughout his history in the detail with which he discusses not only the equipment of the Ottoman army but also the weapons used and their deployment. His history, which exists in two manuscripts, does not have a definitive title, although it is conventionally known as *Tevarih âl-i Osman* [*History of the House of Osman*].[15] The majority of the work is a description of military campaigns that the author participated in, although he also provides information on key political and administrative events, appointment changes, court events such as weddings and celebrations and events happening in Istanbul. It was an important source for later Ottoman historians including Naima. Köhbach argues that Topçularkatibi's style of writing clearly shows he lacked a higher literary education and notes that Topçularkatibi himself acknowledged the stylistic and linguistic defects of his work yet argued that it was still valuable on account of his being an eyewitness to many of the events he narrates.[16]

Ibrahim Peçevi, a native of Pécs, in Hungary (Peçuy/Fünfkirchen), came from a family who had a long tradition of military service in Bosnia. In 1593 he joined the imperial army and participated in a number of campaigns during the Long War. After the war he was employed in the provincial financial administration, was appointed *tahrir* [land census] recorder in a variety of Rumelian *sancaks* then clerk to the grand vizier Kuyucu Murad Pasha (1607–11). Over the next few decades he served in a variety of positions including *defterdar* [treasurer] of the Ottoman administrative regions of Diyarbakır, Tokat, Tuna [the Danube], Temeşvar and Anatolia. He also served as *beylerbeyi* [governor] of the province of Rakka.[17] After retiring in 1641 he moved back to Hungary and wrote a history of the Ottoman Empire, *Tarih-i Peçevi* [*The History of Peçevi*]. As with Hasan Beyzade, his work is a combination of information taken from what would today be described as secondary and primary sources, and oral testimony. Although his account uses the histories of Ottoman historians such as Celalzade Mustafa, Ramazanzade, Mustafa Ali and Hasan Beyzade for events that occurred in his lifetime, he also relies on his own experience as a state official and eyewitness to events. Unsurprisingly his work is particularly detailed with regard to events on the Hungarian and Bosnian marches where he was able to supplement material from various sources and his own experiences with that from his family and local acquaintances.[18] Peçevi also used accounts written by Hungarian historians including Kaspar Heltai and N.V. Istvánffy; they were apparently read to him in Hungarian, and he subsequently translated them into Ottoman Turkish.[19]

It is worth noting at this point that the complex interdependency of Ottoman histories as well as the, often un-cited, incorporation of earlier historical works by Ottoman historians should not be viewed as plagiarism, evidence of unoriginality, residual orality or the result of a stunted literacy. Instead it should be understood as a device or means to legitimise and situate the work into an existing system of knowledge. Berkenkotter and Hudin have demonstrated that twenty-first century academic quotation and citation practices function as integration procedures in that they present academic activity as a cumulative, rational enterprise that builds on accepted wisdom yet constantly seeks new knowledge.[20] Citation practices therefore diachronically and teleologically connect a work to a specific field, or body of existing and accepted work, thereby legitimising and contextualising it as new knowledge. For example, in modern historical writing citations set the knowledge of a specific manuscript, tax register or event within, or against, the field of Ottoman history foremost and then within the broader background of the genre of history and the scope of the humanities. However, Ottoman legitimisation and incorporation praxis were different. Ottoman scholars and writers, in particular those writing about the past within the Ottoman genre of history, authorised and integrated their work through the specific inclusion of precedents, the incorporation of previous works and the diffuse use of a shared vocabulary, common patterns of argumentation and shared knowledge schemas rather than through explicit citation practices. The large-scale incorporation of other authors' work was thus employed to both synchronically and diachronically situate or integrate a work into an

The authority of eyewitness accounts reconsidered 23

existing system or network of knowledge and thus to ultimately legitimise it.[21] Murphey in his study of Ottoman historical writing notes that it was expected Ottoman historical practice for historians writing about events before their lifetimes to defer to and use the testimony of earlier historians. This does not mean that the genre of Ottoman history was derivative or that historians lacked the ability or interest in writing interpretative history. Rather, the focus of creative history writing was limited to events of their own time.[22]

At the end of this chapter I will consider the account of the siege provided in the *telhis* [report] written by the grand vizier Yemişçi Hasan Pasha, which was intended to communicate events that occurred during the autumn and winter of 1601 on the Ottoman-Habsburg marches, particularly the defence of Nagykanizsa castle.[23] I will argue that despite being an official state report by an eyewitness in the area, the apparently transparent language and objective facts in the grand vizier's letter are instead complex rhetorical strategies intended to fulfil a specific politico-textual function and encourage a particular understanding of events.

Three historian-administrators: Hasan Beyzade, Abdülkadir Topçularkatibi and Ibrahim Peçevi

One of the most interesting aspects of the narrations of the Nagykanizsa sieges in the works of Hasan Beyzade and Abdülkadir Topçularkatibi is the lack of interest in the second Nagykanizsa siege in 1601. Topçularkatibi describes the defence in half a folio, and Hasan Beyzade does not mention it at all. In this regard they differ from not only the *gazavatname* [campaign narrative] accounts but also from narrations by later historians.[24] This focus on the capture rather than the defence is not a reflection of what 'really happened' or of a general climate of opinion concerning the relative importance of the capture compared to the defence. The earliest extant scriptum in the *Gazavat-i Tiryaki Hasan Paşa* corpus dates from 1616, only fifteen years after the sieges, and in contrast, it focuses almost exclusively on the defence in 1601, giving only a few lines to the capture in 1600.[25] Moreover, the contemporary significance of the defence of Nagykanizsa in 1601 is illustrated by the fact that Tiryaki Hasan Pasha, the commander of the castle, was rewarded with a vizierate and marriage to the sultan's daughter.[26] Numerous references in *telhis* correspondence from the first few years of the seventeenth century also attest to the importance of the defence to contemporaries.[27] Rather, this emphasis on the Ottoman capture of the castle is most coherently explained by reference to the authors' and their implied audiences' political and military interests. Hasan Beyzade and Topçularkatibi are not really more interested in the capture as opposed to the defence per se; they are in fact focused on the activities of the grand vizier, the central administration and the military. Their cartography of war is dictated and constituted by the movement of the bureaucratic elite and the military. The presence of the grand vizier or the imperial army dictates the importance of a place and the attention it consequently receives in their histories. Although the grand vizier oversaw the first siege and capture of Nagykanizsa in 1600, he and the imperial army were trying to regain Szekesfehérvár, while the second siege of Nagykanizsa was prosecuted, and thus it is on Szekesfehérvár that the attention of these historians is concentrated.

This focus on the bureaucratic elite and military to some extent originates from the authors' personal and professional involvement with the viziers and commanders. As noted they were all employed, to varying degrees, in the military-administrative bureaucracy and were enmeshed in client-patron relationships with members of the elite. They were therefore directly affected by its concerns and viewed the world from such a perspective. Hasan Beyzade, as *baş-tezkereci* and later *re'is ül-küttab* to Grand Vizier Ibrahim Pasha, mapped the war politically, and his perspective is one focused upon the activities of the grand vizier. Considerations of his intended audience may also have dictated Hasan Beyzade's focus upon the capture rather than the defence of Nagykanizsa. His work, framed as history, is very decontextualised and includes complex and relatively unusual Arabic and Persian grammatical constructions and vocabulary.[28] This suggests that his intended audience consisted of very well-educated members of the military and administrative elite whose interests and concerns are more likely to have been also focused on the actions of the grand vizier and the capture of castles rather than a successful defence of a castle by a less high-ranking soldier.

Abdülkadir Topçularkatibi's focus on the capture can similarly be explained by his employment in the military-administrative elite. As secretary to the artillery, his perspective is very much dominated by matters relating to the army, especially appointments and provisioning requirements. He was also present at the siege of Szekesfehérvár in 1601, so understandably he directs most of his attention to this event.[29] Topçularkatibi's history is particularly interesting in terms of Ottoman literacy practices and exemplifies a different type of literacy to that employed by Hasan Beyzade. His narrative is linguistically uncomplicated and exhibits a fluid orthography and grammar, very little direct speech and a simple sentence structure dominated by additive practices. The latter is most explicitly manifested in his predilection for lists. For example, he lists weapons, munitions, provisions, animals, the people present on a battlefield, changes to appointments and those who came to display obeisance to the grand vizier.[30] This tendency to present information in a list format may be a result of a literacy learnt and developed within a context of bookkeeping and military record-keeping. The content of these lists is also illuminative and suggests that Topçularkatibi's perception of the campaign was one dominated by the concerns of provisioning, routes, weapons and formal social relationships and ranks. His narrative reads like an account book or inventory of the campaign rather than as a history, and it seems to have been intended to inform an audience about the practicalities

The authority of eyewitness accounts reconsidered 25

of Ottoman military campaigns rather than entertain or provide didactic instruction. These lists might also provide information about his intended or imagined audiences: middle-ranking military bureaucrats who would want to know not only military details but also who was present and in what capacity. It is precisely this concern for military details that has made him such a valuable primary source for twenty- and twenty-first-century historians. His 'scribal' or secretarial concern with military matters is reflected in his mapping of geographical spatialities as well as political and social ones. His work can be read as a guidebook to Hungarian campaigns because he provides a detailed list of the movements of the imperial army, including dates and halting places. This contrasts with the mapping of space inherent in the *gazavatname* accounts where the geographical references are less concerned with physical places but map instead a spiritual or cultural world located in a shared communal memory.[31]

However, despite his use of a plain style and vocabulary, Topçularkatibi frames his description of events with Persian rubrics. This rubrication practice may reflect his formal training as an administrative scribe: *defters* [registers] were frequently divided into sections by rubrics which summarised the subsequent content. However, the omission of any Persian grammar or vocabulary in his narrative and also the dissonance between the rubrics and the content of the subsequent sections may suggest that they were not actually written by Topçularkatibi himself but were imported from another work. For example, one section which is mainly concerned with the attempt to relieve Szekesfehérvár and which also mentions the death of the grand vizier is rather confusingly captioned with the title: "Concerning the campaign of Kanije castle and Bubofça Castle and other castles and the gathering of the lewd infidel army and the drawing up of a camp and the doing battle and the conquering of the castles and of the camp of the infidels and of the fleeing and of the God-ordained conquest in the time of the commander Vizier Ibrahim Pasha Gazi who was present then."[32] This use of Persian rubrics was therefore more likely intended to frame and authorise the work as history and present it as 'educated' rather than provide an informative description of the section to follow.

Peçevi is similarly cited as an exemplary source by modern historians but for quite different reasons. While Topçularkatibi's history is considered a noteworthy source by virtue of the extensive information on Ottoman military campaigns that it contains, Peçevi is regarded as a prototype of a modern academic historian in his inclusive attitude towards sources and in his 'objective' viewpoint. As noted, Peçevi utilised both Hungarian and Ottoman-language sources in the writing of his history. The dialogism and potential polyvocality arising from his use of Ottoman and Hungarian sources, together with his extensive local knowledge and perspective as an eyewitness to many of the events that he narrates, have led him to be read as offering a historically rigorous, objective account from a balanced viewpoint. However, analysis of his narrative demonstrates that it is as positioned as any other narrative, and the veneer of objectivity arises from its concurrence with the protocols of twenty-first-century academic historical praxis as opposed to any direct correspondence with a putatively existent past. It is this apparent similarity of methodology and presentation that has allowed audiences to elide 'fictive' aspects of Peçevi's account, most notably his inclusion of enemy speeches and his causal attribution of events to divine intervention.[33]

Peçevi's narration, similar to that by Topçularkatibi and Hasan Beyzade, is dictated by the movements and interests of the military-administrative elite. For example, his is the only source, apart from the *telhis*, which offers a semi-detailed account of the grand vizier's attempt to relieve the Habsburg siege of Nagykanizsa in 1601 and the hardships he suffered.[34] However, unlike the accounts by Topçularkatibi and Hasan Beyzade, Peçevi does provide a more detailed account of the 1601 defence of Nagykanizsa castle, giving equal space to both its capture and defence. Although, unlike the *gazavatname* accounts and histories by Katib Çelebi and Naima, Peçevi's narration of the sieges of Nagykanizsa does not centre on Tiryaki Hasan Pasha. For example, in the *gazavatname* accounts Tiryaki Hasan Pasha is depicted as the active agent in events: it is his plan that the grand vizier should attack Nagykanizsa castle and leave him to defend Buda, and it is Tiryaki Hasan Pasha who gives Lala Mehmed Pasha some cannons and then 'orders' him to bombard a number of *palankas* [small wooden fortresses]. In contrast, in Peçevi's account the grand vizier decides that he has other military priorities and appoints Tiryaki Hasan Pasha as governor of Buda. Lala Mehmed Pasha then takes a number of cannons and on his way to the siege of Nagykanizsa successfully captures a number of small forts.[35] This shift in the depiction of Lala Mehmed Pasha's role from the passive to the active reflects Peçevi's political interests and, presumably, his patron-client relationship with Lala Mehmed Pasha.

Peçevi's position as a Hungarian Ottoman has also affected his imagining of the identities of self and other. His naming of the enemy who were killed in the gunpowder explosion during the 1600 siege as Hungarian infidels suggests that that unlike later nineteenth- and twentieth-century historians, he did not exclusively equate 'self' with Ottoman Turk and 'other' with Hungarians: some Hungarians were infidels, and others were not. Equally his imagination of identity does not necessarily appear to be solely orientated along religious lines as his frequent attestations to the bravery, loyalty and prowess of the *Frenk* soldiers who were allied with the Ottomans suggests.[36] However, Peçevi is most certainly writing from an Islamic perspective, and he occupies a world in which God is frequently imagined to directly intervene: Ottoman victory and the inability of the enemy to make progress are all the result of divine intervention. While Katib Çelebi narrates the gunpowder explosion in one of the castle towers as an instance of Ottoman heroism and sacrifice, for Peçevi it exemplifies the power of God and his Prophet to assist those who are favoured.[37]

The *telhis*

A deconstructive analysis of Grand Vizier Yemişçi Hasan Pasha's *telhis* to the sultan of events occurring during the defence of Nagykanizsa in 1601 reveals a number of narrative tensions which imply that the grand vizier did not objectively report what really happened but reinterpreted and restructured events common to all accounts to achieve specific political and textual aims.[38] In particular, I will argue that his account of the role played by the weather, his arrival in Szigetvár (Sigetvar) and the sortie against the enemy by the defenders of Nagykanizsa cannot automatically be assumed to be less constructed and consequently more 'true' than the versions given in the other narratives such as the *gazavatnames*. By framing and structuring his description of events and selecting the content to include, he manages and thus 'fictionalises' the narrative – his account is therefore no less firmly situated within a network or matrix of subjective values and perspectives than more 'literary' narratives.

Superficially, the function of the *telhis* is to communicate to the sultan events on the Ottoman-Habsburg marches that occurred in the autumn and winter of 1601, specifically, the Ottoman defence of Nagykanizsa. In brief, it describes how, despite the fierce winter, the grand vizier and his soldiers set off to relieve the Habsburg-led siege of Nagykanizsa. A small group of experienced soldiers were sent ahead to attack the besiegers' trenches, and they captured forty or fifty of the enemy before returning to Szigetvár. However, before they reached the grand vizier and the rest of his men, they were counter-attacked by the enemy, the prisoners rescued, a *mirza* [prince] killed and two Tatars captured. When the enemy interrogated the captured Tatars, they learnt that the grand vizier and the imperial army were at Szigetvár castle, panicked and decided to abandon the siege. Subsequently, the weather turned nasty, and the enemy were forced to retreat without their cannons. At this point the defenders came out from the castle and killed six or seven thousand of the enemy. The grand vizier then states that the weather was so bad that he had to break camp, abandoning his pavilions and leaving provisions and munitions in Szigetvár, which were later taken to Nagykanizsa castle by the *bey* [lower-level governor or military administrator] of Pozsega (Pojega). He also mentions that he has received a letter from Tiryaki Hasan Pasha, which he has forwarded to the sultan. The rest of the *telhis* provides a description of the hardships he and his men suffered in returning over Osijek Bridge to Belgrade and concludes with a request to return to Istanbul to make preparations for the following year's campaign.[39]

Inter- and intra-textual evidence indicates that the grand vizier was less concerned with solely relating events than with narrating them in such a manner that his actions were justified and a positive image of himself and his capabilities was projected. While the year before, his predecessor, Ibrahim Pasha, had captured Nagykanizsa castle, not only had he, Yemişçi Hasan Pasha, failed to make any significant acquisitions during this campaign season, but he had failed first to protect and then recapture Szekésfehérvár castle. Furthermore, he was not even able to reach Nagykanizsa to relieve the siege. In addition to these failures, he appears to have lacked the full support of the army, which following *ruz-i kasim* [November 7 – traditionally the last day of the campaigning season], returned to winter quarters despite his protestations and his desire to relieve the siege of Nagykanizsa. This suggests that he would have had good reason to be worried about his position and perceptions of his military and administrative competence. Evidence of this concern is present in the text in the litany of excuses for his lack of military success: namely that the weather was atrocious and the *bey* of Silistre and the *beylerbeyi* [governor] of Egypt were derelict in their duties. Throughout the *telhis* the grand vizier is keen to stress the effort that he has expended and the hardships he has suffered. Indeed, the narrative is framed with instances of the difficulties and trials that he endured: it begins with a description of the harsh weather that beset his attempt to retake Szekesfehérvár and concludes with an account of the miseries that overtook him on his journey back from Szigetvár to Belgrade. He also pleads to be allowed to return to Istanbul, no doubt to more effectively persuade the sultan of his abilities and to personally counter any negative speculation about his actions.

> Is there any benefit in this slave sitting in Belgrade when the word of the commander who is sitting in Belgrade is held thus? The affairs will not be accomplished by the preparations of people who don't know and aren't experienced in the campaign circumstances. If affairs had been accomplished in this manner, [if] for the last ten years the commanders had not wintered in this region, this business would have been finished – it would have been completed. But what kind of affairs were accomplished?[40]

Through a manipulation of both the form and content of his narrative, the grand vizier repeatedly emphasises his achievements and downplays the importance of the siege of Nagykanizsa and the actions of the defenders. In the first paragraph he argues that he raised the siege of Szekesfehérvár not because he was unable to capture it but because "a fierce winter fell and because of the raining and snowing, and because of criers continuously coming from the direction of Nagykanizsa".[41] He then continues that it was important to remove the big cannons to safety and *then* to relieve Nagykanizsa.[42] By repeatedly positioning the siege of Nagykanizsa as less important than other border events or occurrences, he not only mitigates his failure to effectively relieve the siege but also emphasises his achievements: namely the safe removal of the cannons.

On a number of occasions the grand vizier employs a single narrative strategy both to emphasise his own accomplishments and concomitantly diminish those of the defenders. The best example of this is his account of the retreat of the enemy besiegers. In contrast to the *gazavatname* narratives that suggest that the enemy retreated due to a combination of the cunning tricks of Tiryaki Hasan Pasha, the final brave sortie from the castle by the defenders and the appalling weather, the grand vizier implies that it was his presence at nearby Szigetvár castle that was the catalyst. While the grand vizier does describe a sortie by the defenders of the castle and also mentions that they were very courageous, through a careful structuring of the narrative he conveys the impression that the defenders made their raid essentially after the defeat of the besieging Habsburg army. As noted, the enemy apparently learn of the presence of the grand vizier and his men at Szigetvár while interrogating two captured Tatars. The 'conversation' between the Tatars and the enemy are partially recounted in the letter in the form of direct speech.[43] This very 'literary' device serves a specific and crucial narrative function because the enemy, upon hearing that the grand vizier is nearby, is so disturbed that it decides to abandon the siege, saying "in any case let's rise and go".[44] The grand vizier notes in the *telhis* that it is *after* the decision has been made by the enemy to "rise and go" that the weather turned nasty and "the soldiers of Islam who were inside the castle came out and put six or seven thousand of the accursed to the sword [. . .] and the accursed left all of their tents and camp and munitions and provisions and much gunpowder and fled."[45] By suggesting that the sortie occurred after the enemy had already decided to leave, he presents the defenders of Nagykanizsa castle as simply taking advantage of an already retreating enemy rather than instigating the withdrawal. The grand vizier further attempts to deflect attention from the actions of the defenders by refraining from mentioning the name of the commander Tiryaki Hasan Pasha: he names him simply as "the *beylerbeyi* of Nagykanizsa". Moreover, he refers to a letter that he received from Tiryaki Hasan Pasha "on this matter" and notes that it has been summarised and forwarded to the capital. He may have decided not to include the summary in his *telhis* because it no doubt narrated events from a conflicting perspective.[46]

The role the weather played in events according to the grand vizier's narrative similarly demonstrates how he constructed his account of events to encourage a positive reception of his actions and abilities. According to the *telhis*, the weather was apparently so severe that it resulted in him having to abandon the siege of Szekesfehérvár, prevented him from actually reaching Nagykanizsa castle and forced him to abandon his pavilions and provisions. However, in the very next sentence he suggests that he deliberately left provisions and munitions in the castle that were subsequently successfully transported to Nagykanizsa castle by the *bey* of Pozsega and the people of Pécs and Szigetvár. How was it possible for the weather to be so appalling that he was forced to abandon his pavilions, but he could deliberately leave provisions and munitions in the castle? And why were the *bey* of Pozsega and the people of Pécs and Szigetvár able to travel to Nagykanizsa but not the grand vizier? Similarly, he glosses over the apparent rebellion of the army by insisting that he offered the soldiers the choice whether to accompany him to Nagykanizsa, thereby effectively stalling any accusation that they disobeyed his command. He also attributes their reluctance to accompany him to the lateness of the season and the terrible weather.

30 *The authority of eyewitness accounts reconsidered*

To conclude, rather than read and consequently privilege contemporary official documents such as *telhis* and histories by eyewitness historian-administrators as unproblematic sources of objective documentary evidence, it should be acknowledged that they are just as positioned and 'fictional' as many 'literary' sources. Although they may ultimately be deemed to be more useful historical sources for specific, present-focused, cultural purposes, this does not imply a more accurate correspondence with the past through transparent language and a less constructed nature but rather that the perspective and function of the document accords more with twenty-first-century academic historical praxis than that of other potential sources.

Notes

1 Arthur Marwick, *The Nature of History*, 3rd ed. (Basingstoke: Macmillan, 1989), 208–210, lists ten different types of primary sources with documents of record in first place, followed by surveys and reports and concluding with oral traditions then observed behaviour. Deborah A. Symonds, "Living in the Scottish Records Office," in *Reconstructing History*, ed. Elizabeth Fox-Genovese and Elizabeth Lasch-Quinn (London: Routledge, 1999), demonstrates a slightly fetishistic attitude towards archival sources, "I am inclined to argue that historians must hold the original documents of whatever they study, look at the paper, and smell everything. Only by coming face to face with surviving documents, seals, letters, maps, accounts, and receipts can one, I believe, fully weigh the meaning of terms like intention, falsification, and truth," 165. Reconstructionist is a term coined by Alun Munslow, *Deconstructing History* (London: Routledge, 1997), 18, and describes historians who believe that by properly analysing sources, we can get closer to finding out what happened (and what it means). Reconstructionists adhere to a representationalist or realist conception of knowledge as outlined in the introduction to this work. I follow Richard Rorty in preferring the term representationalist to realist.

2 As an example, oral testimony is often regarded as being a less reliable source – selective and prone to interpretation, influence and misremembering – of use only when corroborating written documents, to fill in the gaps left by more traditional sources or to give voice to those left out of documentary or written sources. As Peter Claus and John Marriott, *History: An Introduction to Theory, Method and Practice* (Harlow: Pearson, 2012), note "no historian would dream of building a history of modern South Africa on oral history sources alone," 413, whereas conversely it is more than acceptable to base a history solely on written sources. However, as they point out, at the end of their section on oral history, these accusations can be equally levelled against written sources, 423.

3 Gabriel Piterberg, *An Ottoman Tragedy: History and Historiography at Play* (Berkeley: University of California Press, 2003), 31.

4 I. H. Mordtmann and V. L. Ménage, "Hasan Bey-zade," in *The Encyclopaedia of Islam*, ed. Peri J. Bearman, T. Bianquis, C. E. Bosworth, E. van Donzel and W. P. Heinrichs, 2nd ed., vol. 3 (Leiden: Brill, 1971), 249.

5 Hayden White, "The Fictions of Factual Representation," in *Tropics of Discourse: Essays in Cultural Criticism*, ed. Hayden White (Baltimore: The John Hopkins University Press, 1978), 121. See the introduction to this book for White's use of *literary writing*.

6 Mordtmann and Ménage, "Hasan Bey-zade," 248.

7 Ibid., and Piterberg, *An Ottoman Tragedy*, 46.

The authority of eyewitness accounts reconsidered 31

8 *Tarih* and its plural *tevarih* are variously translated as annals, history or chronicles depending on the translator's assessment of the text. I have chosen to use the English terms history and histories unless otherwise stated.
9 Mordtmann and Ménage, "Hasan Bey-zade," 249; Ş. Nezihi Aykut, "Hasan Beyzade Ahmed Paşa," in *Historians of the Ottoman Empire*, ed. C. Kafadar, H. Karateke and C. Fleischer, https://ottomanhistorians.uchicago.edu/en/historian/hasan-beyzade-ahmed-pasa-hamdi (accessed 26/6/16) Turkish version October 2005, English version 2008.
10 Aykut, "Hasan Beyzade Ahmed Paşa."
11 Markus Köhbach, "Der osmanische Historiker Topçılar Katibi 'Abdü'l-qadir Efendi. Leben und Werk," *Osmanlı Araştırmaları* 2 (1981): 77.
12 The last date mentioned in his work is Muharram, 1054, thereby providing a *terminus post quem* for his death, ibid., 78, 88.
13 Ibid., 79, 81.
14 Abdülkadir Topçularkatibi, *Tevarih-i âl-i Osman* Vienna: National-bibliothek, fol.139r.
15 The conventional title was ascribed by Flügel in his catalogue entry for Mxt.130, Gustav Flügel, *Die arabischen, persischen und türkischen Handschriften der kaiserlich-königlichen Hofbibliothek zu Wien* (Wien: K. K. Hof-und Staatsdruckerei, 1865–1867), vol. 2, 260–261; see Köhbach, "Der osmanische Historiker," 88–90. The Istanbul manuscript has not apparently been recorded in a catalogue, Köhbach, 89.
16 Köhbach, "Der osmanische Historiker," 76–77 and 85–86.
17 Franz Babinger and Christine Woodhead, "Pecewi," in *The Encyclopaedia of Islam*, ed. P. J. Bearman, Th. Bianquis, C. E. Bosworth, E. van Donzel and W.P. Heinrichs, 2nd ed., vol. 8 (Leiden: Brill, 1995), 291.
18 Ibid.
19 Ibid., and Bernard Lewis, "The Use by Muslim Historians of Non-Muslim Sources," in *Historians of the Middle East*, ed. Bernard Lewis and P. M. Holt (London: Oxford University Press, 1962), 180–191 and 185–186.
20 Carol Berkenkotter and Thomas Huckin, *Genre Knowledge in Disciplinary Communication: Cognition/Culture/Power* (Hove, UK: Lawrence Erlbaum Associates, 1995), 46–47.
21 Piterberg, *An Ottoman Tragedy*, 53, 119 discusses Ottoman historians' citation practices and the importance of not interpreting them in accordance with modern academic expectation. See Chapter 5 for a more detailed example of Ottoman incorporation practices. See also Donald P. Little, "An Analysis of the Relationship between Four Mamluk Chronicles for 737–745," in *History and Historiography of the Mamluks*, ed. Donald P. Little (London: Variorum Reprints, 1986), 256, for a discussion of the "relationship of borrowing" among Mamluk chronicles. Similarly, in Little, *An Introduction to Mamluk Historiography: An Analysis of Arabic Annalistic and Biographical Sources for the Reign of al-Malik an-Nasir Muhammad ibn Qala'un* (Wiesbaden: Franz Steiner Verlag GMBH, 1970), where he outlines the reliance of Mamluk histories on three key sources for information on the early reign of al-Malik an-Nasir. There was a similar brevity of citation in Ottoman religious texts, where it was expected that readers would have read, mastered and importantly memorised the relevant texts, and as such detailed citation information would not be necessary. I thank Nur Sobers-Khan for this information.
22 Rhoads Murphey, "Ottoman Historical Writing in the Seventeenth Century: A Survey of the General Development of the Genre after the Reign of Sultan Ahmed (1603–1617)," *Archivum Ottomanicum* 13 (1993–1994): 283.
23 I have used both ITSM: Revan.1303 and *telhis* no.52 in Cengiz Orhonlu, *Osmanlı Tarihine âid Belgeler: Telhisler (1597–1607)* (Istanbul: Edebiyat Fakültesi Basımevi, 1970), 44–46, for the text of this report.

24 Katib Çelebi, *Fezleke-i Katib Çelebi*, vols. 1–2 (Istanbul: Ceride-i Havadis Matbaası, 1286–1287/1869–1870) and Naima, *Tarih-i Naima* (Istanbul: Matbaa-i Âmire, 1281–1283/1864–1866) both allot more than three times as much space to a discussion of the defence than the capture, as does Namık Kemal, *Kanije* (Istanbul: Matbaa-i Ebüzziya, 1311/1893–1894). The *gazavatnames* and twentieth-century accounts however provide the most dramatic contrast. For example, Cavid Baysun, *Tiryaki Hasan Paşa ve Kanije Savunması* (Istanbul: Milli Eğitim Bakanlığı Köy Kitaplığı no.15, Milli Eğitim Basımevi, 1950), describes the capture in two pages and the defence in thirty pages. Similarly, the *gazavatnames* summarise the capture in a few lines but provide extensive coverage of the 1601 defence; see Chapters 3 and 4.
25 Berlin: Preußische National-Bibliothek, O.R.3442, *Hatha Kitab-i Tevarih-i Kanije* fols 1b–37b (1025/1616).
26 I. H. Danişmend, *Osmanlı Tarih-I Kronolojisi*, 4 vols. (Istanbul: Türkiye Yayınevi, 1947–1955), 250, notes that he became a vizier in 1608 as does Mehmed Süreyya, *Sicill-i Osmani*, 4 vols. (Istanbul: Matbaa-i Amire, 1308–1316?/1891–1899?). A. D. Alderson, *Structure of the Ottoman Dynasty* (Oxford: Carendon Press, 1956), 169, Flügel, *Die arabischen*, 248, and C. M. Kortepeter, *Ottoman Imperialism during the Reformation: Europe and the Caucasus* (London: University of London Press Ltd., 1972), 249, note that Hasan Pasha married the daughter of Mehmed III (the sister of Ahmed I) but do not give a date.
27 *Telhis* no. 68 and 142 in Orhonlu, *Telhisler*, refer to "Vizier Hasan Pasha who was in Kanije" and "Vizier Hasan Pasha who defended Kanije," 59 and 114, respectively.
28 Features that illustrate the level of decontextualisation include less direct speech, more varied speech act verbs, fewer dietics and more relative clauses.
29 Topçularkatibi, *Tevarih*, fol.147v and Köhbach, "Der osmanische Historiker," 80.
30 For example, Topçularkatibi, *Tevarih*, fol.142a, for types of rope; fol.129b for the different soldiers inspected; fol.130b for lists of weapons.
31 See Claire Norton, "Sacred Sites, Severed Heads and Prophetic Visions," *Journal of the Anthropology of the Contemporary Middle East and Central Eurasia* 2/1 (2014), for more on how the *gazavatname* accounts constructed a religious or cultural cartography.
32 Topçularkatibi, *Tevarih*, fol.128b.
33 Ibrahim Peçevi, *Tarih-i Peçevi*, Istanbul, 1283/1866–1867, 240 and 233, respectively.
34 Ibid., 240.
35 Ibid., 232.
36 Ibid., 232–233.
37 Ibid., 233, and Katib Çelebi, *Fezleke*, 138.
38 Following the death of Ibrahim Pasha in 1601, Yemişçi Hasan Pasha was appointed grand vizier.
39 ITSM: Revan.1303, fols.2b–5a, and Orhonlu, *Telhisler*, no. 52, pages 44–46.
40 Ibid., fol.5a
41 Ibid., fol.2b
42 Ibid.
43 Ibid., fol.3a.
44 ITSM: Revan.1303, fol.3b.
45 Ibid.
46 The inclusion of letters or summaries of correspondence in *telhis* was not unusual, see Orhonlu, *Telhisler*, nos. 49, 51, 64–65, pages 38–40, 40–44, 55 and 55–56, respectively.

2 *Fethnames*
Not just literary bombast

Introduction

Between 26 January and 4 February 1601 CE [the last decade of *Receb* 1009H.], approximately three months after the capture of Nagykanizsa castle, two *fethnames* [victory missives] were sent simultaneously to Queen Elizabeth I in the name of the Ottoman sultan and grand vizier.[1] They both bear the same date and place of composition and were written by the Ottoman historian and administrator Hasan Beyzade.[2] These constitute the earliest extant Ottoman narratives of the 1600 siege of Nagykanizsa.

Victory-letter style *fethnames* are relatively short, official documents of only a few folios in length, written very soon after the conflict described and sent to Ottoman governors, vassals and foreign rulers. These were also disseminated to a wider Ottoman public through oral proclamations on the streets of major Ottoman cities as part of more general victory celebrations and included in histories and *inşa* collections [collections of Islamic cultural writings].[3] Such Ottoman *fethnames* have rarely been the subject of academic inquiry. Despite being official state documents and in the case of the Nagykanizsa *fethnames* being composed and written by a respected Ottoman historian-administrator who was an eyewitness to events, scholars of Ottoman history have tended to perceive *fethnames* as less-than-reliable historical sources. This is partly a consequence of the scarcity of extant *fethnames* and partly a result of their perceived worth as academic sources.[4] Both genres of *fethname* have tended to be overlooked and are not considered to "belong to the first rank of sources available to the historian of events" because they were not intended to be "impartial factual accounts" and their "literary and/or religious-political character" tends "to blur or distort the facts".[5] Consequently they have been categorised as "rather unhistorical" and "halfway between political propaganda and heroic saga".[6] It is assumed that any potential documentary evidence will have been compromised by their literary or propagandistic tendencies.[7] For example, Lewis argues that *fethnames* do not really provide accurate reports; they "are as unreliable as the publicity handouts of any other belligerent, ancient or modern", whereas Schmidt complains that "the literary and/or religious-political character of

Ottoman histories, which tend to blur or even distort the facts" is "very obviously [...] the case in a propagandistic work like the "Letter of Victory" (Fethname)."[8] The categorisation of *fethnames* as political propaganda by Lewis and others is more reprobatory than descriptive in that rather than inform the audience of a potential function of these documents, it is instead designed to signal that they do not constitute reliable sources of evidence by twenty- and twenty-first-century Western academic standards. For example, there is no discussion as to what type of propaganda the *fethname* represents and to what end.

The implied conflation of the term *propaganda* with the idea of texts written from a biased, perspectival or 'religious-political' viewpoint also suggests that there exist non-propagandistic, impartial, factual accounts which represent the past 'as it really happened'. Schmidt asserts that it is "rather easy to sift fact from fiction because we are able to use archival data to 'scrape off' the literary layer", but my contention throughout this book is that we have no foundational, privileged information that we can use to epistemologically or ontologically separate fact from fiction: the literary layer goes all the way down.[9] From the perspective of a putative correspondence with reality, archival, official or 'documentary' texts are just as positioned, subjective and therefore 'literary' as other narratives. Moreover, categorising *fethnames* as merely literary or fictional propaganda and then dismissing them inhibits any analysis into the diverse functions and audiences that these texts had.[10] To argue, as some historians have done, that the reliability of such information is dubious from the point of view of twenty-first-century academic historical scholarship misses the point: *fethnames* contain a description of the victorious battle or campaign framed in a manner congruent with the aims and needs of the Ottoman state. That one of these aims may be propaganda is not in dispute and indeed the primary function of most *fethnames*, both those intended for internal and for external audiences, may be considered to be that of celebrating the victory while glorifying and extolling the power and might of the Ottoman Empire. A concomitant, but no less desired, function may have also been to instil awe in audiences (both foreign and domestic) and thus ensure their continued submission, or obedience to, the Ottoman state. However, to assume these were the only functions of *fethnames* is to ignore the importance of their various framings and textual differences.

The narration of a victory in a *fethname*, at a very basic level, marks the event as significant: it is a victory worthy of note. It thus helps to inscribe a particular history: a history articulated, or marked, by victories of the Ottoman Empire over its enemies. Through this potential to appropriate the past within an official framework, *fethnames* can participate in the process of determining a particular version of events as the true or correct version and thus also legitimise the actions of particular protagonists. This is further emphasised when the *fethname* is subsequently included in an official history of the Ottoman Empire, as is exemplified by the Eger (Eğri) *fethname* included in Selaniki's history. This *fethname* depicts the sultan as a fearless warrior remaining resolute on the battlefield in contrast to other accounts of the battle that noted his apparent indecision and fear in the midst of the battle. It also attempts to justify the appointment and argue against the subsequent dismissal of Çigalazade Sinan Pasha as grand vizier through a rather eulogistic description of his actions and achievements during the battle.[11]

Fethnames could also have played a role in the process of identity construction. The reading aloud of a *fethname* on the streets of Istanbul, for example, would not only have presented the Ottoman Empire as powerful and magnificent, thus both legitimising the rule of the sultan and also justifying what was probably an expensive war, but it would also have had a socially cohesive function through the creation of shared public memories and the reinforcement of a shared identity of self in opposition to that of an enemy other. *Fethnames* sent to foreign rulers and domestic elites could have participated in a similar process of identity formation. Although they may not have desired to establish completely coextensive identities of self, they did attempt to create, or reinforce, a set of common interests, or goals and, perhaps more importantly, worked to establish a shared imagination of an enemy other. Lastly, *fethnames* sent to foreign rulers and Ottoman vassals and governors had a diplomatic function in that they worked, in a variety of ways, to promote the interests of the Ottoman state in their inter- and intra-state relations.[12]

The lack of interest in the functions of *fethnames*, together with a scarcity of extant *fethnames* actually sent to foreign rulers and vassals, has been compounded by the assumption that all inscriptions of *fethnames* celebrating a particular victory are copies of a single original and are "basically the same text" despite their "sometimes considerable differences".[13] As a result any differences among them are ignored or glossed over. Schmidt argues that the four versions he has studied of the Eger *fethname* despite "sometimes considerable differences" are "basically the same text", and he treats them as such, extracting documentary evidence from them to assist his (re)construction of the battle of Eger.[14] In contrast, Lewis explains textual differences by using the model of an originary work and later degenerations. He argues that there exists one true original *fethname* for each victory, the discovery of which would be extremely useful for Ottoman military history, while the value of later variations (deviations?) is mainly literary.[15] For example, he describes the *fethname* issued upon Mehmed II's victory over Uzun Hasan as "the genuine article and not a literary exercise".[16] This distinction between the original, genuine and thus valuable *fethname* and less valuable copies or literary exercises recalls a Derridean lost 'presence' and effectively ignores the variations among *fethnames*.[17] In contrast, I contend that *fethnames* were in fact often deliberately rewritten and revised to accommodate different audiences and functions and that these differences are in fact crucial for understanding the various ways in which Ottoman *fethnames* were understood and used by the state administration and others. These variations, rather than being insignificant or the result of later literary flourishes, provide important evidence concerning the diverse audiences and functions that the *fethnames* had.

Rather than read the Nagykanizsa *fethnames* sent to Queen Elizabeth I for documentary evidence about the sieges, I focus on the framing of the *fethname*, the textual variations, reception context and the expectations of the intended audience with the aim of foregrounding their politico-diplomatic functions and elucidating why the Ottoman state dispatched two separate *fethnames* celebrating the capture in the name of the grand vizier and the sultan.[18] Specifically, I will argue that although the two Nagykanizsa *fethnames* are textually almost identical and were, on first sight, addressed to the same audience, Queen Elizabeth I, the implied audience of the two documents was significantly different. In other words, it was assumed that Queen Elizabeth I would read the *fethnames* with two different sets of expectations regarding their function and meaning. I will thus argue that while the sultanic *fethname* was intended to be read as an 'iconograph of power' within a discourse of imperial sovereignty and imagined the audience as a sovereign leader, the grand vizierial *fethname* was intended to be read within the discourse of non-ambassadorial diplomatic correspondence and was addressed to an implied audience perceived in more friendly terms – a peer, someone with whom one could negotiate.[19] I thus elucidate the means by which these two very similar accounts of the capture of Nagykanizsa castle provided a vehicle for the Ottoman state to perform and thus legitimise its claims to sovereignty and power while simultaneously engaging in informal diplomatic negotiation with the English.

The sultanic *fethname*

The sultanic *fethname* sent to Queen Elizabeth I was intended to be read within a discourse of imperial sovereignty, an assumption reinforced by the 'codicological aesthetics' of the text.[20] It is an impressive, imposing three-foot-long document, embossed with gold, with an ornate sultanic *tuğra*, which when delivered would have been wrapped in silk and placed in a satin purse. The introductory remarks describing Queen Elizabeth as "the select among modest Christian women, the preeminent of those honoured in the whole body of Christians, the one who puts to rights the affairs of the commonwealth of Christian nations, the one who trails the skirts of pomp and stateliness" remind us that while the *fethname* functioned to communicate Ottoman imperial claims and legitimacy to their rivals, both friends and foes, it is also the formal correspondence between two heads of state.[21] The decontextualised language of the *fethname*, a profusion of Arabic and Persian grammatical constructs and vocabulary and its orthographic and grammatical fixity, work to create a sense of distance contributing to the overall sense of formality, awe and majesty.

The standard *inscriptio* and *salutatio* are followed by a *narration* consisting of two sections. The first details the purpose of the campaign, eulogises the grand vizier and refers to the previous year's rout of the enemy and the capture of towns and castles up to Uivar (Uyvar/Ujvár), Buda and Prague. The second section focuses on the current year's campaign, noting that while it was initially directed towards Buda, it was then turned aside in favour of Nagykanizsa upon the discovery of the destruction of the bridge at Osijek and the oppression of *reaya* [subjects of the Ottoman Empire who are not part of the ruling elite] and *beraya* [free citizens] by "the brigands from the military castles of Bubofca and Kanije".[22] It then mentions the capture of Babócsa (Bubofca) castle before providing a description of the 1600 siege of Nagykanizsa, including comment on the enemy commanders, the number of soldiers and amount of equipment. It also relates the battle against the Habsburg relief army, their flight, the eventual surrender of the fortress and the retreat of the people of the castle. A summary is given of the other castles captured that year, and lastly it introduces the bearer of the letter as Bartholomew, one of the sultan's physicians, and exhorts the queen to convey the news of the victory to her subjects.[23]

I will first consider the interpretative naming of the enemy and the justifications given for the military campaign in the sultanic *fethname* with the intention of demonstrating that the document, far from being "halfway between political propaganda and heroic saga", was in fact carefully crafted to fulfil a specific function and to take into account the expectations and sensibilities of its intended English, Protestant audience.[24] The prevalent Ottoman state rhetoric predicated upon continuous *jihad* against an infidel enemy that was frequently employed to narrate and explicate conflicts is toned down in the Nagykanizsa *fethnames* sent to Queen Elizabeth: the term *infidel* is only used three times to designate the enemy.[25] Instead, more religiously neutral terms such as "the enemy", "the soldiers to whom defeat is habitual", "the lords of lewdness", "the confounded accursed", "the enemies of ill-judgment" and "the vile enemy of religion" are used.[26] This contrasts with the naming practices employed in many of the *gazavatname* accounts of the siege, various Ottoman histories as well as in the Eger *fethname* sent to the Yemeni Emir.[27] This naming strategy, and consequently the constructed identity of the Habsburgs, does not presume a cartography of antagonism predicated upon religious difference: the English audience is not automatically conceptualised in the same religious category as the enemy Habsburgs, thereby militating against potential tensions and divisions between the English and Ottomans. Instead, the naming practices allow more complex and nuanced readings. The phrase "the vile enemy of religion", rather than reinforcing a dichotomous distinction between the Islamic and non-Islamic (infidel) worlds, permits the imagination of a shared ontological identity between the English and Ottomans: both the Protestant English and Muslim Ottomans can conceive of the Catholic Habsburgs as "the vile enemy" in religious terms.

38 Fethnames: *not just literary bombast*

The use of the phrases "lords of lewdness" and "enemies of ill-judgment" for the enemy other also implies that the Habsburgs have not become the enemy as a consequence of their religion, as the term *infidel* suggests, but rather as a result of their ill judgment or immorality. This interpretation for the existing enmity between the Habsburgs and Ottomans is reinforced through the explanations given in the *fethname* for the wider Ottoman military campaign in Hungary at this time, which was to "to draw the sword of revenge against the vile enemy of religion" and to ensure "the elimination and eradication of the sedition and wickedness of the enemy".[28] The enemy, the Habsburgs, have acted wickedly, and therefore revenge must be taken; they must be punished. Their actions, not their religion, have motivated the conflict: specifically, they are not being aggressed against because they are Christian. Moreover, this explanation of the conflict is reinforced when the reason for that particular year's action against Nagykanizsa castle is stated: the burning of Osijek bridge and the oppression of Ottoman subjects were apparently the catalysts.

> [T]he brigands from the military castles of Bubofca and Kanije burnt the bridges that were situated on the Buda road and with oppression and the fire of tyranny rendered weak and without strength the *re'aya* and *beraya* and because their removal was mutually deemed a necessary matter and an important undertaking, he deflected the leading rein of departure to that region and he turned the bridle of endeavour to that neighbourhood [for the] conquering and capturing of those aforementioned castles.[29]

This contrasts with the explanations given in other accounts of the sieges. For example, in the *gazavatname* narratives, as well as in Naima's and Namik Kemal's accounts, it is the military implications of the burnt bridge, rather than concern for the local inhabitants, that is of significance for the Ottoman commanders: they are anxious that the destruction of the bridge will make the road unsafe for the returning Ottoman army.[30] In contrast, in this *fethname*, the Ottomans are presented as primarily concerned about the tyrannous actions of the Habsburgs and their oppression of Ottoman subjects.

In terms of articulations of self and other, the use of the phrase *re'aya ve beraya* implies an interesting inclusiveness. Although the primary sense of this phrase is not specifically understood in religious terms, it is an inclusive term generally used to signify 'everyone'; to a Christian, English audience, it may also have had the secondary significance of connoting not only the Muslim subjects of Ottoman Hungary but Christian subjects as well.[31] It therefore could be read as presenting the Ottoman sultan as concerned with *all* his subjects regardless of religion: it is the fight against tyranny and oppression of his population, rather than the fight against infidelity, that concerns him most. This again emphasises the point that the Ottomans are not attacking Christian Europe per se but are instead reacting to an attack upon their lands, not from infidels but from enemies of religion, from the persecutors of Muslims and (Protestant) Christians, the Catholic Habsburgs. The English Protestant audience is being encouraged to read the document, and thus the event, as an example of the Ottoman Empire defending its subjects, including Orthodox and Protestant Christians, against the depredations of their Catholic Habsburg aggressors: something that the queen of England could, to some extent, identify and empathise with.

This all contrasts with the Eger *fethname* sent to the English queen five years earlier. In this *fethname* the *casus belli* for the Ottoman campaign is articulated in the traditional Ottoman, Islamic rhetoric of religious difference and jihad against the unbeliever.

> [A]s his majesty the Lord God commands 'and strive on the path of God' [and] by way of conforming to this great command I have placed before myself *gaza* and jihad materially and spiritually for the sake of Allah by concluding victorious *gazas* and on the auspicious augury this year with prosperity and luck and felicity and awe I was directed against Egri castle.[32]

This difference between the *fethnames* can be explicated, I believe, with reference to the politico-military context against which the conquests occurred and the letters were sent. In 1596, the English, French and Dutch were all at war with the Habsburgs: a situation that benefited the Ottomans as it not only forestalled any chance of a potential pan-European, anti-Ottoman crusade, but it also detracted the Spanish Habsburgs from assisting the Austrian Habsburgs in their war with the Ottomans. It therefore probably did not seem necessary to the Ottomans to significantly alter the standard rhetorical *casus belli* expressed in terms of the Ottoman sultan's duty to fulfil God's command to defend Islam against rival religious ideologies by waging *gaza* and jihad against infidels and heretics. However, by 1601, actualised, or proposed, alliances between the Habsburgs and their Christian European counterparts may have begun to cause the Ottomans some concern.[33] In this context, imaginations of the enemy and explanations of conflict that used the discourse of Christian-Muslim antipathy and the vocabulary of jihad would be imprudent and would not necessarily encourage, or foster, a closer Anglo-Ottoman relationship, something I believe that the grand vizierial *fethname* particularly wanted to achieve. Therefore the Ottomans not only rather judiciously substituted the traditional *casus belli* based upon the rhetoric of jihad with one that foregrounded the defence of all Ottoman subjects against Habsburg tyranny but also reimagined the enemy, still in religious terms but terms which the English could share.

Another textual flourish which indirectly affects presented conceptions of self and other, as well as further fosters cordial relations with the Christian English, are the two references to the *Frenk* soldiers garrisoned in the

Habsburg-held fortress of Pápa who defected to the Ottomans in 1600 and subsequently participated in the capture of Nagykanizsa castle.[34] Two such references in such a brief document not only imply that alliances between Christians and the Ottomans are possible and beneficial, but also reinforce the impression that the Ottomans do not see Christians per se as the enemy. Loyalty to the Ottoman Empire, rather than religion, determines one's status as a friend or foe of the Ottoman Empire.[35]

This concern about a pan-European, anti-Ottoman crusade also explains an interesting omission from the *fethname*. First, although many of the commanders of the relief force are mentioned by name, the commander in chief, Phillipe-Emmanuel of Lorraine, the Duke of Mercoeur, is not.[36] That the Ottomans would not have been aware of his presence is unlikely as Lefaivre notes that the sight of the French commander leading Austrian troops against the Ottomans caused a great shock throughout Europe, and the Ottomans dispatched in March 1601 Barthélemy de Cœur, the envoy who presented, and probably translated, the *fethnames* both to the Venetian doge and Queen Elizabeth I, to the French king to protest about the duke's activities.[37] Stein suggests that this omission was "in order not to reveal Ottoman anxiety about their French allies and, thus, weaken their position vis á vis the English".[38] However, in the earlier *fethname* celebrating the capture of Eger Castle, the Ottomans do not seem concerned about French participation in the Habsburg military forces as they note that the soldiers of "the kings of Austria and Spain and of the pope and of the French duke and of Transylvania and of all the seven kings gathered in the Egri region."[39] Moreover, there were also a number of prominent Englishmen allied with the Habsburg forces fighting against the Ottomans in the conflict.[40]

However, if we read this *fethname* from the perspective of Ottoman concern over a French and potentially English alliance with the Habsburgs, this omission becomes more understandable. While most of Europe was allied against the Habsburgs, it was of no great importance to the Ottomans whether 'renegade' Englishmen or Frenchmen fought alongside the Habsburgs against them in Hungary. However, when these same European countries began concluding treaties with the Habsburgs, not only were they now not engaging the Habsburgs on a second front, but they could potentially ally with them in a crusade against the Ottomans. I will argue that it was this anxiety that prompted the Ottomans to send a second *fethname*, as a diplomatic tool, to try and cement their relationship with the English and to implicitly advise against an alliance with the Habsburgs. Therefore, perhaps the omission of the duke's name in both *fethnames* should be read as an oblique indicator of Ottoman concern rather than as an attempt to disguise it.

The formal tone of the *fethname* is also evidenced in the laudatory remarks that stress the grand vizier's martial and statesman-like qualities. Not only is he "the lion of the day of war and the fearless, courage-inciting lion" and the "commander and chief of so many hundred thousand enemy-hunting soldiers", but he is "the basis of order in the world, the one who manages the affairs of the nations with penetrating thought".[41] This emphasis on his role as a statesman helps to foster the impression of the Ottoman polity as just, dignified and peaceable and to disparage the notion that there is an ideological impetus or desire on their part to be embroiled in perpetual war against Christian states. This idea is stressed again in the following sentence when an oblique reference is made to the attempt to negotiate an Ottoman-Habsburg peace treaty at Esztergom the previous year.

> And last year (7) it was previously revealed and communicated to your ever noble presence in our imperial letter of joyful association how, when we sent [our army] against the soldiers to whom defeat is habitual who stood in ranks opposite Östürgün [Esztergom], the king of reversed circumstances was conquered and broken and routed and crushed by irresistible might and to what degree the towns and cities up to Uivar and (8) as far as Buda and Barağa [Prague] were routed.[42]

There were two attempts at peace made in 1599. The first instigated by the Austrian Habsburgs was conducted at Vác [Vaç/Waitzen] on 11 October 1599 CE / 21 *Rebi'ül-evvel* 1008 H. The second was held at Stúrovo [Ciğerdelen/ Párkány] across the river from Esztergom. The Ottoman army arrived, and the Habsburgs retreated across the river, destroying the bridge. After the failure of the peace negotiations, the Ottoman army and Tatars advanced further north and raided the lands up until Uivar.[43] This reference to peace negotiations does not occur in the grand vizierial *fethname*, nor in any of the *gazavatnames*, and its inclusion here seems designed to aid the Ottoman representation of themselves as a peace-loving, law and treaty-abiding state that does not wish to attack their Christian neighbours but are forced to because of the latter's unreasonableness and aggression.[44]

The desire to present the Ottoman sultan and empire as embodying imperial sovereignty, as powerful yet munificent and just, also explains why the *fethname* mentions the Ottoman capture of some minor fortresses including Bulundvár and Lak, following the siege of Nagykanizsa, but does not record the subsequent execution of the garrison because they were supposedly rebellious.[45] A similar elision occurs in the Eger *fethname*: here the slaughter of the Eger garrison after their surrender at the hands of Ottoman soldiers is not mentioned.[46] Stein suggests that the Ottomans omitted these details as they were keen not to offend the sensibilities of the English by referring to the deaths of their co-religionists.[47] This does not seem very plausible though, considering that the Eger and Nagykanizsa *fethnames* both mention the deaths of thousands of Christian soldiers during both sieges. I argue instead that the omission is best explained in terms of the discourse of the *fethname*; a munificent and just sultan probably does not order or condone the mass killing of the enemy regardless of the circumstances, and so this information is conveniently omitted from the *fethnames*.

The precepts of formal interstate communication as exemplified in the genre of *fethnames*, also explains a discrepancy in the two accounts of the siege by Ottoman historian Hasan Beyzade. In the Nagykanizsa *fethname* he describes the occupants of the besieged castle stubbornly holding out for a few more days following the defeat of the Habsburg relief force before eventually surrendering just before the fortress was about to be taken. However in his history written sometime later, he notes that the occupants of the castle requested quarter as soon as they realised that the relief force had fled.[48] Which of these accounts represents the truth? This is an impossible question to answer. Even if we ask not which account corresponds most accurately to reality but instead which coheres most closely with the other available evidence – with other extant texts – we are no closer to a solution. İbrahim Peçevi, and Abdülkadir Topçularkatibi, both eyewitnesses to events, disagree in their accounts concerning the surrender of the garrison. Peçevi writes that the occupants of the castle requested quarter as soon as they realised that the relief force had fled, but Topçularkatibi claims they held out for a few more days.[49] I suggest that the discrepancy between Hasan Beyzade's narratives can best be explained most usefully in terms of the function of the two texts. The *fethname* has a more propagandistic role, and thus it would be more suitable in this narrative to exaggerate the fortitude of the defenders to further eulogise the achievements of the Ottomans.

The sultanic *fethname* concludes with a reference to the "loving affection and agreement and love and sincere friendship" held by the English towards the Ottomans. It then commands that the English should "be fearful . . . [and] cause this felicitous conquest, this prosperity filled conquest, to be known and believed by the people in your provinces and our other friends" so that it will be "the cause of their gladness, rejoicing, cheerfulness and happiness".[50] Such language and sentiment provides further evidence that one of the key functions of *fethnames* sent to foreign rulers was to fulfil official and imperial protocol *and* glorify the Ottoman Empire.

The grand vizierial *fethname*

I now want to turn to the grand vizierial *fethname*: why was it sent? Why were two virtually identical missives dispatched to celebrate the successful capture of Nagykanzisa castle? Furthermore, what explains the few textual differences between both documents? I argue that these questions can best be answered if the grand vizierial *fethname* is read as having a diplomatic and mediatory, rather than a predominantly propagandistic, function. Suraiya Faroqhi has noted that in the Venetian archives, sultanic rescripts are often found accompanied by letters written in the grand vizier's name. She argues that these more informal letters evidence a distinct difference in tone and allow a glimpse of the negotiating and political bargaining process between the Ottoman state and foreign governments.[51] I suggest therefore that the two Nagykanizsa *fethnames* operated in a similar manner: although superficially they are textually identical, they were framed differently, created distinct expectations in their audiences and were read as having separate intentions. The grand vizierial *fethname*, in contrast to the sultanic *fethname*, was not addressed to a sovereign in his or her official or ceremonial capacity but was addressed to an audience imagined in more friendly terms, as a peer, someone with whom to negotiate and correspond. Similarly, its function was not as an iconograph of power but as a tool of diplomacy.

This, however, begs the question as to why it was necessary to co-opt the grand vizierial *fethname* as a tool of diplomacy and why the grand vizier could not just write directly to the English queen and court. *Telhis* correspondence between the grand vizier and sultan suggests that there were specific protocols involved in interstate correspondence.[52] *Telhis* no.86 implies that despite the Ottoman desire for information concerning the new king of England, James I (1603–1625), and their concern as to the status of the country and whether it had been invaded by the Spanish Habsburgs, they were deliberately waiting for the new English king to formally request shelter and offer his service to the threshold of felicity.[53] This determination not to commence any new communication until the protocols of accession had been adhered to resulted in the Ottomans refusing to send a new 'trade' document to the English king and the dispatch of a copy of the old one written previously to Queen Elizabeth I instead. Communicating at an official level outside the boundaries established by protocol may have been interpreted as signalling weakness. The capture of a castle such as Nagykanizsa however, would provide a suitable opportunity to correspond with the English queen, and consequently the *fethname* is appropriated by the grand vizier to a diplomatic function as it provides an ideal opportunity to raise shared concerns in an indirect manner and to reconfirm English opposition to the Habsburgs. The grand vizierial *fethname* can therefore, most heuristically, be interpreted if read against a frame of European peace movements and shifts in alliances which were of concern to both the Ottomans and the English.[54]

The first section of the grand vizierial *fethname* consists of the customary *salutatio* and is identical to that in the sultanic *fethname*. The *narratio* of this text is best considered as two distinct sections: the first references an earlier English victory, whereas the second details the Ottoman victory at Nagykanizsa. This latter section is, with only a few differences, the same text as the *narratio* in the sultanic *fethname*. The letter then concludes in a friendly manner and wishes for continued correspondence. The fact that the *fethname* is addressed from the grand vizier, the physical appearance of the document, and the friendly introduction to the *narratio* conditions the audience's horizon of expectations and indicates that the primary function of the text is not as an iconograph of imperial power.[55] The whole tone of the document is more informal and presupposes a different relationship between implied audience and author: one of greater intimacy and cordiality, which also alters the expectations of the audience with regard to what will follow.

There are a number of points of interest in the first section of the *narratio*. First there is an extended section in which the English ambassador is eulogised and described as "the model of the leaders of the Christian nation" and as a "faithful friend and well-wisher of all of our affairs" who "sends letters in a friendly manner to this region" which are "full of fidelity and loyalty", thereby foregrounding the cordial and personal relationship between the two countries.[56] This ongoing recursive diplomatic communication and correspondence between the English and the Ottomans is reinforced by a further reference to letters that "continually come to one from your region" and works to articulate ideologies of commensurability that envisage both states as possessing similar political systems as well as shared diplomatic practices and goals.[57]

Secondly the *fethname* mentions that the English ambassador has informed the *Porte* that the queen's "famous commander set about fighting and battling face to face in the province of Flanders with the accursed Archduke Alberte who is the brother of the perverted king" and that "the brother of the perverted king was crushed by irresistible might and routed and the commander was made victorious and successful."[58] The "perverted king" referred to is the Habsburg Emperor Rudolf II and the battle that of Nieuwpoort [Nieuport] in Flanders on 2 July 1600, where a mixed army of Dutch, Germans, Scots, English and others fought and defeated the archduke and Spanish Habsburgs. This reference seems a little surprising at first glance because the English and Dutch army was caught by surprise and forced into battle, and the resultant victory was considered a barren one by many contemporaries who invoked divine favour as the only explanation for what, given the commander's blunders, should have been a defeat. Indeed it is often thought to have dramatically illustrated to the English and Dutch the extent of Spanish control over the Flanders coast and the difficulty in removing them.[59] Moreover, the combined army was in fact commanded by Prince Maurice of Nassau and not by Sir Francis Vere, who was actually only commander of the rear guard.

The reference to this English victory in the grand vizierial *fethname* and not in the sultanic *fethname* can be explained if the two documents are understood as serving different functions and essentially being directed at two distinct audiences. Praising another country's victory, even if that country is an ally, is not appropriate to the discourse of an official *fethname* where the emphasis is on promoting the greatness of the Ottoman Empire. On the other hand, the grand vizierial *fethname* is written within a more mediatory frame and in this more personal discourse mention of the battle serves a number of functions. It demonstrates Ottoman awareness of current English affairs and a concern for English matters and victories, all of which helps to foster a friendly tone.

Mention of this battle has a more specific function though: it works to further develop the construction of shared imaginations of otherness by foregrounding a key similarity between the Ottomans and English: they are

Fethnames: *not just literary bombast* 45

both fighting the Habsburgs and have both been victorious against them. This then implicitly foregrounds the commonality between the English and the Ottomans and indirectly emphasises the Ottoman-English alliance against the Habsburgs. The suggestion, ever present in this *fethname*, that the English should continue to fight the Habsburgs, is re-stressed in the subsequent exhortation: "let it not cease from being that you are always victorious and dominant over your enemies and those who are from your opposing side are inverted in this manner."⁶⁰ However, mention of this battle does not only bring to mind an English-Ottoman alliance, it also evokes and reminds the audience of the futility and inappropriateness of an English-Habsburg alliance because the battle at Nieuwpoort coincided with Habsburg-English peace negotiations at Boulogne, which subsequently faltered and came to nothing. Lastly, by exaggerating and emphasising the rather pyrrhic English-Dutch victory, the Ottomans may be trying to persuade Queen Elizabeth I that the Spanish Habsburgs can still be defeated in Flanders and that they should not abandon the fight and agree to an alliance with them.

The few differences between the *narratio* section of the grand vizierial and sultanic *fethnames* can also be explicated as a result of their different functions and intended audience. First, there is no reference to the attempted peace negotiations at Esztergom the previous year in the grand vizierial *fethname*. Reading the *fethname* against a background of concern over the French-Habsburg alliance and as having a function of strengthening Ottoman-English ties at the expense of a possible Habsburg-English alliance, the omission of reference to Ottoman-Habsburg peace negotiations makes sense. The Ottomans could hardly expect the English to refrain from concluding a peace treaty with the Habsburgs while they themselves were attempting to negotiate such an accord. Obviously, the English audience would be aware of Ottoman peace overtures if not from other sources then at least from the sultanic *fethname*. However, what I want to emphasise here is that although there is benefit in positively drawing attention to it within the framework of the sultanic *fethname*, within the diplomatic frame of the grand vizierial *fethname*, such an allusion would not be meaningful or pertinent and thus is erased.

The second section of the *narratio* of both *fethnames* is virtually identical. The main divergence between the two accounts occurs when describing how the lives of the people from Nagykanizsa castle and their belongings were spared. In the sultanic, but not the grand vizierial, *fethname* it is specifically mentioned that the sultan granted them freedom, thus emphasising his personal munificence.⁶¹ The next difference occurs with regard to the second mention of the *Frenk* soldiers from Pápa. The sultanic *fethname* has "the *beylerbeyis* of Rumeli and Bosnia with the *Frenk* soldiers who had come from Pápa, conquered the castle of Lak and Bulundvar", but the grand vizierial *fethname* has, "the *Frenk* soldiers who had come from Pápa, conquered the castle of Lak and Bulundvar with the *beylerbeyis* of Rumeli and

Bosnia".[62] I find it hard to believe that the scribe who managed to copy this entire section verbatim should fail to do so here unless it was deliberate. Perhaps this can be explained again in terms of the two different functions of the *fethname*: the sultanic *fethname* was intended to promote the official glory of the state and therefore would be expected to emphasise the activities of its officials, whereas the grand vizierial *fethname* aimed to foreground examples of European cooperation and alliance with the Ottomans and therefore cites the *Frenks* from Pápa first.

The grand vizierial *fethname*, in contrast to the sultanic *fethname*, concludes in a friendly manner with references to the enduring, long-term friendship between the countries and monarchs.

> From the old days until this present moment as a consequence of your faithfulness to the threshold of the sublime [the sultan's court] whose mark is felicity, and of your well wishing [to] this region and your long friendliness and loving affection, the events of this side, at length, have been communicated to the side of your noble self.[63]

This phrase marks in the text, or makes explicit, the real reason for the communication: the Ottomans have confided, albeit implicitly, their fears and hopes to the English about a potential English-Habsburg alliance precisely because of the longevity and closeness of their relationship. That the Ottoman state is requesting or hoping that the English continue to fight the Habsburgs or at least refrain from concluding alliances with them is further reinforced by references to various congruities between the English and the Ottomans: their simultaneous victories over the Habsburgs, their common friends and enemies –

> both on your side and in our region, honour like this has occurred. Always may our enemies not be free from being conquered and broken in this manner and our friends not be lacking victory and triumph[64]

– and by their wish that the English will "not cease from giving your enemies continually a reprimand in this manner".[65] A reading of the two Nagykanizsa *fethnames* as either neutral repositories of documentary fact by virtue of being official state documents inscribed by an eyewitness to events or unhistorical examples of Ottoman literature or propaganda misunderstands one of the key functions that these texts had. I argue that they can perhaps be more profitably read as embodying both imperial ceremonies of legitimation and as instances of non-ambassadorial diplomatic mediation.

Notes

1 The term *fethname* was, and still is, commonly used to describe two different genres or categories of written text. The first describes literary works which celebrate Ottoman victories in general terms, and examples can be found in A. S.

Fethnames: *not just literary bombast* 47

Levend, *Gazavat-nameler ve Mihaloğlu Ali Bey'in Gazavat-namesi* (Ankara: Türk Tarih Kurumu Yayınlarından / XI. Seri, No. 8, Türk Tarih Kurumu Basımevi, 1956). Such literary *fethnames*, often written months or years after the campaign, tend to focus on the narration of a single victorious campaign or battle and often eulogise the Ottoman sultan or commander. Christine Woodhead, "Ottoman Historiography on the Hungarian Campaigns: 1596 The Eger Fethnamesi," in *VII. CIÉPO Sempozyumu [Proceedings of the VIIth Conference of the Comité des Études Ottomanes et Pré-Ottomanes (CIÉPO), at Pécs, Hungary, 1986]*, ed. J. L. Bacqué-Grammont, İ. Ortaylı and E. van Donzel (Ankara: Türk Tarih Kurumu Basımevi, 1994), 469–477, discusses one such example – that of Ta'likizade's *Eger Fethnamesi*. Murat Cem Mengüç, "A Study of 15th Century Ottoman Historiography," (PhD diss., Cambridge University, 2007), 27–30, discusses this genre of literary *fethnames* in a fifteenth-century context. He comments that while such works may have had their origins in the earlier tradition of *gazavat-names*, by the fifteenth century they constituted a linguistically more ornate and religiously-orientated genre and probably were solely for palace consumption and not aimed at a more popular audience as they are extant only in single copies. The second type of *fethname* is perhaps best described as a victory letter and is the focus of this chapter. Christine M. Woodhead, "Fetihnāme," in *Encyclopeadia of Islam, THREE*, ed. Kate Fleet, Gudrun Krämer, Denis Matringe, John Nawas and Everett Rowson (Leiden: Brill Online. 2014), available online http://dx.doi.org/10.1163/1573-3912_ei3_COM_27035 (accessed 22/7/16), offers a useful overview of the genres.

2 Hasan Beyzade, *Telhis-i Tacü't-tevarih*, fol.468a. According to I. H. Mordtmann, and V. L. Ménage, "Hasan Bey-zade," in *The Encyclopaedia of Islam*, ed. Peri J. Bearman, Th. Bianquis, C. E. Bosworth, E. van Donzel and W. P. Heinrichs, 2nd ed., vol. 3 (Leiden: Brill, 1971), there are five extant Nagykanisa *fethnames* written by Hasan Beyzade. Three of these are described as being in a *mecmu'a* [compendium of writings] previously in the possession of Cavid Baysun, but I have been unable to locate them. The remaining two are located in the National Archives, London. The *fethname* in the name of the grand vizier is London: National Archives, SP.102/61 fols 87–88 and that in the name of the sultan is London: National Archives, SP.102/4 21. These will from now on be referred to in the main text as the grand vizieral *fethname* and sultanic *fethname*, respectively; citations will be abbreviated to NA: SP.102/61 and NA: SP.102/4.

3 The first few lines of the Eger *fethname* in Mustafa Efendi Selaniki, *Tarih-i Selaniki*, ed. M. İpşirli, vol. 2 (Istanbul: İstanbul Üniversitesi Edebiyat Fakültesi yayınları, 1989), 643–644, and the version of the Eger *fethname* in the *inşa* collection in Berlin: Staatsbibliothek Preußischer Kulturbesitz, ms.or.fol.3332 fol.187b iterate the sultan's command to ensure the document is read aloud and news of the victory made public. See also Suraiya Faroqhi, "Ottoman Victory Celebrations," unpublished manuscript. I thank the author for kindly sending me a copy of this article.

4 To date I have established that there are three extant *fethnames* which were sent to Queen Elizabeth I of England: two celebrating the capture of Nagykanizsa in the name of the sultan and the grand vizier, respectively, see n.2, and one celebrating the capture of Eger, London: National Archives, SP 102/4 11. Maria Pia Pedani, "Ottoman *Fetihnames*: The Imperial Letters Announcing a Victory," *Tarih Incelemeleri Dergisi* 13 (1998), notes in an extremely useful article that in the Venetian State Archives she has located six extant copies of Ottoman-language *fethnames* and two Greek *fethnames* sent to the doge as well as Italian translations of seven others. Of the Ottoman-language *fethnames*, one celebrates the capture of Eger, Venice: State Archive, Lettere e sciture turchesche. f. 5, cc. 187; one celebrates Süleyman's capture of Tabriz, Venice: State Archive,

Documenti turchi n.640; three celebrate victories in Hungary in 1541 and 1543 (two victories), Venice: State Archive, Documenti turchi nos. 463, 507, and 509; and one an earlier victory in Persia, Venice: State Archive, Documenti turchi n.342. See also the archival catalogue compiled by Maria Pia Pedani Fabris, ed., *I 'Documenti turchi' dell'Archivio di Stato di Venezia* (Roma: Instituto Poligrafico e Zecca dello Stato, 1994). Of the thirty-eight works in Levent, *Gazavat-nameler* with the title of *fethname*; only three could possibly be considered examples of official victory-letter style *fethnames*: Kazasker Raşid, *Fetih-name-i Cezire-i Mora* [*The Victory Letter of the Island of Mora*], described as a *fethname* which was sent by the sultan; a *fethname* sent by Prince Selim (later Selim II) to his father, Kanunî Süleyman, after the battle of Konya Meydan; and the *Fetih-name-i Kara Boğdan* [*The Victory Letter of Kara Boğdan*], which is described by Levend as being located in a collection of letters, 137, 51 and 173, respectively. Geoffrey L. Lewis, "Fathname," in *The Encyclopaedia of Islam*, ed. P. J. Bearman, T. Bianquis, C. E. Bosworth, E van Donzel and W. P. Heinrichs, 2nd ed., vol. 2 (Leiden: Brill, 1971), 839, mentions a Uygur-language *fethname*; Caesar Farah, "Announcing an Ottoman Victory in Hungary to a Yemeni Amir," in *A Miscellany of Middle Eastern articles: In Memoriam Thomas Muir Johnstone 1924–1983*, ed. A. K. Irvine, R. B. Sergeant and G. R. Smith (Harlow: Longman, 1988), discusses and provides an English translation of an Arabic translation of an Ottoman-Turkish *fethname* sent to the Ottoman governor of Kawkaban, Emir Ahmad b. Muhammad Shams al-Din, celebrating the capture of Eger castle. The Arabic translation can be located in an anthology described in the article notes as: Entry History 1576 in *Fihrist Makhtutat al-Jamiʿ al-Kabir*, ed. Ahmad ʿAbd al-Razzaq, ʿAbdallah M. al-Hibshi, and ʿAli Wahhab al-Anisi (Sanaʿa: Ministry of Awqaf, 1984); the Ottoman Turkish original is not known to be extant. Re-inscriptions or versions of *fethnames* purportedly sent to foreign rulers and Ottoman governors can be found in various Ottoman histories and in collections of *inşa* works. However, these cannot uncritically be accepted as identical to actual *fethnames* sent to rulers and governors.
5 Woodhead, "Ottoman Historiography," 469; Jan Schmidt, "The Egri-Campaign of 1596: Military History and the Problem of Sources," in *Habsburgisch-osmanische Beziehungen – Relations habsbourg-ottomanes Wien, 26.-30. September 1983: Colloque sous le patronage du Comité international des études pre-ottomanes et ottomans*, ed. Andreas Tietze (Wien: Wiener Zeitschrift für die Kunde des Morgenlandes. Beiheft 13, 1985), 129.
6 Schmidt, "The Egri-Campaign of 1596," 140, n.15; and Bernard Lewis, *Istanbul and the Civilisation of the Ottoman Empire* (Oklahoma: Norman, Centers of Civilization series 9, 1963), 166.
7 Geoffrey L. Lewis "The Utility of Ottoman Fethnames," in *Historians of the Middle East*, ed. Bernard Lewis and Peter Malcolm Holt (London: Oxford University Press, 1962), 196, argues that one cannot seek in *fethnames* "accurate reports of events"; instead they provide "clues to the *persona* of the Ottoman Empire [...] and a picture of how the Empire wanted to be regarded by its friends and enemies".
8 Ibid., 192 and 196; Schmidt, "The Egri-Campaign of 1596," 129.
9 Schmidt, "The Egri-Campaign of 1596," 130. This is not to say that we cannot and do not distinguish fact from fiction, the real from the imagined, but when we do it is on the basis of genre-specific criteria that arise from particular socio-cultural contexts and not any immanent characteristics to which particular texts correspond. See Claire Norton and Mark Donnelly, "The Siege, the Book and the Film: *Welcome to Sarajevo* (1997)," in *The Fiction of History*, ed. A. L. MacFie (London: Routledge, 2014), for a more detailed discussion of the fact/fiction distinction in the context of both historical discourse and film.

10 To date, no systematic study of the various audiences and functions of *fethnames*, and the possible use they may have for historians, has been undertaken. No real attention has been paid to what the Ottoman state hoped to achieve by sending these documents to their various recipients or the motivation behind the re-inscription of the 'same' *fethname* in multiple, different textual contexts. J. M. Stein, "A Letter to Queen Elizabeth I from the Grand Vezir as a Source for the Study of Ottoman Diplomacy," *Archivum Ottomanicum* 11 (1986): 234, analyses the grand vizierial *fethname* NA: SP.102/61 fols.87–88 in terms of its potential diplomatic function, arguing that it is "an instrument in the Ottoman effort to establish a friendship of alliance with England" and was "principally [. . .] intended to serve the ends of Ottoman diplomacy", but he does not consider it to be a *fethname*, unlike Mordtmann and Ménage "Hasan Bey-zade" and myself. This raises the problem of what constitutes the genre of Ottoman letter-type *fethname*s. I would argue that because it was written at the same place and time as the sultanic *fethname* and because it not only resembles the *fethname* in form and content but in many places is identical to it, it can, most usefully, be considered to be an example of a letter-type *fethname*. It is possible that Stein declined from classifying it as a *fethname* because of the commonly associated expectations of a *fethname* document: that it is a literary piece of laudatory propaganda. I agree with Stein that the function of this document is diplomatic but suggest that rather than reclassify the document as a letter, we should instead reformulate and broaden our conception of the genre and function of *fethname* to include diplomatic uses among others. Woodhead "Fetihnāme," notes that *fethnames* could have diplomatic as well as propagandistic functions. Although the main focus of Woodhead, "Ottoman Historiography," is an examination of a literary *fethname* of the siege, she does, in an introduction to her article, briefly discuss some of the differences between the Eger *fethnames* sent to Queen Elizabeth and that sent to the Yemeni Emir, Ahmad b. Muhammad Shams al-Din. She also acknowledges that such documents "should not be considered as mere inaccurate rhetoric, but that they can express otherwise unwritten attitudes and calculations" 470–471, but she does not explore what these might be. In Claire Norton, "'Lords of Lewdness': Imagining the Infidel 'Other' in Ottoman *Fethnames*," in *Osmanischer Orient und Ostmitteleuropa*, ed. Robert Born and Andreas Puth (Stuttgart: Steiner Verlag, 2014), I explore in more detail the interpretative significance of the differences between the various extant Eger *fethnames* in the context of a wider discussion of Ottoman imaginations of self and other in a diplomatic context.

11 See Schmidt, "The Egri-Campaign of 1596," 132 and 137; Mustafa Efendi Selaniki, *Tarih-i Selânîki*, ed. M. İpşirli (Istanbul: Edebiyat Fakültesi Basımevi, 1989). The literary style of *fethname* was also used, at times, to justify the actions of statesmen and to establish an official, or agreed-upon version of events; see Murat Cem Menguc, "Safai, the Poet, the Sheikh and the Collector of Memories," a paper given at the MESA conference, Montreal, 2007. I thank the author for allowing me to read a copy of the paper.

12 For more on the diplomatic function of *fethnames*, see Claire Norton "Iconographs of Power or Tools of Diplomacy? Ottoman *Fethnames*," *Journal of Early Modern History* 20/4 (2016).

13 Schmidt, "The Egri-Campaign of 1596," 141, n.20.

14 Schmidt, "The Egri-Campaign of 1596," compares versions of the Eger *Fethname* in the following works: Selaniki, *Tarih-i Selânîki*, Istanbul: Topakı Sarayı Müzesi, ms. Revan 1137, fol.313a; Feridun Bey, *Mejmu'a-i munşe'at al-selatin* [*The Collection of the Sultans' Writings*], vol. 2 (Istanbul: Takvimhane-yi Amire, 1265–1274/1848–1858)), 100–101, and the *inşa* collections, Leiden: Leiden University Library, ms.cod.1090 fols 50b–52a and Berlin: Staatsbibliothet Preussischer Kulturbesitz ms.or.fol.3332 fols 187b–189a.

15 Lewis, "Fathname," 840. When Lewis describes some of the *fethnames* as literary exercises, he is still referring to the genre of *fethname* defined as an official document or letter and not the first category of literary works; see n.1. As Lewis used collections of *fethnames* in *inşa* works, by original *fethname* he may have meant a *fethname* that was actually sent to a foreign ruler or Ottoman governor.
16 Ibid., 839.
17 See John Dagenais, "That Bothersome Residue: Toward a Theory of the Physical Text," in *Vox Intexta: Orality and Textuality in the Middle Ages*, ed. A. N. Doane and C. Braun Pasternack (Madison: The University of Wisconsin Press, 1991), 246–259, for the problems that this can create and especially 249 for the idea of a Derridean lost "presence".
18 Two *fethnames* celebrating the capture of Nagykanizsa were also sent to the doge of Venice, one in the name of the grand vizier and the other in the name of the sultan. Lajos Fekete, "A velencei állami levéltár magyar vonatkozású fethnāméi," *Levéltari közlemények* 4 (1926): 154–157; see also Pedani, "Ottoman Fetihnames," 185, for a reference to these two *fethnames*. Unfortunately, from the beginning of the 1950s, these two *fethnames* cannot be found in the Venetian archives (I thank Dr Pedani for providing me with this information in a personal email dated 25/02/08). However, Fekete provides a summary in Hungarian of the sultanic *fethname* and from a brief consideration of an Italian translation of Fekete's summary, kindly provided by Dr Pedani, the *fethname* presented to the doge seems remarkably similar to that given to Queen Elizabeth, and it might not therefore be unreasonable to assume that two *fethnames* were sent to Venice for the same reason as two were sent to England.
19 The phrase is adapted from one used by Gülrü Necipoğlu, "Süleyman the Magnificent and the Representation of Power in the Context of Ottoman-Habsburg-Papal Rivalry," in *Süleyman the Second and His Time*, ed. Halil İnalcık and Cemal Kafadar (Istanbul: Isis Press, 1993), 170. In this article she argues that particular items commissioned by the Ottomans and ceremonies performed by them were intended to demonstrate, to western European states, Ottoman claims to be a world empire and the legitimate heirs of the Holy Roman Empire. Sultanic *fethnames* sent to foreign rulers partook of a similar discourse and were intended to demonstrate Ottoman legitimacy and imperial standing.
20 Ralph Hanna, "Producing Manuscripts and Editions," in *Crux and Controversy in Middle English Textual Criticism*, ed. A. J. Minnis and Charlotte Brewer (Cambridge: D. S. Brewer, 1992), 129. Medieval scholars have for many years explored how the presentation of a text affects its reception.
21 NA: SP.102/4 21 line 1.
22 Ibid., lines 8–11.
23 This is probably a reference to Barthélemy de Cœur, who was one of Mehmed III's doctors. Albert Lefaivre, *Les Magyars pendant la domination ottomane en Hongrie: 1526–1722*, vol. 1 (Paris: Perrin Et Cie, 1902), 255, and n.2 notes that he was a 'renegade' Frenchman who was sent by the sultan to the French king in March 1601 to protest about the duke of Mercoeur commanding the Habsburg army against the Ottomans. The date of his travel to Europe and the similarity of the names suggest that it was he who also delivered the *fethnames* to Queen Elizabeth I. A letter from the English ambassador at Constantinople, Lello, dated January 1601 (NA: SP. 97/4 fol.155a) also notes the dispatch by the Ottomans of a doctor to Venice and France. The doctor is referred to as "d.hert" – an Anglicised version of de Coeur perhaps? It is reasonable to speculate that he delivered the *fethnames* commemorating the capture of Nagykanizsa to the Venetian doge as well.
24 Lewis, *Istanbul*, 166.
25 NA: SP.102/4 21 lines 13, 18 and 22.

Fethnames: *not just literary bombast* 51

26 Ibid., lines 4, 7, 12 and 30, 22, 24 and 3, respectively.
27 Naima, *Tarih-i Naima*; Katib Çelebi, *Fezleke*; İbrahim Peçevi, *Tarih-i Peçevi*; Topçularkatibi, *Tevarih*; and Hasan Beyzade, *Telhis-i Tacü't-tevarih*; Farah, "Announcing an Ottoman Victory in Hungary to a Yemeni Amir."
28 NA: SP.102/4 21 lines 3–4.
29 Ibid., lines 9–11. See what follows for a discussion of the meaning of *re'aya* and *beraya* in the context of this *fethname*.
30 See for example any of the *gazavatnames* in the *Gazavat-i Tiryaki Hasan Pasa* corpus, i.e., Istanbul: Millet Kütüphanesi, A.E.Tar.187 fol.3a (henceforth IMK: A.E.Tar.187); Naima, *Tarih-i Naima*, 236; and Namık Kemal, *Kanije* (Istanbul: Matbaa-i Ebüzziya, 1311/1893–1894), 14–15.
31 *Re'aya* is often translated as 'peasant' or 'subjects of the Ottoman Empire who are not part of the ruling elite' and *beraya* as 'free citizens', but Virginia Aksan, "Military Reform and Its Limits in a Shrinking Ottoman World, 1800–1840," in *The Early Modern Ottomans: Remapping the Empire*, ed. Virginia Aksan and Daniel Goffman (Cambridge: Cambridge University Press, 2007), 122, includes a quote by Mahmud II originally cited in Viorel Panaite, "The *Re'ayas* of the Tributary-Protected Principalities: The Sixteenth through the Eighteenth Centuries," *International Journal of Turkish Studies* 9 (2003), in which Mahmud II argues that it is his wish "to ensure the peace and security of all inhabitants of our God-protected great states, *both Muslim and raya*" [emphasis mine]. The implication here is that *raya* (or *re'aya*), in this context, signifies non-Muslim subjects of the Ottoman Empire. Franz Babinger, *Mehmed the Conqueror and His Time* (Princeton: Princeton University Press, 1978), 412, refers to non-Muslim Ottoman subjects as *re'aya*. A similar use of *re'aya* can be seen in the Serbian folk song, "*Pocetak bune protiv dahija*," cited in Milne Holton and Vasa Mihailovich, eds, *Songs of the Serbian People* (Pittsburgh: University of Pittsburgh Press, 1997). Here the *raja* (the non-Muslims) are juxtaposed against the *Turci* (Muslims); I thank Alex Drace-Francis for this reference. The term *re'aya* is also used in a similar manner in a variety of Ottoman state documents concerning Cyprus from the late eighteenth and early nineteenth centuries: in another official rescript by Mahmud II, there is the phrase *müslim ve re'aya* (Istanbul: Başbakanlık Osmanlı Arşivi: Hatt-i Hümayun, HAT.25303, dated 1226H); in a summary of a *takrir* sent by the Kapudan Pasha to the Porte, the entire inhabitants of Cyprus are referred to as *ahali-i cezirede* [the people of the island], but on occasion we have *ehl-i islam ve re'aya* [the people of Islam and the *re'aya*], where presumably *re'aya* signifies the non-Muslim population (Istanbul: Başbakanlık Osmanlı Arşivi: Cevdet Maliye, C.ML.3801 dated 1231H); and in a *defter* [register of taxes] there is *ehl-i Islam ve ehl-i zimmet re'ayalar* (Istanbul: Başbakanlık Osmanlı Arşivi: Cevdet Maliye, C.ML.6251 dated 1204H). I kindly thank Antonis Hadjikyriacou for bringing these documents and their use of the term *re'aya* to my attention. I argue that in a similar manner *beraya* could be read here as referring to Muslim and *re'aya* to non-Muslim Ottoman subjects.
32 NA: SP.102/4 11 lines 2–3.
33 The Spanish had negotiated a peace treaty with the French in May 1598. The French had pressed for the English and Dutch to be included in their peace treaty, but when the inclusion of the Dutch was ruled out, Queen Elizabeth I had refused to negotiate. Overtures for a negotiation between the Habsburgs and English were put forward by the Brussels government in 1598 but were postponed until late summer 1599. Meanwhile hostilities were not suspended. In January Queen Elizabeth I sent an English emissary to discuss a possible venue for a meeting, and negotiations began again at the end of February 1600, although the main conference did not happen until the summer, when the Flemmish envoy suggested a defensive and offensive pact be agreed between the English queen and Habsburg

52   Fethnames: *not just literary bombast*

archduke. Negotiations faltered and came to nothing. See W. MacCaffrey, *Elizabeth I: War and Politics 1588–1603* (Princeton, NJ: Princeton University Press, 1992).

34   NA: SP.102/4 21 lines 21: "The next day again they fought in like manner and the *Frenk* soldiers who had left Pápa castle and who were with the soldiers in the trenches shared in the happiness" and 36: "Besides this, the *beylerbeyis* of Rumeli and Bosnia with the *Frenk* soldiers who had come from Pápa, conquered the castle of Lak and Bulundvar. . . ." For more on the *Frenk* soldiers from Pápa who deserted see Caroline Finkel, "French Mercenaries in the Habsburg-Ottoman War of 1583–1606: The Desertion of the Papa Garrison to the Ottomans in 1600," *Bulletin of the School of Oriental and African Studies* 55/3 (1992): 465–468.

35   The Hungarian translation of the sultanic *fethname* sent to the doge of Venice also includes a reference to the *Frenk* soldiers in Pápa, see Fekete, "A velencei." We can only speculate, but presumably the *fethnames* sent to Venice were also reinscribed with the aim of subtly reimagining identities of self and other to foster good relations with the Venetians.

36   Those mentioned by name include: Zirinoğlu, Banatı, Nadajdi, General and Kara Hersek. Stein, "A Letter," 237, describes Banatı as Batthányi and Nadajdi as Ferenc II Nádasy (1555–1604), who served as Royal Master of the Horse, Lord Lieutenant of the country of Vasvár and member of the imperial delegation to the abortive peace negotiations in 1599. He translates *Kara Hersek* as 'unlucky dukes' but also offers another reading of it as '*kıra hersek*' or 'royal dukes from the Hungarian Királyı Herceg'. For Zirinoğlu see Chapter 3. I have been unable to locate a specific referent for the individual named as General Philipp Emanuel. The duke of Mercoeur was called in the autumn of 1600 from the Low Countries to take over the high command of the imperial troops; see Franz Pichler, "Captain John Smith in the Light of the Styrian Sources," *The Virginia Magazine of History and Biography* 65 (1957): 351. Lefaivre, *Les Magyars*, 254, also mentions his arrival in Vienna in 1600, whereas Finkel, "French Mercenaries," 453, gives the date of arrival as 1599. The duke of Mercoeur could not really be considered as a loyal French subject nor as under the control of the French king and state. For many years he had been an ally of the Habsburgs and had set himself up in Brittany as a "local satrap under Spanish auspices" as part of the Spanish Habsburg strategy to assail Henry IV by encouraging regional magnates to assert their autonomy against his central authority, MacCaffrey, *Elizabeth I*, 253. For a detailed discussion of the duke of Mercoeur's engagement in the imperial army against the Ottomans from 1599 to 1602, see Marco Penzi, "From 'Frenchman' to Crusader: The Political and Military Itinerary of Philippe Emmanuel Duke of Mercoeur (1558–1602)," in *Türkenkriege und Adelskultur in Ostmitteleuropa vom 16. bis zum 18. Jahrundert*, ed. Robert Born and Sabine Jagodzinski (Ostfildern: Jan Thorbecke Verlag, 2014).

37   Lefaivre, *Les Magyars*, 255.

38   Stein, "A Letter," 235. Lefaivre, *Les Magyars*, 255–256, offers an alternative explanation of Ottoman concern at the duke's behaviour. Quoting from the *Extrait des mémoires, journaux de Pierre L'Estoile – Mars 1601*, he reports an alleged conversation between the sultan's emissary Barthélemy and the French king during which Barthélemy states that the pashas fear that with the duke fighting against the Turks, he might fulfil a prophecy that the sword of a Frenchman will chase the Turks from Europe and reverse their empire. Penzi, "From 'Frenchman' to Crusader," 163, notes that this prophecy can be found on pages 7–8 in the 1958 edited edition of L'Estoile's journal: Pierre de L'Estoile, *Journal de L'Estoile pour le règne de Henri IV (1589–1600)*, ed. André Martin, vol. 2 (1601–1609) (Paris: Gallimard, 1958).

Fethnames: *not just literary bombast* 53

39 NA: SP.102/4 11 line 16. The referent for this French duke may have been Baron de Bonparc. Théodore de Gontaut-Biron, *Ambassade en Turquie de Jean de Gontaut Biron, Baron de Salignac 1605 a 1610 correspondance diplomatique & documents inédits* (Paris: Honorè Champion, 1888), notes that the baron recruited the Frenchmen in Pápa in 1597, when the Habsburg emperor asked him to send troops to aid him against the Ottomans. He may have erroneously dated his arrival to 1597 after the siege of Eger – also cited in Finkel, "French Mercenaries," 453.
40 Captain John Smith participated in a number of battles during this war. Most notably he participated in the relief of Fort Olumpagh, which was besieged by the Ottomans shortly after their capture of Nagykanizsa. He claims that he contributed to the success of the Habsburgs with his use of torch telegraphy and a fake attack using pyrotechnics. He was subsequently honoured and made captain over two hundred and fifty cavalry and proceeded to the Habsburg siege of Székesfehérvár in 1601 under the command of the duke of Mercoeur. See John Smith, *The True Travels, Adventures and Observations of Captain John Smith, in Europe, Asia, Affrica, and America, from Anno Domini 1593 to 1629* [. . .] (London: printed by J. H. for Thomas Slater, and are to bee sold at the Belw Bible in Greene Arbour, 1630), chs. IV and V, and Pichler, "Captain John Smith," 333. Pichler also notes the presence of English Jesuits in Esztergom around this time (335) and that "many noble youths and adventures mainly from the Dutch war school of Alexander de Parma and Maurice of Orania . . . came from all lands to 'practice in the conduct of war and in fighting with the Turks, who heretofore had been so superior'," 351. The quote he cites is from A. H. Löbl, *Zur Geschichte des Türkenkrieges von 1593–1606*, vol. 1 (Prague: Rohlíček und Sievers, 1899–1904), 43.
41 NA: SP.102/4 21 lines 5, 6, and 4, respectively.
42 Ibid., lines 6–7.
43 İ. H. Danişmend, *Izahlı Osmanlı Tarih-I Kronolojisi*, vol. 3 (Istanbul: Türkiye Yayınevi, 1947–1955), 197–198.
44 The reference to a continuing correspondence between the two states further situates the document within an ongoing discursive and dialogic process and reinforces the impression that the Ottomans are not intrinsically antagonistic towards Christian states.
45 Katib Çelebi, *Fezleke*, 137, and Naima, *Tarih-i Naima*, 237, both mention the subsequent execution of the garrison.
46 Feridun, *Mejmu'a-i munşe'at al-selatin*, 3, line 10. See Katib Çelebi, *Fezleke*, 141, for an allusion to this event and also Danişmend, *Kronoloji*, vol. 3, 170.
47 Stein, "A Letter," 234, n.18.
48 Hasan Beyzade, *Telhis-i Tacü't-tevarih*, fol.467b.
49 Peçevi, *Tarih-i Peçevi*, 235; Topçularkatibi, *Tevarih*, fol.138b.
50 NA: SP.102/4 21 lines 38, 39–40.
51 Suraiya Faroqhi, "Ottoman Views on Corsairs and Piracy in the Adriatic," in *The Kapudan Pasha, His Office and His Domain*, ed. E. Zachariadou (Rethymnon: Crete University Press, 2002), 360–361.
52 Cengiz Orhonlu, *Osmanlı Tarihine âid Belgeler: Telhisler (1597–1607)* (Istanbul: Edebiyat Fakültesi Basımevi, 1970), 76–77. The *telhis* is not dated in Orhonlu, but all the *telhis* in this book date from between 1597–1607. Reference to the new English king, James I, means that the *telhis* is from 1603 at the earliest.
53 Ibid., 77.
54 See n.33.
55 Stein, "A Letter," 234–235 compares it to other letters. It is also physically smaller, the flourishes on the letters are less noticeable and the writing is not so well thought out in that some of the words are obviously squashed onto the ends

of lines. The introduction to the grand vizierial *fethname* begins "after prayers suitable to friendship and congruent to friendly affection it is communicated in a friendly manner that [. . .]" NA: SP.102/61 line 2, whereas the sultanic *fethname* commences in a more ostentatious manner, "when the exalted imperial seal arrives let it be known that [. . .]" NA: SP.102/4 21 line 2.
56 NA: SP.102/61 lines 2–3.
57 Ibid., line 3. Natalie Rothman, "Afterword: Intermediaries, Mediation, and Cross-Confessional Diplomacy in the Early Modern Mediterranean," *Journal of Early Modern History* 19 (2015): 250, cites Sanjay Subrahmanyam's notion of commensurability as outlined in *Courtly Encounters: Translating Courtliness and Violence in Early Modern Eurasia* (Cambridge: Cambridge University Press, 2012), xiv.
58 Ibid., lines 4–5.
59 MacCaffrey, *Elizabeth I*, 291–292. The English suffered heavy losses with the death of eight hundred of their one thousand six hundred men present. Following the victory, the Dutch began negotiations with the Spanish Habsburgs, and it is likely that it had a similar impact on English-Spanish diplomacy.
60 NA: SP.102/61 lines 6–7.
61 NA: SP.102/4 21 lines 34–35: "by surrendering the keys of the castle the high sovereign brought mercy into existence and safety was bestowed to the lives, possessions, children and households of those in ruined circumstances who were the remnant whom the sword had spared." cf. NA: SP.102/61 line 30: "by surrendering the keys of the castle mercy was given to the lives, possessions, children and households of those in ruined circumstances who were the remnant whom the sword had spared."
62 NA: SP.102/4 21 line 36 and NA: SP.102/61 line 31.
63 NA: SP.102/61 lines 33–34.
64 Ibid., lines 32–33.
65 Ibid., line 35.

3 The *gazavatnames*
Erasing oral residue and correcting scribal error

The *gazavatnames*

The most detailed Ottoman description of the retaliatory Habsburg siege of Nagykanizsa in 1601 is contained in a corpus of twenty-five Ottoman manuscripts dating from 6 *Muharrem* 1025 H. [25 January 1616 CE] to 16 *Receb* 1230 H. [24 June 1815 CE], which are today known collectively in library catalogues by the rubric *Gazavat-i Tiryaki Hasan Paşa* [*The Campaign of Tiryaki Hasan Pasha*].[1] These manuscripts can be considered as examples of a *gazavatname* or *gazaname* [campaign narrative] genre of writing; that is to say they provide accounts of Ottoman military campaigns.[2] Woodhead argues that there is a clear continuum between the accomplished literary *gazanames* written by authors such as Talikizade and presented to the sultan and the less sophisticated "leaner, slimmer" anonymous examples exemplified by the *Gazavat-i Sultan Murad b. Mehemmed Han* [*The Campaign of Sultan Murad b. Mehemmed Han*].[3] However as there are significant differences not only in the style and language, but also in the intended audience, function and genre expectations of the texts, it might be useful to conceptualise them as belonging to two distinct generic literary types. While the former are, and were, often extant only in a few copies, most notably individual presentation copies, the latter are more prevalent, do not have a cited author (although the scribe responsible for inscription is often mentioned) and were not primarily intended for presentation to a patron. The *Gazavat-i Tiryaki Hasan Paşa* manuscripts are examples of the latter group.

Gazavatnames are often read and categorised by scholars today as being generically closer to literature than history. Their primary functions are seen as didactic or entertaining; they "were not primarily written to contribute to the historical record".[4] As such, historians frequently treat *gazavatname* accounts as if they are less reliable than other historical sources because of their supposed pronounced eulogistic and semi-fictional, literary or epic character. Consequently, their usefulness for the historian is considered limited and restricted to helping fill in the gaps in the historical record, the provision of evidence for the development of Ottoman literary genres, or descriptions of the virtues that the Ottomans regarded as suitable for their rulers to exhibit.⁵ This attitude is particularly exacerbated with regard to 'popular' *gazavatnames*.

There is much of interest that can be said about this corpus of Nagykanizsa *gazavatname* manuscripts – it is an exciting and reasonably long tale, full of drama; brave Ottoman soldiers; despicable, often drunk, infidels; graphic accounts of violent confrontations; and seemingly limitless cunning tricks and ruses employed by the eponymous hero with which to confound and ultimately defeat the enemy. It is animated by colourful language, dialogue and frequent scene changes. However, it also provides an insight into Ottoman literacy strategies: the importance and significance of rubrication and framing, the reading practices and preferences of different individuals and audiences, the process of manuscript re-inscription and the ways in which intertextual references not only condition the possible meanings available to audiences but also reflect the conceptual schemas of interpretative communities. It also offers an opportunity to explore the theoretical concepts of residual orality, interiorised literacy, the authorial work, textual stability and plural literacy practices as applied in the context of manuscript variation and other textual or narrative characteristics. As such, in this chapter I will outline three interpretative tools that I will use in my analysis. The first argues for reading the manuscripts within a performative rather than a typographic framework of analysis: an approach in which many, but not all, of the individual manuscripts are viewed as unique instances of creation and not as derivative or degenerative copies of a privileged originary text. The second model problematises the preeminence ascribed to linear reading in a twenty-first-century academic context and instead suggests that the concept of ethical reading might more profitably explain sections of apparent incoherence in some of the manuscripts. Lastly, I contend that rather than ascribe residual orality to an entire culture on the basis of specific textual features, it might be more useful to focus on the reception of particular texts. I therefore posit the idea of a vocality-ocularity spectrum upon which texts can be located depending on whether they were more or less likely to be read or heard. In Chapter 4 I undertake a close textual analysis of three of the manuscripts in the corpus. In so doing I illustrate how the narrative was variously read, appropriated and reinscribed to reflect more or less politically or religiously heterodox perspectives.

The typographic model and oral characteristics

The dominance of the typographic model in manuscript scholarship together with an over-reliance by scholars on nineteenth-century printed editions of manuscripts and scholarly editions has led to a tendency in Ottoman studies to assume that there exists a conceptual object that can be termed the 'authorial work' which is semantically and physically constant among manuscripts. This is reflected in cataloguers' and historians' desire to rubricate the corpus of the Nagykanizsa *gazavatname* manuscripts with a single, all-encompassing title, implying that they are all copies of the same work. However, the corpus does not consist of identical copies of one work, and although many of the manuscripts possess striking and extensive similarities, not only in terms of narrative events but also of linguistic structure, they also exhibit interesting and significant lexical and semantic variations. For example, they possess different introductions and conclusions, and they narrate the sieges from more or less religiously and politically orthodox or heterodox perspectives.[6] They are therefore not really 'copies' but are also not original and distinct works, so how should they be categorised? Should we look for and privilege the original version and ignore subsequent iterations with their introduced changes? Should we try and erase the 'damage' done by scribal variation? What sense do the concepts of author, work, scribe and copy have for this corpus of manuscripts and our analysis of it?

The modern typographic paradigm takes as its archetype the printed book – a fixed, original, written work by a single author. In a manuscript context such a model implies an a priori distinction between author and copyist, original work and copy. It also interprets variations among manuscript recensions of a particular work, the presence of what have been termed oral characteristics, fluid grammar and orthography, and textual incoherence as evidence either of the oral transmission of the work, a more general residual orality in the culture or scribal illiteracy.[7] Ottoman society was characterised by a vibrant 'oral' culture: *aşıks* [oral storytellers] extemporised oral performances of well-known epic tales and stories to listening audiences; the memorisation and oral recitation of religious and legal texts was prevalent; a wide variety of written texts including romances, fables, jokes, poetry, sermons, songs and newspapers were read aloud by the *kissa-khan* [professional recitor or reader] and listened to in the *kıraathane* [coffee-shop], the mosque, public squares and other venues; and there was a tradition of the recitation, or performance, by authors of their written historical, geographical, religious and literary works to gatherings in the *meclis* or salon.[8] This cultural 'orality' together with the fact that quite a few Ottoman texts exhibit a variety of 'oral-formulaic' characteristics, variation among individual manuscript recensions of a particular 'work' and grammatical or orthographic fluidity superficially position the Ottomans as a prime example of a Muslim, Arabic-script using, recitational, logocentric culture that had not fully interiorised literacy.[9] In an Ottoman context a number of scholars have glossed the presence of manuscript variation and oral characteristics as symptomatic of oral transmission, residual orality, scribal error or the 'popular' or 'folk' nature of the work. This contrasts with their assessment of texts that do not possess such characteristics as the output of a more educated elite who have more effectively interiorised literacy.[10] Such an approach disregards or ignores the multiple audiences, functions and meanings suggested by the manuscript differences and their various framings, and provides an incomplete picture of Ottoman literacy practices, genre classifications and the role played by narratives of the past in identity formation. I contend that explanations deriving from the application of a typographic model of analysis not only present a picture of Ottoman literacy practices as monolithic, degenerative and flawed by incompetence but they also problematically interpret the practices of glossing, translating, commenting, annotating and copying as derivative and unoriginal.

In addition, utilising the typographic model leads to a number of problematic and incoherent conclusions.[11] It seems contradictory to argue that scribes who were literate enough to copy, amend or add significant sections to their manuscripts were really virtually illiterate because of their spelling and grammatical practices and their verbatim inclusion of incoherent passages of text. More importantly, there is rarely any critique of the sense in which a work is considered to be 'oral'.[12] Are scholars referring to oral composition, transmission or performance or a combination of all three?[13] In what circumstances and for whom is the work oral? Linguists such as Chafe and Danielewicz, Zellermayer, Denny and Tannen have argued against the existence of a clear difference between spoken and written discourse in terms of the presence, or absence, of particular characteristics.[14] Tannen has demonstrated that the presence in a text of characteristics which are often described as 'oral-formulaic' is not exclusively determined by the media of the text, its method of composition nor the societal level of interiorised literacy but is instead determined by the degree of contextualisation or decontextualisation of the text, which is in turn affected by transcription systems utilised, the communicative needs of the society, cultural preferences and the function of the work.[15]

The linear model of literacy implied by the typographic model assumes a gradual progression from orality to a fully interiorised literacy where the different states also engender cognitive differences. Arguing that some cultures, and Ong includes Arabic-language-using societies here, have a stalled or incomplete literacy implies that they are less developed and do not process information in the same way as more 'advanced' societies.[16] In the case of Arabic-language cultures, this seems unlikely given the highly developed calligraphic traditions. Messick acknowledges that many Muslim and especially Arabic-language-using communities have a preference for recitational practices but argues that this does not necessarily indicate an inadequately interiorised literacy. It could be more profitably understood as evidence of there existing different literacy practices.[17] This idea of plural literacy practices and reading strategies, in conjunction with an acknowledgement that audiences have different expectations concerning texts and that particular genres of text require different standards of orthographic regularity and fixity in transmission, is a more heuristically beneficial means of explaining manuscript variation and the presence of 'oral-formulaic' characteristics than derogatory references to semiliterate scribes, stalled literacy or an elusive orality.

Scribal re-inscription: discourses of authority and performance

If orthographic and grammatical fluidity and textual variation among manuscripts in the same corpus are not to be explicated as evidence of scribal incompetence or a stalled literacy, then how can they be coherently explained? Why have some scribes assumed a licence to retitle, abridge, expand and reorder, whereas others have copied their exemplars verbatim?[18] Machan, working in the context of medieval European manuscript culture, has suggested a model that explains such variation. He argues that manuscripts were produced and received within two different textual discourses, each embodying or possessing its own concomitant expectations concerning literary style, authorship, textual production and textual stability or fixity.[19] Discourses concerned with religious or state functions tend to import a much greater importance to the fixity of language because an incorrect reading resulting from orthographic or grammatical variations could result in an erroneous understanding of tradition, culture or God. These texts, written in Latin, therefore acquired an a priori assumption of permanence and fixity, a lexical and thematic prestige and a degree of stasis and regularity. They were, in effect, situated within a different cultural and textual framework to texts in the vernacular. The textual discourse within which texts in the vernacular were produced and consumed, Machan argues, was one more akin to oral improvisation whereby each text was understood as a unique or original performance of the individual scribe. The variety of conscious alterations that the scribes made as they 'copied' the works can thus be compared to the improvisations, or changes, of extemporaneous performers as they re-created songs or narratives, as described by Lord.[20] Within this more fluid, vernacular discourse, there is no object text but rather a continuous tradition of text making and remaking. No 'work' exists until a 'performance', and then each 'performance' is understood as a unique and original work.[21] Many variations between manuscripts can therefore be redefined as the result of conscious scribal 'performance' or reinterpretation and re-inscription.

Pearsall and Dagenais have similarly argued that variant 'copies' of manuscripts should be understood as 'recompositions' rather than as 'decompositions' from a more valuable original and valued accordingly.[22] Dagenais, like Machan, argues that the unit of study should be each codex, not some postulated archetype of a work, and that all codices should be seen as equally legitimate. Therefore, he suggests replacing the original authorial work paradigm of traditional philology, which is modelled on the printed book (the typographic model), with a reader or manuscript-centred model.[23] Such a reader-centred paradigm would enable one to explore the wider world of manuscript textuality and to examine how one manuscript is transformed into another though accretions of gloss, commentary, marginalia and other textual emendations.[24] It would also allow one to analyse how different rubrics, textual divisions, marginal notations and the presence of other works in a manuscript all gloss a text in alternative ways and thus offer the possibility of different potential meanings. Orthographic and grammatical variations can similarly be explained. Just as copies of manuscripts inscribed within the discourse of fluidity were not understood as being immutably fixed, neither were grammar and spelling conventions. Thus what editors and scholars frequently interpret as scribal error – dittography, elision, hyper- and hypometric lines, and grammatical and spelling variations – is only one interpretation of the phenomena. They could perhaps be more profitably interpreted as providing evidence of the irrelevance of such fixity to particular audiences within certain genres, discourses or contexts. It might also suggest that audiences had other strategies for negotiating texts and different expectations of a text. Is it possible that such audiences expected indeterminacy, and were conditioned to skip over inconsistencies or used, to a greater extent, systems outside of the letter of the text as a way of investing the text with meaning?[25]

I would argue that the study of Ottoman manuscripts would benefit from the application of a model of analysis predicated on the idea of there being two fundamental textual discourses: a discourse of authority and a more fluid or performative discourse. The positioning of a work in one or other of these discourses would depend on a cluster of variables including language, considerations of genre, the implied audience and the intended or perceived function of the text. One would therefore expect legal, religious and state or bureaucratic texts to exhibit a greater concern for fixity and to be written within a discourse of authority whatever their language. Similarly, texts by a well-known or renowned author may also possess a greater degree of *authoritas* and stability. However, other Ottoman texts do seem to have been produced and were intended to be consumed within a more performative discourse of fluidity, and these include many but not all of the manuscripts in the *Gazavat-i Tiryaki Hasan Paşa* corpus.[26] Within such a discourse the search for an original author and ur text makes little sense. Instead, the manuscript should be the focus of study because it was this that audiences encountered and it was this that determined their understanding of the work.

It is, however, important not to surreptitiously reimpose the author/original work model upon these manuscripts by classifying each manuscript as an original work in its own right and figuring the scribe as commensurate with an author. Rather, we need a different vocabulary to describe works produced within more fluid, performative discourses, one in which the uniqueness of the manuscript is acknowledged together with its relation to the other manuscripts in the corpus. In this book I have chosen to adopt Dagenais's term *scriptum* (pl. *scripta*) to describe such works and to use the term *scribe* to describe the activities of the producer of the scriptum. For works written in a discourse of fixity and authority, I will continue to use the terms *author* and *work* and for those copied within such a framework the terms *copyist* and *manuscript* or *recension*. For example, Katib Çelebi wrote the *Fezleke* within the more fixed discourse of authority and thus is correctly identified as its author, whereas scribes copying his work are copyists and not 'performers' or scribes. The case is similar for Câfer Iyânî and his *Cihadname-i Tiryaki Hasan Paşa*.[27]

In the context of the *Gazavat-i Tiryaki Hasan Pasha* manuscripts, while it is useful to conceptualise the majority as performative scripta, the copyists of a couple of the manuscripts make a clear distinction between their actions and those of an 'original' author.[28] The copyist of Bub.3459 (1668–9) writes "however this poor one wrote the Kanije *gazavat* such that those who are read to in the *meclis* shall pray for this poor one and also let the one who wrote it not be neglected from [their] prayers."[29] A similar distinction between copyist and author is made in H.O.71d (1754): "Whoever reads the noble *fatiha* let them forgive the soul of the deceased Hasan Pasha and the *gazis* who were present in this great *gaza* and this scribe of letters Süleyman Efendi and that of Edirnevi Seyyid Abdullah ibn Ali ve ibn Veli who wrote this book in 1168 and also firstly, spare the soul of the scribe Mehmed Halife."[30] These manuscripts also exhibit a far more stable orthography and grammar and in the introductory section utilise to a greater degree the languages of authority in an Ottoman context – Persian and Arabic. I would therefore argue that they were copied, transmitted and intended to be received within a discourse of authority rather than fluidity. Although it is not possible to establish a copying schema of interrelatedness among the majority of the Nagykanizsa *gazavatname* scripta because the fluid or performative discourse within which they were inscribed does not make them amenable to such an analysis, it is possible to establish a tentative schemata with regard to a small group copied within a discourse of authority.[31] In this group of manuscripts, there are two instances of identical copies, one being No.5070 (1757), which is an identical copy of H.O.71d (1754), although written by a different copyist, and the other being O.R.393 (undated) and Nr.525 (undated), which were probably written by the same copyist as the hand appears the same.[32] O.216 (1716), although much closer overall to No.5070 (1757) and H.O.71d (1754), does share some features in common with Bub.3459 (1668–9), O.R.393 (undated) and Nr.525 (undated), so I suggest, therefore, that it might represent an intermediary inscription.[33]

It appears as if later readers also read these manuscripts within a discourse of authority exhibited by their concern for orthographic and grammatical fixity and factual coherency as evidenced through their interventions in the text. The copyist of Bub.3459 (1668–9) left gaps in the text to which someone later added in red ink certain narratorial interjections and religious phrases. Of interest in the context of a discussion on textual stability is the fact that they took this opportunity to grammatically 'correct' the text and add in 'missing' words.[34] Furthermore, a later reader subsequently made further amendments to two sections of red text, providing short vowels and some grammatical corrections.[35] For these readers there was a fixed, correct grammar and orthography, and the application of it to this text was deemed appropriate. This contrasts with the 'uncorrected' fluidity present in many of the other scripta.[36] Two readers of O.R.393 (undated), and A.E. Tar.188 (1810) have corrected the name of the sultan, changing it from Ahmed to Mehmed.[37] The reader of O.R.393 (undated) has also written in the margin next to one of their corrections, "accession 1003, length of reign 9 years, Sultan Mehmed the conqueror of Egri. This conquest victoriously occurred in the year 1011, because in [10]12 it was the time of Sultan Ahmed."[38] For these readers, reading for historical accuracy was important. However, such corrections are unusual. In the scripta in which the sultan is named, the majority name him erroneously as Ahmed – yet it is corrected in only two manuscripts. The widespread occurrence of this inaccuracy and the fact that there is considerable evidence of other scribal re-inscription and emendation in these scripta suggests that the inaccurate naming of the sultan demonstrates a lack of concern as to the sultan's identity rather than scribal ignorance: the person of the sultan is abstract and marginal to the narrative and interests of the scribes and their implied audiences.[39]

Ethical reading

I argue that the idea of readers and writers approaching a text with different expectations concerning orthographic, grammatical and 'factual' stability is a more plausible explanation of instances of 'error' than the notions of the Ottomans being a culture beset with residual orality. However, it does not address the problem of scribes and copyists faithfully copying apparently incoherent passages while simultaneously rewriting or 'correcting' other perceived 'errors'. This can be explained though in terms of different literacy strategies. Rather than read problematic sections of text as incoherent and the result of poor or inadequately interiorised literacy or scribal error, we could re-evaluate them as evidence of different literacy practices.[40] Dagenais has argued that although many contemporary models of literature are based upon the notion of linear narratives, which move the narrative forward and encourage reading strategies that privilege the unravelling of the meaning of the work, there are alternative ways of reading. He suggests that medieval reading practices were different to contemporary practices and describes a strategy or practice he terms *ethical reading*.[41] He argues that medieval reading practices were far more interpretative than contemporary Western practices and that audiences did not expect to reduce texts to a single 'coherent' reading but sought to engage a text rhetorically and to elicit or construct a system or network of values or ethical models from texts.[42] In other words, they did not simply read to extract the meaning from the text but rather to inspire personal meditations.[43]

I suggest that this notion of ethical reading could help explain some apparent incoherencies in the *Gazavat-i Tiryaki Hasan Paşa* corpus of manuscripts. There are a number of examples of 'confused' passages in the scripta

The gazavatnames: *erasing oral residue* 63

which, if read ethically, could be seen as providing meditations or commentaries on issues of authority and power.[44] One of the most significant of these centres on a stratagem that Tiryaki Hasan Pasha employs while besieged in Nagykanizsa castle to try and convince the Habsburgs that he does not have any cannons.[45] In brief, the narratives state that on a Thursday, the Habsburg army commanded by King Ferdinand II was encamped a day's march from Nagykanizsa. The king sent a scouting party of five thousand men to assess the situation of the castle and to gather information. When Tiryaki Hasan Pasha obtained news of this, he commanded his men not to fire the castle's cannons and prevented the cavalry from going outside the gates, although he did send out foot soldiers. His men obeyed, and after a brief skirmish with the Habsburgs, the latter returned to their camp. The next day, Friday, another scouting party was sent to the castle. Again Tiryaki Hasan Pasha ordered the cannons to be silent and hidden and only sent out foot soldiers to fight. At noon the enemy came beneath the castle walls and beseeched the Ottomans to fire a cannon at them. Tiryaki Hasan Pasha instructed his men to inform the enemy that there were no cannons in the castle, and if there had have been, they would have definitely fired them as the Ottomans love killing infidels. His men, however, were devastated by this command and protested, begging that they not be ordered to give such vile news to the enemy. They argued that if the intention of the enemy was previously not to attack the castle, then once they heard this news, they would change their minds and definitely besiege it. Tiryaki Hasan Pasha, then said, 'Obey my words. You don't know what I know. I have hidden the cannons in a secret place.' His men were mollified by this answer and dutifully obeyed his command and conveyed his answer to the enemy soldiers. The next day, the same thing happened, but the Ottomans also told the Habsburg scouts that they were planning on abandoning Nagykanizsa castle in a few days. This resulted in the Habsburgs not only moving their camp within cannon range of the castle walls, but they also allowed a wagon train into the castle which they mistakenly assumed had come to remove the inhabitants' possessions but which, unbeknownst to them, was full of provisions and Ottoman soldiers. Tiryaki Hasan Pasha, having thus lured the enemy army within cannon range and enabled the supply wagons to enter the castle, instructed the commander of the artillery to fire the cannons at the Habsburgs, causing considerable destruction and loss of life. The wisdom of his decision not to fire the cannons earlier becomes apparent, and the siege begins in earnest.

Upon close study of this passage, there appears to be a number of narrative inconsistencies. The most important of these centres on the cannons, the soldiers' awareness of their existence and the reasons Tiryaki Hasan Pasha gives for not firing them. Why are his soldiers happy to hide the existence of the cannons from the enemy on Thursday and Friday morning but not on Friday afternoon? How did Tiryaki Hasan Pasha move a hundred cannons to a secret place without anyone knowing? Why move them anyway? Moreover, his soldiers' concern about telling the enemy that they have no cannons is assuaged when Tiryaki Hasan Pasha informs them that he knows more than they do and that he has hidden the cannons in a secret place. This suggests that they are not so much concerned with the enemy being told that they have no cannons but are worried that they really have no cannons, even though they were expressly told that morning not to fire them. Lastly, we know that Tiryaki Hasan Pasha's intention in not firing the cannons is to lure the enemy right beneath the walls of the castle and also to permit the entrance of the wagon trains, so why does he not just tell his men that this is his plan? The whole passage just does not seem to make sense when read in terms of linear narrative.

If, however, this section is read as an ethical meditation on the subject of authority and power, its incoherence is erased.[46] In this passage Tiryaki Hasan Pasha attempts to exercise the power he possesses derived from his position as an imperial *beylerbeyi* [governor]. This attempt to exercise power is challenged; his men are reluctant to do something which they believe to be illogical, incomprehensible and deleterious to their situation on the basis of his position as an official of the state military-administrative structure. However, when he counters their challenge with a reference to his personal knowledge and competence, they agree to obey him. Thus the authority he possesses as an experienced border commander is more persuasive than the power he possesses by virtue of his position as a *beylerbeyi*. Yet, Tiryaki Hasan Pasha could have simply justified his command by providing information to his men about the stratagem. In doing so he would have appeared as an experienced general, competent at warfare and possessing military and strategic knowledge. So why doesn't he? By mentioning secret places and information that his men do not know, he figures himself as having mystical or divine rather than temporal knowledge. By meeting the challenge of his men with a claim to mystical knowledge, it is implied that some commanders should be obeyed *because* they possess divine approbation. This reading parallels other places in the narrative where Tiryaki Hasan Pasha is figured as having divine knowledge through intertextual references to *menakibname* literature – narratives which concern the exploits and miracles of divinely inspired warrior-saints.[47] A third possible reading stresses the importance of obedience to those in authority as the ethical focus of this passage. The challenge to Tiryaki Hasan Pasha and his reassertion of power foregrounds the question of obedience: it is through blindly obeying Tiryaki Hasan Pasha that his trick is rendered successful and the ultimate victory of the castle and soldiers is secured.[48]

The plurality and diversity of Ottoman reading practices is evidenced by the alterations made to this section by various other writers who, because of their employment of different reading strategies, determined that the passage was incoherent and therefore rewrote it so that it became meaningful to them and compatible with their ways of reading. The two most obvious examples of this are Katib Çelebi's reinterpretation in the *Fezleke* and that by the scribe of O.R.6442 (1815).[49] In O.R.6442 (1815) when Tiryaki

The gazavatnames: *erasing oral residue* 65

Hasan Pasha's men complain that they do not want to tell the enemy that they have no cannons, Tiryaki Hasan Pasha answers,

> You don't know what I have taken into account. Now you hold the words that I said, first of all I have hidden those cannons in a place and if I fire the cannons now the infidels will say that, 'the Turks will not give the castle to us.' But the reason for my not causing the cannons to be fired is this, that the infidels will say, 'they will give the castle to us' but I have to play a trick for the provisions.[50]

This answer, although similar to those given in the other *gazavatnames*, does not pose any difficulties for comprehension when read for linear narrative. Tiryaki Hasan Pasha states that he has hidden the cannons somewhere, but from the context of these words, we assume that he means he has hidden them from the enemy. He then explains that he has done this to trick the enemy into believing that the Ottomans are about to surrender the castle so that he can get the extra provisions inside. These extra lines clarify the passage and make explicit an element of Tiryaki Hasan Pasha's plan. A scribe has obviously, at some juncture, added these additional lines to the standard *gazavatname* version of the cannon event to make the passage comprehensible when read for linear narrative for the implied audience.

The vocality-ocularity continuum

Redundancy, repetition, digressions and the absence of titles have often been taken to indicate that a text was originally 'oral', that the scribe was barely literate or that the culture in which the text was produced and consumed had not fully interiorised literacy and exhibited a degree of residual orality. To avoid the assumptions and problems concomitant with the term *orality*, Zumthor and Schaefer have argued for a new term, that of *vocality*.[51] Schaefer uses the term to classify works that utilise the oral-aural medium for reception regardless of whether the text was originally an oral or written composition.[52] Works that were recalled from memory, those composed extemporaneously and the reading aloud of written texts would all therefore be classified as received in vocality. I therefore suggest reinterpreting certain characteristics previously understood as signalling the 'oral' nature of a work as instead being determined by its intended reception. All written texts can, of course, be read aloud, but what determines the inclusion of a text under the heading of vocality is the mode of reception by the implied and actual audience as determined from cues in the text and/or performances of the work. It may be useful to think of there existing a continuum ranging from texts that were definitely read aloud to those read silently, with many existing in between.

Graphical marks which attempt to replace lost illocutionary force such as punctuation, under- or overlining, the use of different-coloured inks and

66 *The* gazavatnames: *erasing oral residue*

paragraph indentation can generally be interpreted as indicating that a text was read silently rather than read aloud to a listening audience because such marks provide information pertinent to a reader and not a listener.[53] Titles can also be interpreted as evidence that the text was read and not heard: vocal performances of texts rarely commence with a spoken title; instead they begin with an address to the audience or nothing. An index or a contents page are, similarly, primarily tools useful to a reader and not to a listener. But possibly the graphemes that most definitively indicate a reading, rather than listening, audience are marginal comments: listening audiences do not make marks in texts. Conversely, redundancy and repetition in a text might indicate its position further along the vocality axis. As Ong noted, the nature of oral performances or readings of a text encourages repetition as audiences may miss certain points due to physical factors in the environment.[54] In addition, repetition is often used to stress a particular point or to elaborate difficult or complex ideas because back scanning and rereading are not possible in a listening context. Direct addresses to the implied audience have also traditionally been interpreted as indicating the oral performance of a work. However, caution must be exercised in interpreting such comments because as Machan has demonstrated many works exhibit such 'oral' characteristics for rhetorical or aesthetic purposes.[55] It may therefore be preferable to adopt a cluster-theory approach where no one example or characteristic is sufficient, or necessary, to determine the mode of performance; rather, a cluster of indicators may be interpreted as demonstrating the probable method of reception of the text.

In the context of the *Gazavat-i Tiryaki Hasan Paşa* corpus, many of the scripta contain ocularity cues, such as the use of red ink, overlining and short vowelling.[56] The use of red ink and overlining usually tends to illuminate religious phrases, the name of God, quotes from the Qur'an and sometimes the names of important personages such as Tiryaki Hasan Pasha. However, in Bub.3459 (1668–9) the copyist has used red ink to highlight interjections which function to move the story on and to indicate the end of digressions and particular scenes.[57] These interjections were added into specially left gaps after the initial inscription.[58] Likewise, occurrences of the term *ba'dehu* [after that] in O.R.33 (undated) are inscribed in red ink, thus suggesting that they performed a similar managerial function and spatially divided up the text.[59] On other occasions, perceived difficult or unfamiliar words are short vowelled to indicate the pronunciation. While the presence of such marks does not preclude the work predominantly being read aloud or heard, they are best interpreted as evidence for the works being read, especially when they occur in conjunction with other ocularity cues (titles, ornamentation, complex grammatical phrases and a lack of repetition) together with an absence of vocality cues (e.g., repetition, the absence of titles or titles in the form of incipits).

Lastly, sometimes Ottoman reading and reception practices are referenced in the narrative itself. At the end of the narrative, the scribe/copyist generally

The gazavatnames: *erasing oral residue* 67

requests that those who are read the tale in the *meclis* say prayers for him and sometimes for Tiryaki Hasan Pasha and the *gazis* besieged with him: "let those who are read the *gazavat* of the deceased and forgiven Gazi Tiryaki Hasan Pasha in *meclises* remember also this poor one."[60] Not only is the verb 'to read' in the passive, which implies a listening audience, but the reference to *meclises* or gatherings also implies a listening audience because such gatherings were often convened for the purpose of listening to 'oral' performances of works. Interestingly, scripta T.F.46 (1689), A.E.Tar.188 (1810) and H.O.71a (undated) refer to both those who are read to (or listen) and those who read, thus including both reception practices.[61] However, three of the scripta have written only "*okuyan*" ["those who read"], perhaps indicating that they had a different experience of reception practices and conceived of an audience who would be primarily reading the text. For example, No.235 (undated) describes "those sincere brothers who read the *gazavatname*".[62]

These postscripts also provide information on how the scribe or copyist perceived his role and why he rewrote the text. Two mention that they inscribed the text in order that a work by them would remain.[63] Although some specify directly that they wrote the text in order that those who are read to will pray for them, most state that they wrote it and then subsequently request that they be prayed for.[64] O.216 (1716) makes a brief reference to a patron when he asks for forgiveness for "the souls of Gazi Hasan Pasha, the *gazis* who participated in this great *gaza*, and the one who caused this to be written, and the one who wrote it".[65] The idea of an ocularity-vocality continuum upon which manuscripts can be placed with regard to their intended or actual reception, I argue, is a far more useful way of classifying manuscripts than utilising the rather problematic notions of oral and literate cultures or the idea that particular written works exhibit more or less residual orality. In Chapter 4 I undertake a more detailed analysis of individual scripta and manuscripts using the conceptual models already outlined: the idea of there being performative and authoritative discourses, the notion of ethical reading and the ocularity-vocality continuum.

Notes

1 A list of the manuscripts can be found in the bibliography. For the sake of brevity, when referring to the corpus as a whole, I will often describe them simply as the *gazavatnames*.
2 For a very brief overview of this genre see Christine Woodhead, "The Ottoman Gazaname: Stylistic Influences on the Writing of Campaign Narratives," in *The Great Ottoman-Turkish Civilization*, vol. III *Philosophy, Science and Institutions*, ed. Kemal Çiçek, Ercüment Kuran, Nejat Göyünç, Halil İnalcık, İlber Ortaylı and Güler Eren (Ankara: Yeni Türkiye, 2000). A.S. Levend, *Gazavatnameler ve Mihaloğlu Ali Bey'in Gazavat-namesi* (Ankara: Türk Tarih Kurumu Yayınlarından / XI. Seri, No. 8, Türk Tarih Kurumu Basımevi, 1956), is the iconic work on this subject and provides an introduction, a bibliography of *gazavatnames* and an analysis and transcription of the *Gazavat-name-i Mihaloğlu 'Ali*

68 The gazavatnames: erasing oral residue

Beğ. It is worth noting that neither Ottoman authors nor modern scholars were or are able to clearly distinguish or agree on the categorisation of Ottoman works rubricated as *gazavatname, fethname, zafername, şehname* and *tarih* – the genre boundaries are very fluid.

3 Woodhead, "The Ottoman Gazaname," 66. See also Christine Woodhead, "Taliqizade Mehmed," in *Historians of the Ottoman Empire*, ed. C. Kafadar, H. Karateke and C. Fleischer (2005), available online https://ottomanhistorians.uchicago.edu/en/historian/taliqizade-mehmed (accessed 26/6/16), for a brief overview of the four main *gazanames* of Talikizade: Talikizade, *Şeyname-i Hümayun* (Istanbul: Türk ve İslam Eserleri Müzesi, no. 1965), narrates events from the Ottoman-Habsburg Long War, including the capture of the fortresses of Veszprém and Pápa in 1593 and 1594, respectively. Talikizade, *Şeyname-i Sultan-i Selatin-i Cihan* (Istanbul: Topkapı Sarayı Kütüphanesi, Hazine 1609), narrates events from the capture of Eger Castle; Talikizade, *Gürcistan Seferi* (Istanbul: Topkapı Sarayı Kütüphanesi, Revan 1300), narrates the Ottoman capture of Turmanis in the Ottoman-Safavid war of 1578–1590. Talikizade, *Tebriziyye* (Istanbul: Topkapı Sarayı Kütüphanesi, Revan 1299), describes Özdemiroglu Osman Pasha's capture of Tebriz in 1585. See also Christine Woodhead, ed., *Talikizade's Şehname-i Hümayun: A History of the Ottoman Campaign into Hungary 1593–1594* (Berlin: Klaus Schwarz Verlag, 1983). Halil İnalcık and M. Oğuz, ed, trans. and intro., *Gazavat-i Sultan Murad b. Mehemmed Han: İzladi ve Varna Savaşları (1443–1444) Üzerinde Anonim Gazavâtnâme* (Ankara: Türk Tarih Kurumu Basımevi, 1978), describes the exploits and adventures of Sultan Murad in Europe.

4 Woodhead, "The Ottoman Gazaname," 60.

5 Levend, *Gazavat-nameler*, 1. Woodhead, "The Ottoman Gazaname," 57, contrasts the "dry and unembellished" account of Ottoman historian Selaniki with the account given in Talikizade's *gazaname*. This suggests that the latter narrative was embellished. It also echoes the view outlined at the beginning of Chapter 1 that perceives narratives by historians as being in some way more factual and less literary.

6 Many of the manuscripts also display fluid orthographic and grammatical practices, include 'incoherent' passages and contain a range of 'oral-formulaic' characteristics outlined below.

7 Such 'oral-formulaic' characteristics include: a prevalence of paratactic construction; additive rather than subordinative tendencies and a rather ambiguous syntax when subordination does occur; a proclivity for aggregative rather than analytic thought; an extensive use of direct speech and dialogues; repetition and redundancy; direct addresses to the audience; orthographic and grammatical variation; apparently incoherent phrases and passages, including confusion as to who is doing what to whom; episodic narrative; the presence of standardised themes; digressions; formulaic or colloquial language; a high proportion of proverbs, aphorisms, epithets, clichés and alliteration; and a tendency towards conservatism and homeostasis. These characteristics have been variously described by Walter Ong, *Orality and Literacy: The Technologizing of the Word* (London and New York: Methuen, 1982), 37–45 and 48–49; Ursula Schaefer, "Hearing from Books: The Rise of Fictionality in Old English Poetry," in *Vox Intexta: Orality and Textuality in the Middle Ages*, ed. Alger N. Doane and Carol Braun Pasternack (Madison: The University of Wisconsin Press, 1991), 121; and Dennis Tedlock, "The Speaker of Tales Has More Than One String to Play on," in *Vox Intexta: Orality and Textuality in the Middle Ages*, ed. Alger N. Doane and Carol Braun Pasternack (Madison: The University of Wisconsin Press, 1991), 13. See also P. M. Holt, "Al-Jabarti's Introduction to the History of the Ottoman Empire," *Bulletin of the School of Oriental and African Studies* 25 (1962): 41.

8 İlhan Başgöz, "The Epic Tradition among Turkic Peoples," in *Heroic Epic and Saga: An Introduction to the World's Great Folk Epics*, ed. F. Oinas (Bloomington: Indiana University Press, 1978), 324; Nora K. Chadwick and Victor Zhirmunsky, *Oral Epics of Central Asia* (Cambridge: Cambridge at the University Press, 1969), 316–317; Palmira Brummett, *Image and Imperialism in the Ottoman Revolutionary Press 1908–1911* (Albany: State University of New York Press, 2000), 46–47, quoting Ahmet Rasim, *Şehir Mektupları*, vol. 1 (Istanbul: Milli Eğitim Basımevi, 1971), 40, and Ahmet Eken, *Kartpostallarda Istanbul* (Istanbul: Büyükşehir Belediyesi, 1992), 182; Wolfgang Eberhard, *Minstrel Tales from South-Eastern Turkey* (Berkeley and Los Angeles: University of California Press, 1955), 7; Suraiya Faroqhi, *Approaching Ottoman History: An Introduction to the Sources* (Cambridge: Cambridge University Press, 1999), 144, quoting Cornell Fleischer, *Bureaucrat and Intellectual in the Ottoman Empire: The Historian Mustafa Ali (1541–1600)* (Princeton, Guildford: Princeton University Press, 1986), 22–23; Woodhead, "The Ottoman Gazaname," 58.

9 Ong, *Orality and Literacy*, 26 and 68–69. Brinkley Messick, *The Calligraphic State: Textual Domination and History in a Muslim Society* (Berkeley: University of California Press, 1993), 25, uses the phrase *recitational logocentrism*; Derrida coined the word *logocentrism* to describe the privileging of the spoken word.

10 Holt also argues that an abrupt, colloquial text, highly ungrammatical sentences, recurrent cliches and sparse and imprecise dating suggest to a reader that the works in question were records of colloquial, oral narrations. Silay and Başgöz also both assume that the presence of digressions in a work indicates an oral origin: Kemal Silay, "The Usage and Function of Digression in Ahmedi's History of the Ottoman Dynasty," *Turcica* 25 (1993): 149 and İlhan Başgöz, "Digression in Oral Narrative: A Case Study of Individual Remarks by Turkish Romance Tellers," *Journal of American Folklore* 99/391 (1986): 8 and 15. Başgöz, "The Epic Tradition," 314, describes such textual features as the use of traditional formulas, syntactical parallelism, repeated images and symbols and formulaic narration as 'oral characteristics' and argues that their presence in *Dede Korkut* is sufficient to indicate its orality. He also argues that one of the functions of the extended epithets given to the various protagonists is to help the narrator remember the story, and thus he suggests an oral mode of performance. Barbara Flemming, "Public Opinion under Sultan Süleyman," in *Süleyman the Second and His Time*, ed. Halil Inalcık and Cemal Kafadar (Istanbul: Isis Press, 1993), 49–58, also argues that the presence of addresses to the audience demonstrate that the work was intended for oral recitation. Gabriel Piterberg, "A Study of Ottoman Historiography in the Seventeenth Century," (PhD diss., Oxford University, 1992), 149–152, and "Speech Acts and Written Texts: A Reading of a Seventeenth-Century Ottoman Historiographic Episode," *Poetics Today* 14/2 (1993): 402–403, also contends that the colloquial nature of a work, and the occurrence of direct speech, passages addressed to a listening audience and the use of formulaic language to introduce and conclude digressions indicate the oral nature of a work. Holt, "Al-Jabarti's Introduction," 41, argues that 'popular' works were characterised by a colloquial style and flawed grammar. See also Cornell Fleischer, "From Sehzade Korkud to Mustafa Ali: Cultural Origins of the Ottoman *Nasihatname*," in *Proceedings of the Third Congress on the Social and Economic History of Turkey Princeton 1983*, ed. H. Lowry and S. Hatto (Istanbul: The Isis Press, 1990), 60–61, who argues that "egregious spelling errors demonstrate a scribe's acquaintance with Arabic and Persian was rudimentary at best and that he was only partly literate."

11 I discuss the problems inherent in traditional explanations of the presence of oral-formulaic characteristics and manuscript variation in more detail in Claire Norton, "Erasing Oral Residue and Correcting Scribal Error: Re-interpreting

the Presence of Mnemo-Technical Practices in Ottoman Manuscripts in the Early Modern Period," in *Culture of Memory in East Central and in the late Middle Ages and Early Modern Period*, ed. Rafal Wojcik (Poznan: Biblioteka Uniwersytecka, 2008).

12 This contrasts with much recent work in the fields of European medieval and South Asian literary cultures. I am more familiar with examples from the former, and these are cited in the discussion that follows. However, Sheldon Pollock has done a lot of work problematising the oral-literate dichotomy in a South Asian context; see Sheldon Pollock, ed., *Literary Cultures in History: Reconstructions from South Asia* (Berkeley: University of California Press, 2003), among other works.

13 Silay, "The Usage and Function of Digression," 149, although mentioning orality does not explain what 'the oral discourse is' nor why it is singular; Başgöz, "Digression in Oral Narrative," mentions the "oral origin" of works, "oral literature" and "folklore" as if they are definite and meaningful things. Woodhead, "The Ottoman Gazaname," 58, argues that the presence of certain key phrases that serve a managerial function in the text such as *ez-in-canib* and *ama bu yana* indicate that the *gazavatname* in question is much closer to the oral tradition of *gazi* legends without stipulating what this is. However, Flemming, "Public Opinion," 51, and Piterberg, "A Study of Ottoman Historiography," 145, do specify that the characteristics they have identified point to the oral recitation or performance of the work.

14 W. L. Chafe and J. Danielewicz, *Properties of Written and Spoken Language* (Berkeley and Los Angeles: University of California, 1987); Michal Zellermayer, "An Analysis of Oral and Literate Texts: Two Types of Reader-Writer Relationship in Hebrew and English," in *The Social Construction of Written Communication*, ed. B. Raforth and D. Rubin (Norwood, NJ: Ablex, 1988); J. P. Denny, "Rational Thought in Oral Culture and Literate Decontextualization," in *Literacy and Orality*, ed. David Olson and Nancy Torrance (Cambridge: Cambridge University Press, 1991); Deborah Tannen, "Oral and Literate Strategies in Spoken and Written Narratives," *Language* 58 (1982); Tannen, "The Oral/Literate Continuum in Discourse," in *Spoken and Written Language: Exploring Orality and Literacy*, ed. Deborah Tannen (Norwood, NJ: Ablex, 1982); Tannen, "Oral and Literate Strategies in Spoken and Written Discourse," in *Literacy for Life: The Demand for Reading and Writing*, ed. R. W. Bailey and R. M. Fosheim (New York: Modern Language Association, 1983); Tannen "Relative Focus on Involvement in Oral and Written Discourse," in *Literacy, Language and Learning: The Nature and Consequences of Reading and Writing*, ed. David Olson, Nancy Torrance and Angela Hildyard (Cambridge: Cambridge University Press, 1985); Tannen, "Spoken and Written Narrative in English and Greek," in *Coherence in Spoken and Written Discourse*, ed. Deborah Tannen (Norwood, NJ: Ablex, 1984).

15 Tannen has also described these characteristics in terms of strategies reflecting a relative focus on the message or interpersonal involvement. See Norton, "Erasing Oral Residue," 34–36, for more information.

16 Ong, *Orality and Literacy*, 68–69.

17 Messick, *The Calligraphic State*, 25.

18 Laurence De Looze, "Signing Off in the Middle Ages: Medieval Textuality and Strategies of Authorial Self-Naming," in *Vox Intexta: Orality and Textuality in the Middle Ages*, ed. A. N. Doane and C. Braun Pasternack (Madison: The University of Wisconsin Press, 1991), 176 n.2. He refers the reader to G. L. Bruns, "The Originality of Texts in a Manuscript Culture," *Comparative Literature* 32 (1980). See also D. Embree and E. Urquhart, "*The Simonie*: The Case for a Parallel Text Edition," in *Manuscripts and Texts: Editorial Problems in Later Middle English Literature*, ed. D. Pearsall (Woodbridge: D. S. Brewer, 1987), 53.

The gazavatnames: *erasing oral residue* 71

19 Tim W. Machan, "Editing, Orality, and Late Middle English Texts," in *Vox Intexta: Orality and Textuality in the Middle Ages*, ed. Alger N. Doane and Carol Braun Pasternack (Madison: The University of Wisconsin Press, 1991).
20 Ibid., 236–237.
21 See J. M. Foley, "The Oral Theory in Context," in *Oral Traditional Literature: A Festschrift for Albert Bates Lord*, ed. J. M. Foley (Columbus: Slavica, 1980), 26.
22 John Dagenais, "That Bothersome Residue: Toward a Theory of the Physical Text," in *Vox Intexta: Orality and Textuality in the Middle Ages*, ed. A. N. Doane and C. Braun Pasternack (Madison: The University of Wisconsin Press, 1991), 252. Derek Pearsall, "Texts, Textual Criticism, and Fifteenth-Century Manuscript Production," in *Fifteenth-Century Studies*, ed. R. Yeager (Hamden: Archon, 1984), 126–127.
23 John Dagenais, *The Ethics of Reading in Manuscript Culture: Glossing the Libro de Buen Amor* (Princeton, NJ: Princeton University Press, 1994), xvii, xix, xvi and 12.
24 Ibid., 17–18.
25 Ibid., *The Ethics of Reading*, 111, 131 and 151. This is not to say that all audiences would have read in this way. Not only contemporary scholars but also medieval readers often complained that texts were full of fragments; indeterminacy; unusual grammar and spelling; missing words, sections and chapters; bad rhymes; unrelated marginalia; and an indeterminacy about who was speaking or what the object of the verb was. The point is that we should not assume that all audiences necessarily reacted in this way. An example of how Ottoman audiences themselves would have had to navigate through often confusing texts is evidenced in the introductory section of one of the *Gazavat-i Tiryaki Hasan Paşa* scripta London: British Library: O.R.6442 (1815) (henceforth referred to as LBL: O.R.6442). Although it gives the appearance of being inscribed by an educated, competent scribe with a clear hand, it is very confused. In particular the inscription of Qur'anic quotation 2.249 is problematic and essentially reverses the meaning of the quote. Similarly, the scribe's plea "to be known with a good name in the transitory world" presumably unwittingly reverses the request to be known with 'a good name' in the eternal world or after life, fol.54b. In addition there are numerous half-finished sentences and changes of subject which make deriving any meaning from it particularly difficult.
26 It would be interesting to read the various extant manuscripts of the *Menakib-i Mahmud Paşa-i Veli* within a fluid, performative model of analysis. On three occasions this work is bound with copies of the *Gazavat-i Tiryaki Hasan Paşa*: Manisa: İl Halk Kütüphanesi No.5070 (1757) (henceforth referred to as MIHK: No.5070) *Feth-i Konstantiniye ve Mahmud Paşa-i Veli ve Tiryaki Hasan Paşa Cihadı*; Vienna: National-bibliothek H.O.71d (1754) (henceforth referred to as VNB: H.O.71d) *Menakib-i Mahmud Paşa-i Veli*; and Vienna: National-bibliothek A.F.234 (1720) (henceforth referred to as VNB: A.F.234) *Merhum Mahmud Paşanın zaman-i şebabetinde vefatına değin vaki olan ahval-i şerifleri ve menakib-i latifleri zikr olunur*. The title of manuscript no. 5070 probably occurred because the *Menakib-i Mahmud Paşa-i Veli* also contains an account of the capture of Constantinople; a preliminary reading of the inscriptions of *Menakib-i Mahmud Paşa-i Veli* in these three manuscripts indicates that although No.5070 and H.O.71d are identical, A.F.234 differs in a number of ways. See Halil İnalcık and M. Oğuz, "Yeni Bulunmuş bir "Gazavat-i Sultan Murad," *Ankara Üniversitesi Dil ve Tarih-Coğrafya Fakültesi Dergisi* 7 s.2 (1949): 494, and Franz Babinger, *Die Geschichtsschreiber der Osmanen und ihre Werke* (Leipzig: Otto Harrassowitz, 1927), 25 n.1. İnalcık and Oğuz note that there are many extant copies of the work including two in their faculty library and a fragment at the end of İnalcık and Oğuz, *Gazavat-i Sultan Murad b. Mehemmed Han*. They also note that the various extant versions show considerable differences with regard

72 *The* gazavatnames: *erasing oral residue*

to chronological displacement of people and events. See Théoharis Stavrides, *The Sultan of Vezirs: The Life and Times of the Ottoman Grand Vezir Mahmud Pasha Angelović (1453–1474)* (Leiden: Brill, 2001), ch. X, for a detailed discussion of the *Menakib-i Mahmud Paşa-i Veli*.

27 Câfer Iyânî, *Cihadname-i Tiryaki Hasan Paşa* (Istanbul: Millet Kütüphanesi A.E.Tar.190, undated) (henceforth referred to as IMK: A.E.Tar.190).

28 With regard to the other scripta the performative model is more appropriate. At least one scribe seems to have been aware that he was rewriting or reinterpreting a previous work[s] "[I] wrote this *gazavat* anew", Istanbul: Millet Kütüphanesi, A.E.Tar.188 (1810) fol.55b (henceforth referred to as IMK: A.E.Tar.188).

29 Bologna: Biblioteca Universitaria, Bub.3459 (1668–1669) fol.108b (henceforth referred to as BBU: Bub.3459).

30 VNB: H.O.71d (1754), fol.67b. At the end of the next work in the manuscript which details the later exploits of Tiryaki Hasan Pasha, the same distinction is made again, VNB: H.O.71d fol.86a: "the one who wrote this *menakib* [is] the poor one, the humble, and the needy (the mercy of God the all-powerful be on him) Edirnevi al-Seyyid Abdullah Hasib ben Ali ibn Veli, and read the *ihlas* [sura] three times and the *fatiha* once for the soul of this [afore]mentioned one."

31 I discuss in Chapter 4 the fact that these manuscripts all exhibit a quite unique introductory section which has a far more politically and religiously orthodox tone and utilises to a far greater degree of Persian and Arabic linguistic elements.

32 MIHK: No.5070 (1757) and VNB: H.O.71d (1754); and Munich: Bayerische Staatsbibliothek, O.R.393 (undated), Paris: Bibliothèque Nationale, Nr.525 (undated) (henceforth referred to as MBS: O.R.393 and PBN: Nr.525 respectively). BBU: Bub.3459 (1668–1669) is closely related to O.R.393 (undated) and Nr.525 (undated) but has a few scribal additions.

33 Budapest: Magyar Tudományos Akademia Konyvtara, O.216 (1716) (henceforth referred to as BMTAK: O.216). Paris: Bibliothèque Nationale, Sup.Turc.170 (1760) (henceforth referred to as PBN:Sup.Turc.170) appears to be copy of Istanbul: Millet Kütüphanesi, A.E.Tar.189 (1715) (henceforth referred to as IMK: A.E.Tar.189), and both bear a degree of interrelation with O.216 (1716), although for reasons I outline in Chapter 4, they cannot unproblemtically be described as produced and consumed within a discourse of authority.

34 In BBU: Bub.3459 fol.89b the reader has added *kuffar* before the word *asker* and then added ی to the end of *asker*.

35 Ibid., fol.80b.

36 For example, Cambridge: University Library, O.R.700 (1773–1774) (henceforth referred to as CUL: O.R.700), London: British Library, O.R.12961 (1789) and London: British Library, O.R.33 (undated) (henceforth referred to as LBL: O.R.12961 and LBL: O.R.33).

37 For example, MBS: O.R.393 fol.6a and fol.63a; IMK: A.E.Tar.188, fol.1b and 52b. In the former all seven instances of Ahmed have been corrected, whereas in the latter two out of the seven instances have been corrected.

38 MBS: O.R.393 fol.63a.

39 A clue to the origin of this misnaming and why it is Ahmed that is erroneously cited as sultan may be provided by LBL:O.R.12961. On fol.1b, in what is essentially a preface, it is written, "The tellers of news, the transmitters of history and the glorious sayers of past events, wondrous stories and strange dreams, reported that before the accession to the throne of the exalted Sultan Ahmed, from the line of Osman, sultan of both land and sea, may he rest in peace, rebels appeared in the province of Anatolia." It is possible that the scripta which reference Ahmed display the result of an earlier navigational variation and a shift from "before the time of Ahmed" to "in the time of Ahmed".

40 Evidence of different communities' diverse reading practices can be found in the marginal notes in *Piers Plowman* manuscripts among other sources. C. D. Benson, "Another Fine Manuscript Mess: Authors, Editors, and Readers of *Piers Plowman*," in *New Directions in Later Medieval Manuscript Studies*, ed. Derek Pearsall (York: York Medieval Press, 2000), 27–28, has argued that marginalia demonstrates that the concerns of medieval audiences do not concur with those of modern readers. While the latter are concerned with the poet's sources and theological positions, the former mark the seven deadly sins, proverbs, prophecies, different genres of discourse and examples of ecclesiastical abuse. He suggests that this demonstrates different reading strategies, perhaps a reading for future compilations, or *florilecture*, or ethical reading.

41 See also the practice of meditative reading outlined by Sylvia Huot, "A Book Made for a Queen: The Shaping of a Late Medieval Anthology Manuscript (B.N. fr. 24429)," in *The Whole Book: Cultural Perspectives on the Medieval Miscellany*, ed. Stephen G. Nichols and Siegfried Wenzel (Ann Arbor, MI: University of Michigan Press, 1996), 129. Here she describes meditative reading as an expansive reading process or strategy where the reader dwells on a familiar text, repeating it and each time casting an ever wider net of associations until they are led to the contemplation of many different points.

42 Dagenais, *The Ethics of Reading*, 62.

43 This is akin to a process which might be labelled *ethical viewing* described by Robert Rosenstone, *Visions of the Past: The Challenge of Film to Our Idea of History* (Cambridge, MA, and London: Harvard University Press, 1995), 156 and 177. Here he describes how some films provide opportunities for nonlinear readings of the past. Such films do not pretend to describe the literal reality of past events, look for documentary truths, emphasise a linear sense of time nor focus on providing an analysis of cause and effect and naturalistic explanations for why things occur. Rather, they focus on providing different kinds of truths – instead of factual truth perhaps narrative, emotional, psychological or symbolic truths (141) on symbolising personal traits and virtues, people's perceptions of power, authority and morality. In this aspect they prefer morality to chronology and attempt to present different ways of understanding ourselves and the world. Although Scott Troyan, *Textual Decorum: A Rhetoric of Attitudes in Medieval Literature* (New York and London: Garland Publishing, Inc., 1994), does not refer to literacy practices, he does strongly argue that apparent incoherencies and errors should be reinterpreted as deliberate, and consequently one should try and understand what meaning they may have had for a medieval audience. See p.17 for his idea that disjunctions are attempts to modulate responses.

44 I discuss the ethical reading of some apparently incoherent passages in more detail in Claire Norton, "Being Tiryaki Hasan Pasha: The Politico-Textual Appropriations of an Ottoman Hero," in *Frontiers of the Ottoman Imagination: Essays in Honour of Rhoads Murphey*, ed. Marios Hadjianastasis (Leiden: Brill, 2014).

45 A version of this event that describes the trick and outcome can be found in IMK: A.E.Tar.187 fols 7b-13b, fol.8b contains the supposedly incoherent section.

46 I utilise the distinction drawn between power and authority by Greg Dening, *Mr Bligh's Bad Language: Passion, Power and Theatre on the Bounty* (Cambridge: Cambridge University Press, 1992), 80–81. He notes that power is public, impersonal and dependent on rituals of reification and signs of distance, whereas authority is private, personal and dependent on interpretative wisdom and signs of adaptability. A man could have power without authority and vice versa.

47 For example, he is depicted as having the ability to locate fords in previously impassable rivers, he can discern an individual's true intent and he experiences prophetic visions; see IMK: A.E.Tar. 187 2a-b, 5a-b 42a-b. I discuss the

74 The gazavatnames: erasing oral residue

intertextual references to *menakibname* and *kesik-baş* (severed-head) literature in more detail in Claire Norton, "Sacred Sites, Severed Heads and Prophetic Visions," *Journal of the Anthropology of the Contemporary Middle East and Central Eurasia* 2/1 (2014).

48 Which of these readings or ethical messages will appear dominant is dependent upon the frame in which the audience receives the narrative, other aspects of the narrative and the audiences' personal interpretative structures. For example, if the audience is not familiar with *menakibname* literature or their motifs, or the work is framed in terms of orthopraxic religion, thus effectively over-coding any *menakibname* references, then the mystical reading will not be so obviously available.

49 c.f. Katib Çelebi, *Fezleke*, 151–152 and LBL: O.R.6442 fol.60a. I discuss Katib Çelebi's re-inscription of this event and that of later reader-writers in Chapter 5.

50 LBL: O.R.6442 fol.60a.

51 This term was originally coined by Paul Zumthor, *La Lettre et la Voix: De la 'littérature' médiéval* (Paris: Seuil, 1987) and subsequently used and developed by Schaefer, "Hearing from Books."

52 Schaefer, "Hearing from Books," 117. Schaefer conflates the reception of a text in vocality with the presence of a high degree of formula in the text, and although I am not prepared to ascribe formula exclusively to either 'oral' texts in the traditional sense nor solely to texts received in 'vocality' as Schaefer does, her ideas are still immensely useful.

53 In certain situations graphical marks may be designed to provide information, not for a silent personal reader but for a reader intending to read the text aloud to others: short vowelling unknown or unfamiliar words could aid pronunciation, the use of coloured ink or overlining could indicate where one could pause between sections, for example.

54 Ong, *Orality and Literacy*, 40.

55 Machan, "Editing, Orality, and Late Middle English Texts," 236. Flemming, "Public Opinion under Sultan Süleyman," 51, and Silay, "The Usage and Function of Digression," 150, both conclude from the presence of addresses to an audience or reader that a work was intended to be read aloud or possessed a significant oral influence.

56 I use this term as a counterpoint to the concept of vocality to describe a reception context in which the text is primarily read, not heard.

57 BBU: Bub.3459 fols 82a, 82b, 83b, 85b and 87b.

58 Ibid., fol.80b. Interestingly religious phrases, references to God, the Prophet and Qur'anic verses are not written in red in this manuscript, although they are overlined in red. The exception is a Qur'anic quote on fol.80b. This has the effect that the red interjections effectively spatially divide the text, possibly making it easier to search and read.

59 In addition, on LBL: O.R.33 fol.15a when the effects of the first three cannon balls fired by the enemy at Nagykanizsa castle are discussed, the words *ikinci* and *üçüncü* have been written in red, although the latter has been over-inscribed in black at some later time. This again seems to serve an organisational function. There are also intermittently other unusual signs written in red above some words, namely ~ and a short vertical straight line written above words in the manner of the symbols used for short vowels. See fols.1b, 16b–17a, 20a–b, 22b–27b, 35a, 43b, 49a–50a, 51a, 52a, 53a, 55a and 59a.

60 Ibid., fol.59b.

61 Bratislava: Universitätsbibliothek, T.F.46 (1689) fol.53b (henceforth referred to as BU: T.F.46) includes, written diagonally on the left-hand side of the page, a prayer for God's mercy for the one who wrote, the one who read and the one

The gazavatnames: *erasing oral residue* 75

    who listened. Vienna: National-bibliothek, H.O.71a (undated) fol.25a (henceforth referred to as VNB: H.O.71a) and IMK: A.E.Tar.188 fol.55b.
62 Cairo: Dar al-Kutub, No.235 (undated) fol.37a (henceforth referred to as CDK: No.235). See also Vienna: National-bibliothek, H.O.71c (1671) fol.42b (henceforth referred to as VNB: H.O.71c) and BMTAK: O.216 fol.71b.
63 VNB: H.O.71d fol.67a and BMTAK: O.216 fol.71b.
64 See BBU: Bub.3459 fol.108b for an example of the former case and VNB: H.O.71a fol.25a and Berlin: Preußische National-Bibliothek, A.Oct.34 (undated) fol.64a for the latter (henceforth referred to as BPN: A.Oct.34).
65 BMTAK: O.216 fol.71b.

4 The *gazavatnames*
Rewriting the exemplar – individual scripta

Rubrication

Titles possess a complex notational status: they describe, denote, exemplify, advertise and contain potential readings. Nomination identifies the work as a particular script and, by positioning it within a known frame, constructs or modifies audiences' horizon of expectation and thus their consequent reception and interpretation of the work.[1] Modern cataloguers and scholars have categorised the twenty-five Nagykanizsa *gazavatname* manuscripts, despite their variations, within a typographic model as instances, or copies, of one work and have given this now unique work a single title: *Gazavat-i Tiryaki Hasan Paşa* [*The Campaign of Tiryaki Hasan Pasha*].[2] This collective rubrication positions the work as a campaign narrative and assigns it to a single genre, that of *gazavatname*, thereby conditioning the expectations of contemporary audiences in response to the work. So great is the lure of the typographic model and its insistence on a single title and genre that when scholars have encountered alternative titles on these twenty-five manuscripts, they have ignored them or argued that the scribe or rubricator made a mistake.[3]

However, as Maclaverty notes, titles belong to instances of a work and not to the work itself.[4] One of the most important things that these titles and rubrics can tell us is how the scribes perceived these texts, how they categorised them and how they expected their readers to classify and respond to them. Diverse or varied titles are therefore important and should not be erased as a result of overzealous cataloguing. The different titles foreground the fluidity that the terms *tarih*, *hikaye* and *gazavatname* possessed for distinct Ottoman discourse communities: by variously rubricating these nearly identical manuscripts, the scribes reflect different Ottoman understandings of these genre classifications as well as different conceptions of the factual or fictional status of the Nagykanizsa narrative. Although the term *hikaye* is generally understood as connoting a tale or story and thus implying a fictional aspect, it can be applied to narratives with a historical theme and a greater degree of realism than those of other Ottoman literary genres such as epico-religious narratives.[5] On the other hand, *tarih* is usually applied to narratives agreed to be about historical events.⁶ However, for some, but not all, Ottoman audiences the term *tarih* more appropriately signifies the genre of chronicle or dynastic history, which relates the events of a sultan's reign year by year. For such audiences, descriptions of specific military campaigns would perhaps be more properly classified as *gazavatnames*. *Menakibnames*, in contrast, are generally understood as consisting of the narratives detailing the semi-legendary exploits or heroic deeds of heroes framed as warrior-saints and thus often possess a pronounced fictional aspect from the perspective of twenty-first-century Western academia.⁷ The different titles therefore signify the diverse ways in which scribes and their implied audiences responded to and categorised the manuscripts – sometimes as history and sometimes as story – illustrating that generic distinctions are not inherent in the text but are rather a product of the conceptual frameworks of the scribe or implied audience.

Framings

The framings of texts can have a significant effect on the potential meanings available to audiences. The *gazavatname* scribes, through the use of different introductory and concluding sections, as well as other narrative, linguistic and stylistic variations, in effect created different, individual scripta as they read, interpreted and reinscribed their exemplars. These rewritings provide us with evidence of the literacy practices and conceptual frameworks of different interpretative communities: how audiences appropriated, interpreted and read the tale in diverse ways. In this chapter, I will make explicit how the different re-inscriptions display complex and often contradictory attitudes towards the political hegemony of the military-administrative system. While some of the scripta were inscribed from a generally more orthodox, official and authoritative perspective, others were written within a more heterodox or even subversive cartography. Many of the scribes and copyists have read Tiryaki Hasan Pasha as a laudable exemplum of an Ottoman border commander and constructed the lesson that it is obedience and religious faith that ensures victory. Others have situated him politically far more firmly within the central, imperial political elite and religiously within a more orthodox interpretation of Islam – he is the epitome of a good Muslim. However, it is also feasible to read the text in a far more subversive manner, and a number of scribes have rewritten their scripta in such a way that different political interests, constructions of identity and imaginations of religious praxis are foregrounded. These plural readings provide an apposite example that meaning is not unitary and located in the text, but it is constructed by audiences within the protocols, norms and frameworks of their interpretative communities and their previous experiences.

For the purposes of analysis and discussion, it is helpful to divide the Nagykanizsa *gazavatname* scripta into three broad categories. These divisions largely coincide with differences in the introductory sections that the scripta have. Group one scripta all include a virtually identical, short introduction and can be considered for heuristic purposes to constitute a normative or standard version of the tale.[8] Group two manuscripts all possess a longer introduction containing a number of Qur'anic quotations and appear to have been inscribed within a more fixed, authoritative discourse, which not only permits the establishment of possible relationships of inscription or copying but may also explain their politically and religiously more conservative or orthodox interpretation of events.[9] The group three scripta are far more distinct as texts and as such have unique introductions.[10]

Introductions

Group one scripta essentially narrate the same events from a similar perspective, but they are not identical copies and the differences among the various scripta cannot be adequately described in terms of scribal or chirographic variation. Although the variations are more lexical than semantic, there are a few differences in terms of content.[11] The scripta all commence with Qur'anic verse 2:249, which forms part of a series of verses that narrate the story of David and Goliath: "many a time has a small band defeated a large horde by the will of God. God is with those who are patient (and persevere)."[12] This quotation effectively conditions audience expectations of the tale that will follow: it is presented as a heroic fight of the few against the many. Commentaries on this verse stress the following maxims: size and strength are of no avail against truth, courage, faith, determination and careful planning; the hero should use his own weapons and those available against the enemy; if God is with you then the enemy's weapon will become a weapon against him; pure faith brings God's reward; and personality conquers all dangers and puts heart into wavering friends. These are essentially also the fundamental lessons of the Nagykanizsa narrative. It is a tale that emphasises the careful planning of the commander of the besieged castle, Tiryaki Hasan Pasha: his perseverance, faith and cunning stratagems. He has very few men and weapons, but he uses effectively what he has. Through this quotation an intertextual parallel is constructed between David and Tiryaki Hasan Pasha. Just as David killed Goliath with trickery and Goliath's own weapon, thereby causing the Philistine army to flee, similarly Tiryaki Hasan Pasha turns the enemy's greed and suspicion of each other against them to obtain their cannons, which he subsequently uses against them, something that ultimately results in the flight of their army. Following the quotation, an Ottoman-Turkish gloss is provided, which may suggest that the implied audience was not expected either to be familiar with the quotation or to have the required level of Arabic to translate it themselves.[13] There is then a statement from the implied scribe that he has written the work in order that it not be kept secret or forgotten and a plea that he be remembered in the audiences' prayers.

Group two manuscripts all contain a variant of a longer, two-folio introduction that has the effect of situating the subsequent narrative in a religiously orthodox framework. It begins with a discussion of God's creation of the world and the claim that the purpose of life is to worship God as it was for this reason that he created humans. It describes how God made Muslims special by giving them the spirit, which he withheld from synthesists, infidels and hypocrites. This suggestion that non-Muslims are lesser in God's eyes is an idea continued in the next section, where it is argued that infidels can never be true friends of the believers. A clear distinction between Muslims and non-Muslims is thus being delineated, preparing the reader for the next passage which, despite a few caveats, essentially exhorts the virtues of waging war on non-believers, arguing that it is a more noble action than the perambulation around the *Kaba* while on the Hajj. The introduction then lists the duties incumbent upon every Muslim, including praying five times a day and the obligation to undertake *gaza* [war]. The implicit message of this introduction is that *gaza* against the infidel, because of their status as the infidel, is a religious duty incumbent upon all Muslims.

This theme is continued and emphasised through the use of a number of Qur'anic quotations. The introductory section begins with a partial quotation from Qur'anic verse 4:84: "So fight on in the way of God, [. . . b]ut urge the believers [to fight]. It may well be that God will keep back the might of the infidels." The use of this Qur'anic quotation to begin and thereby frame the narrative as opposed to verse 2:249 used in group one scripta alters the horizon of expectations of audiences. Together with two other Qur'anic quotations – "I have not created the *jinns* and men, but to worship Me" and "those who believe should not take unbelievers as their friends in preference to those who believe" – it manipulates the focus of the narrative and helps to situate the audiences' reception of the subsequent narrative as a story of dutiful Muslims, who were created solely to worship God and who fulfill their obligations to God by fighting the infidel.[14] This contrasts with the use of verse 2:249 in the introduction of group one scripta, which emphasises that the few may defeat the many because they are favoured by God as a result of the *justness* of their cause and their *aversion to tyranny*.

By framing the narrative in this way, audiences of the group two manuscripts are encouraged to read the defence of Nagykanizsa and the actions of Tiryaki Hasan Pasha as the story of a good Muslim fulfilling his duty by fighting the infidels. In the cartography of violence mapped out by this introduction, the infidels are the 'other'; infidels can never be associated with self, and it is their status as infidel rather than their actions that determines their subsequent status as an enemy or friend of the Ottomans. Moreover, this introduction also works to over-code the more heterodox elements present in the main narrative. This is not to say that potentially heterodox readings are erased; they are still available to those familiar with *menakibname* [narratives of heroic and miraculous deeds] works and other literature such as *kesik-baş* [severed-head] tales. Rather, there exists more than one possible semiotic system at work in the manuscripts, and this introduction conditions audience expectations, thereby facilitating a more orthodox reading. It is

80 *The gazavatnames: rewriting the exemplar*

interesting that the copyist or a later reader of Bub.3459 has overlined in red the Qur'anic quotations and other religious phrases, thereby not only making explicit their own conceptual framework but also visually conditioning the manner in which future audiences will read the narrative.[15]

Endings: obedience to justice or those in authority?

Just as introductions frame and condition audience responses to a text, so too do conclusions. One of the most significant variations in terms of evidence of different scribal interpretative strategies occurs at the end of the majority of the scripta in a digressionary epilogue added in the voice of the implied scribe on the subject of political authority and the religious obligation to obey one's superiors. The majority of the scripta include a short version of this digression, and although they are not identical, there is an essential commonality which permits them to be classified together.[16] An example of the digression is as follows:

> Hey, believers, after the great have a deep desire and have become pure, God (be he exalted) accepts their prayers. And those who are the community of Muhammad must obey him because obedience to him is one of the articles of faith. The Lord God (be he exalted) shall give help and victory to those soldiers, because these soldiers are the soldiers of God (be he exalted) and he will judge them worthy of a great *gaza* like this. But, the greatest commander is our fortunate and august *padişah*. May his ministers refrain from tyranny because the Lord God (be he lauded and exalted) commanded, "Obey Allah, and the Prophet and those in authority among you" this means: obedience to them is part of Islam.[17]

This concluding passage stresses the necessity of obedience to military commanders if victory is to be obtained, thereby creating an indirect intertextual link to the Qur'anic passage concerning the defeat of Goliath from which Qur'anic verse 2:249 is taken. The soldiers in Saul's army are tested and told not to drink water from a stream. Those that obey their commander are given strength by God, so they are therefore able to defeat Goliath and his army.[18] It also establishes an intra-textual link to the ethical readings of the tricks and stratagems employed by Tiryaki Hasan Pasha earlier in the narrative and their emphasis on the importance of having blind obedience to one's superiors.[19]

Four scripta have, however, added a few extra lines to this passage, suggesting that the scribes interpreted the work in a significantly different way to other scribal readers:

> If those in authority do not act in accordance with the law code of Muhammad and [instead] act according to their own desire and if they stretch out the hand of tyranny, that which is suitable for Muslim

The gazavatnames: *rewriting the exemplar* 81

believers is that they should bring him [that person] forcefully and by compulsion to [obedience to] the command of God and the traditions of the exalted Prophet and to the law code of Muhammad and let them prevent him from [perpetrating] tyranny. If he will not turn away, that person is not one of those in authority: May it be thus known.[20]

The passage now preaches obedience only to *just* rulers and advocates violent rebellion against and the usurpation of unjust or tyrannical rulers.[21] This additional phrase repositions the emphasis of the narrative on the virtue of justice rather than obedience. The metaphor of rulers stretching out the hand of tyranny in this passage also provides an intra-textual link to the earlier textual digression on the importance of justice, King Nüşirevan and the enemy. In this digression, the narrator reiterates the opening Qur'anic quotation then comments that the kindness and favour of God will only be bestowed upon a commander who does not stretch out the hand of tyranny but is just and fair. "There is no help [and thus victory] nor favourable opportunities for oppressors. The infidels are victorious."[22] He then asserts that if the commander himself does not commit tyranny, but turns a blind eye to that committed by his subordinates, then God will also not grant him victory because "to bring blasphemy into the world is better than to bring tyranny". God will therefore favour the infidel rather than an unjust Muslim ruler. As an example, the narrator refers to King Nüşirevan, ostensibly the greatest king of the Sasani line of Persian sovereigns, and comments that the Prophet himself praised him for his justness.[23] The addition of these few lines to the digressionary epilogue reframes the narrative and suggests that certain scribes read and interpreted the actions of Tiryaki Hasan Pasha within an interpretative political frame that stressed the importance of justice and *not* the necessity of blind obedience to one's superiors. The addition also strongly implies that the Habsburgs are the enemy, not because of their status as infidels but because of their tyrannical actions, a view that is implicit in the *fethname* account of events as sent to Queen Elizabeth I and discussed in Chapter 2.

That the potentially subversive nature of this additional passage was not lost on a scribe nor, more probably, a later reader, is evidenced by the short-vowelling (the addition of diacritics to indicate the vowels) practices in one of the manuscripts. The short vowelling of whole passages is uncommon in non-religious texts that employ Arabic-based alphabets and is usually restricted only to the Qur'an and other religious or legal works.[24] However, scripta A.Oct.34 (undated) is short vowelled throughout, with one exception: the passage already noted that advocates violent opposition to unjust rulers. The short vowelling subsequently recommences with the concluding remarks requesting prayers be said for Tiryaki Hasan Pasha and the scribe.[25] A possible explanation of this anomaly centres on an alternative function of short vowelling: to aid students who are learning to read languages that employ the Arabic alphabet. Perhaps the person responsible for short vowelling the text thought that this section was potentially too subversive for students?

Three manuscripts have, in contrast, rewritten the digression to emphasise the importance that obedience to the *padişah*, Tiryaki Hasan Pasha and Islam played in the successful defence.[26]

> Hey believer, brethren, be aware, that is to say, know about the victory and success of this handful of poor *gazis* against the infidels – O you who believe, obey God and the Prophet and those in authority among you – (it was expressed) and it was because of the perfect level of obedience and submission to the *padişah*, the religion of Islam and to Hasan Pasha and their avoidance and shunning of tyranny – praise be to Allah (be he exalted) – [that] events happened in the manner above.[27]

Each of these three manuscripts also include the two-folio introduction analysed that argues that non-Muslims are the enemy by virtue of their unbelief and that the duties of a good Muslim include the obligation to wage war against the infidel. Working together the introduction and epilogue thus effectively frame the narrative and condition audience responses to the narrative. They situate the cartography of violence in religious terms rather than on an axis of the just and the tyrannical. Although they cannot eliminate or erase other potential meanings, they can over-code them. For example, the digression on King Nüşirevan and the precept that justice is more important than belief, previously outlined, is still present, but when situated in an interpretative framework that emphasises obedience to authority, its interpretative significance is reduced.

The example of this digressionary epilogue illustrates the polysemic potentiality of texts and the dialogic act of reading and re-inscription. It demonstrates the potential problems in using a typographic model predicated on a single original text and multiple identical copies to explicate manuscripts produced and consumed within a more fluid or performative discourse. The search for an original authorial text would result in a disregard for the variety of ways in which the scribes interpreted and appropriated their exempla in accordance with the conceptual schemas of their interpretative communities, ideological agendas and own worldviews. A model in which each manuscript is privileged is a more profitable way of exploring the reading strategies and intellectual paradigms of different early modern Ottoman (and other) audiences.

Budapest: Magyar Tudományos Akademia Konyvtara, O.216: arguments for a more orthodox reading

As suggested, the group two manuscripts appear to have been reinscribed within a politically and religiously more orthodox interpretative frame. O.216 (1716) includes the introductory section already discussed, but it further adjusts audiences' expectations by framing Tirykai Hasan Pasha in a more official, imperial and orthodox manner in its rubric: *This is the treatise of the council official, Tiru Gazi Hasan Pasha*.[28] The phrase 'council official' [*divan efendisi*] is usually translated to mean 'the official secretary of a vizier or governor of a province', but this is not really appropriate in the context of Tiryaki Hasan Pasha, who was himself both a provincial governor and later a vizier, not a secretary. I have therefore read this phrase as suggesting that Tiryaki Hasan Pasha was an official of the *divan* or imperial council.[29] Furthermore, the drug references inherent in his name (*tiryaki* means opium addict) are effaced by changing his nickname from *Tiryaki* to *Tiru*. Such an adjustment is reinforced by the inclusion in this scriptum of another work that narrates the exploits of Tiryaki Hasan Pasha after his successful defence of Nagykanizsa usually titled *The Book of the Other Campaign Narratives*.[30] In this work he is specifically described as abstemious and as an ascetic.[31] This 'sequel' narrative describes Tiryaki Hasan Pasha's relief of the siege of Pest, his raids on the Croatian border with the Crimean Han, various other battles in Hungary and his participation in the attack against the *celali* rebel Canpuladoğlu in Anatolia at the behest of the grand vizier, Kuyucu Murad Pasha.[32] The narrative culminates with the death of Tiryaki Hasan Pasha after he has had built a *medrese* and tomb in Pécs.

The inclusion of other 'works' in individual scripta not only provides an additional interpretative frame for audiences that works to condition their responses to the text but also reflects how actual audiences read. To the extent that such manuscripts are deliberately rather than randomly collated – that is they can be considered as anthologies and not miscellanies – they can inform us of the literacy practices, generic categories and conceptual schemas of the compilers and their implied audiences within which the work was received and interpreted.[33] Was the work bound with other advice works, stories, histories or religious works? What common themes or concerns can be identified? What intellectual, aesthetic or pragmatic decisions and rhetorical strategies determined the contents? In *The Book of the Other Campaign Narratives* Tiryaki Hasan Pasha is presented as a good Muslim, a loyal servant of the sultan who does his duty by fighting the infidel. All traces of liminality; be they social, in his distance from traditional centres of power; spiritual, in his depiction as a more heterodox hero; or personal, in the suggestion that he was a drug addict, are removed. He is reinterpreted in a far more stable, fixed manner. He is also located within the central networks of authority and patronage to a much greater extent in this work, as exemplified by his establishment of a *medrese* [educational institution] and a *vakıf* [charitable endowment that provides support for religious institutions such as schools, mosques, etc.] in Pécs, his kissing the imperial rescript commanding him to go to Anatolia and his subsequent placing of it against his head in a gesture of respect and subservience to the word of the sultan.[34]

There is also evidence that the scribe of O.216 imagined his implied audience as men of religion rather than men of war as he refers to "our religious friends who will read it [the tale]". The use of 'we' creates a psychological link and accentuates the relationship between the implied scribe and the implied audience.[35] The scribe and copyist of H.O.71d and No.5070 similarly ask God's forgiveness "for my religious brethren who read [this] and the compatriots who are warriors of Islam", creating a distinction between the two communities and situating the copyist within the former.[36]

Evidence that actual audiences of group two manuscripts had knowledge of key religious texts and read the work within a religiously informed context is provided by a marginal note in H.O.71d (1754). In this manuscript besides the numerous Qur'anic quotations in the introduction, there is also an Arabic prayer included in the 'sequel' text. An anonymous reader has provided a gloss for the prayer in the margins, writing: "The Sahib-i Keşşaf said about this prayer that 'truly, I have found the name of the greatest'. Now it is this that was said, 'let them read this prayer after every prayer, by his grave, may he be exalted, he will guide it to acceptance. Allah knows best the right words.'"[37] This gloss offers a commentary on the Arabic prayer in the text and, through its rather oblique reference to *Sahib-i Keşşaf*, creates an intertextual link to the Ottoman scholar of *hadith* and Qur'anic commentary, Hayreddin Hızır Atufi's *Keşfü'l-Meşarık*. This work was an explanation of the *Meşariku'l-envari'n-nebeviyye*, which itself was a collection of *hadith* found in the *Sahib-i Buhari*. The writer of the comment obviously expected that future readers would be familiar with not only the exegetical work of Hayreddin Hızır Atufi but also the shorthand reference to it. Such an interpretative community is far removed from that of some of the more heterodox scripta that will be discussed below.

Cambridge: University Library, O.R.700 – a more heterodox reading

O.R.700 (1773–4) offers the potential for a radically more heterodox and politically subversive reading than many of the other scripta.[38] In essence it is a complex site of contestation where numerous authoritative voices and discourses are challenged. Unlike the other scripta, it presents the tale within an oral storytelling frame with the first sentence of the introductory section, including numerous references to a performance in vocality: "the narrators of news and the ones who relate works and the traditionalists of the time relate that in the reign of the exalted Sultan Ahmed Han . . ."[39] This reference to a tradition transmitted, performed and received in vocality is then authorised by the phrase "and it is also recounted from the official letters of the sultan". Here the authority of the sultan and the administrative system, as well as the authority of the written word, is used to legitimise the 'oral' account. This idea of the scribe or author having constructed his work from various accounts performed in vocality is continued throughout the narrative with interjections that reference oral sources and transmitters: "but the oral source states that . . ." and "the oral narrator transmitted . . ."[40]

However, such scribal comments are not sufficient to conclude that the narrative was originally received in vocality; further evidence in the form of vocality cues would be required. Indeed a written Nagykanizsa *gazavatname* scriptum must have served as an exemplar for the scribe because much of O.R.700 is identical to the other scripta in the corpus. Therefore the references to 'oral' sources should probably be interpreted as indicating that the scribe-author had recourse to both written and 'oral' sources or that it was simply a rhetorical device used to create a particular atmosphere or as a validatory mechanism.

Following the standard Qur'anic verse 2:249 and its Ottoman Turkish gloss in the introductory section, the scribe notes that his aim in "expounding the great battles of the vizier and that *gazi* and maker of plans" is to encourage praise for Tiryaki Hasan Pasha.[41] He then continues that he will now make plain how Tiryaki Hasan Pasha conquered Nagykanizsa castle, therefore refiguring Hasan Pasha as a conqueror and not as a defender. Although the scriptum emphasises Tiryaki Hasan Pasha's promotion to vizier, I suggest that it offers a politically more subversive or heterodox reading than many of the other scripta. Specifically, Tiryaki Hasan Pasha is not depicted as an imperially sanctioned hero. Rather he stands alone, outside of the political-military establishment and central imperial networks of power. The scribe complicates the power-authority distinction and figures Tiryaki Hasan Pasha as possessing authority derived from his personal experience and ability rather than simply the power arising from his position within the administrative structure. While in the other *gazavatname* scripta Tiryaki Hasan Pasha is portrayed as the grand vizier's equal, someone worthy of respect, here he is depicted as the superior of the grand vizier. When he meets with the grand vizier prior to the first siege of Nagykanizsa, the *gazis* look to him, not the grand vizier, and ask him what he commands, arguing that he knows best.[42] This is followed by Tiryaki Hasan Pasha giving orders to the grand vizier's own steward to go ahead and besiege Nagykanizsa castle.[43] Tiryaki Hasan Pasha here has usurped the power of his superiors through authority derived from his personal abilities and experience rather than that bestowed upon him by his official position within the military-administrative structure.

The extent of Tiryaki Hasan Pasha's authority is further foregrounded by the scribe deliberately distancing him from the official military-administrative system and hierarchical structures of dependency and networks of power. This is achieved through portraying Tiryaki Hasan Pasha as reluctant to accept praise and gifts and preferring to bestow rewards on his men from his own possessions rather than requesting positions from the central administration. Fish has argued that, "requesting and accepting praise are acts which place their performer in a position of dependence whereas promising and rejecting [. . .] leave the self inviolate."[44] Receiving the sultan's robes, swords and other gifts, therefore, figure one in a subordinate position; one's acts are available to be judged worthy or unworthy by the sultan and rewarded accordingly. Making requests for military-administrative positions for one's men also implies a recognition that the person from whom the request is made is superior, if only in his ability to potentially fulfil the request. Moreover, gifts of clothing integrate the recipient into networks of power and depict social relations on the wearer's body.[45] The investiture of particular clothes including robes of honour is the means by which a person is given a form, shape or a social function as a monarch, lord, office holder or household servant.[46] Clothes thus possess a transnaturing ability and a constitutive power that can be used to enforce conformity. They are persistent reminders of status and incorporation, and as such they function as a material mnemonic that inscribes obligations and indebtedness upon the body.[47] Being given a vizierial robe or *tuğ* inscribed not only the duties of office but an obligation to the sultan and the state structures: it marked the assimilation of the recipient to the Ottoman body politic.[48] In the other *gazavatname* scripta, Tiryaki Hasan Pasha is incorporated into the military-administrative structure through acts of gift giving: the sultan bestows on him a vizierate and gives him horses, robes of honour and a bejewelled sword.[49] At Tiryaki Hasan Pasha's request the sultan also rewards his men, making grants of a *sancak* [administrative district] and giving monetary rewards to all the soldiers who were besieged.[50] In O.R.700, however, Hasan Pasha does not make any requests, nor is he rewarded with robes of honour, swords and horses by the sultan; he thus remains outside of the bonds entailed by gift giving.[51]

However, the most explicit demonstration of the personal authority of Tiryaki Hasan Pasha occurs when he effectively crowns Zirinoğlu (meaning 'son of Zirin') as king of Hungary: "He [Tiryaki Hasan Pasha] caused him [Zirinoğlu] to be invested with a robe of honour. Again he said, "[Y]ou are the Hungarian king" and he put a document in his hand.''[52] Zirinoğlu features in all of the manuscripts as the commander of the Hungarian forces allied with the Habsburgs during the 1601 siege. In all the scripta he enters into correspondence with Tiryaki Hasan Pasha following the defeat of the Habsburg besieging army and the raising of the second siege of Nagykanizsa, but in O.R.700 (1773–1774) he does not write a letter. Instead he visits Tiryaki Hasan Pasha in person and at that time is crowned king of Hungary.[53] Here, Tiryaki Hasan Pasha, rather than being incorporated into, and therefore subject to, a superior's hierarchy and structure, invests another and is a kingmaker.

Although this coronation is not corroborated by any other sources, there is considerable documentary evidence that there existed close relationships between various border commanders, and they frequently came to agreements among themselves that suited local conditions rather than the wishes or dictates of the respective imperial centres.[54] Moreover, through the inclusion of the following comment by the scribe just after the supposed coronation that "he [Tiryaki Hasan Pasha] sent him [Zirinoğlu] away with glory because the Hungarian people are always very much inclined to and supportive of the side of Islam", the demarcation of the self-other dichotomy in purely religious or ethnic terms is destabilised, and an alternative sense of identity based upon local border conditions is affirmed.[55] Tiryaki Hasan Pasha, although Muslim and an Ottoman military commander, fights to install as king a Christian Hungarian. It also shifts the cartography of antipathy of the narrative from one based upon empires (Ottoman and Habsburg) or religion (Christianity and Islam) to one concentrated on local border conditions. The siege is not located in the ideological conflict between Christendom and Islam; it is located in local Hungarian politics. Tiryaki Hasan Pasha is fighting to implement regime change; he wants to remove the Habsburg incumbent, the candidate of the imperial centre, and replace him with Zirinoğlu, the more local candidate. This shift from the imperial to the local is reinforced in a discussion about campaign plans earlier in the narrative between Tiryaki Hasan Pasha and the grand vizier. In all the other scripta Tiryaki Hasan Pasha argues that they should attack Nagykanizsa as then they will only be two or three days' journey from the Austrian king's capital. However, in O.R.700 he argues that Nagykanizsa is only two or three days from the capital of the Hungarian king.[56] This alteration has the effect of modifying the cartography of war implicit in the narrative: it is not a conflict between imperial rivals but one focused on local border conditions in Hungary. Lastly, the crowning of Zirinoğlu as the king of Hungary may also indicate the culturally heterogeneous nature of the implied audience: the heroes of this narrative are those of 'both sides', not only the Ottoman, Muslim Tiryaki Hasan Pasha but also the local Christian, Hungarian Zirinoğlu, who gains much of his prestige from being literally the son of Miklós Zrínyi, who achieved mythic status as a Hungarian hero when in 1566 he died leading a last, desperate charge from Szigetwar castle against the Ottoman sultan, Süleyman I.[57] In a similar manner, scriptum O.R.6442 (1815) imagines the Hungarians as if not sympathetic to the Ottomans then at least rather hostile to the Habsburgs. When the enemy are discussing capturing Nagykanizsa, Zirinoğlu is described as laughing up his sleeve in a secret, cunning manner, adding to the portrayal of Hungarian-Habsburg relations as full of mistrust and hostility.[58] Moreover, the European map of antipathies of this scribe is such that when citing the allies of the 'king of the Lutherans', he can read اینکلوس (*Ingiliz* -English) as انکروس (Engurus – Hungary) and thus envision Hungary taking sides with the 'King of the Lutherans' against the Habsburgs – a change that neatly reflects, and continues, the Habsburg-Hungarian rift that Tiryaki Hasan Pasha makes use of, and exacerbates, in the narrative.[59]

Zirinoğlu's investment as king in O.R.700 (1773–1774) also reifies the dominant maxim of the narrative: the importance of justice and need to refrain from tyranny. Zirinoğlu is the local Hungarian instantiation of King Nüşirevan, the just infidel who was favoured by God because of his aversion to tyranny and his renowned justice. Moreover, the idea that God favours the just is particularly foregrounded in this scriptum through the positioning of the section on Nüşirevan as a speech by Tiryaki Hasan Pasha rather than as a digression by the implied narrator or author. Furthermore, the 'digression' is extended with the claim that God will ensure that for the unjust commander, "his eyes will not see, his horse will not run, his sword will not cut."[60] This foregrounding of the importance of justice over obedience is also reasserted through the omission of the obedience digressionary epilogue found in many of the other scripta.

Lastly, the language used in this scriptum is very colourful. When Tiryaki Hasan Pasha's concealment of the castle's cannons is revealed with their sudden firing at the unsuspecting besiegers, it is described thus:

> [T]he cannon ball, the divine servant, after splitting one of the four commanders in half, severing the head of another and the arm of another caused the crown to fall to the ground from the head of the king. He himself fell like a mangy dog from the roof of a church and fainted like a swine.[61]

Other interesting descriptions include the castle with its cannons sticking out from the battlements being compared to a porcupine, the bombed and devastated houses in the confines of the castle being described as "the house of father woe" and the rather gory assertion that when the Ottomans pursued the enemy after the latter's defeat, so many were killed that one could cross over the ford on a bridge of corpses.[62] This colourful language in combination with some other similarities that will be discussed suggests a possible congruence between the implied audiences of O.R.700 (1773–1774) and the next scriptum I will look at: O.R.12961 (1789).

London: British Library, O.R.12961

O.R.12961 (1789), inscribed by Salih Ağa Divitdar on 21 March 1789, is the longest and possibly the most distinct of the manuscript corpus *Gazavat-i Tiryaki Hasan Paşa*. Not only does it include an additional and apparently unique thirty-folio narrative of Tiryaki Hasan Pasha's exploits in the region prior to his famous defence of Nagykanizsa, but it provides much longer descriptions of the weather and condition of the besiegers in the last few days of the siege, the capture of the enemy camp, distribution of booty, pursuit of the fleeing enemy by Kara Ömer Ağa and the battle between the Christian rulers at the end. With regard to the transmission and origin of the work, there is a strong suggestion that it may have originated as two separate tales. The first third of the narrative, which concerns Tiryaki Hasan Pasha's adventures before the siege of Nagykanizsa, features Arab Oğlu as his trusted deputy. However, with the commencement of the Nagykanizsa narrative, Arab Oğlu vanishes and is replaced by Kara Ömer Ağa. The fact that these two heroes both remain in their 'own' sections of the tale suggests that it may have originally been two distinct narratives.[63]

The gazavatnames: *rewriting the exemplar* 89

Differences in vocabulary, narrative and framing practices also intersect to present a different ideological position and suggest that the politico-cultural cartography of the scribe and intended audience was very different to that, for example, of O.216 (1716) – O.R.12961 (1789) offers a much more heterodox, earthy, politically liminal perspective. The articulation of self and other in this scriptum is also unusual because it includes alternative voices that imagine identity in opposition to the spatial and political imaginings inherent in both Ottoman and Habsburg imperial rhetoric. Moreover, the main theme in O.R.12961 (1789) is not the importance of justice or obedience to one's superiors, rather the moral lesson to be derived is that God helps the *just defender*. Although it is still possible to derive the moral of God aiding the just few in their fight with the many, the effect is lessened by the absence of both supporting Qur'anic quotations and the King Nüşirevân digression. These elements are replaced instead with proverbs concerning the danger of waking the sleeping snake. The idea that God helps or favours those who are attacked is given further support in the discussions at the end of the scriptum between the Swedish king and the pope in which the former argues that it would have been his Christian duty to aid the Austrian king in battle against the Ottomans if the Ottomans had been the aggressors, but as the Habsburgs attacked Ottoman lands, crushing peasants beneath their feet, the fault lies not with the Ottomans but with the Habsburgs.[64] This theme is revisited in Tiryaki Hasan Pasha's answer to the pope's query as to whether the Qur'an permits the slaughter of so many Christians. He answers that the Qur'an would prohibit it if the Ottomans had been the aggressors, but as it was the Habsburgs who were the besiegers and desired to invade Ottoman lands, then his actions were legitimate.[65] Such an emphasis on defence may reflect the time and place in which the work was inscribed and received – 1789. Over the course of the previous twenty years, Ali Bey had declared himself sultan of Egypt; in 1770 Russia had defeated the Ottomans on the Danube and in 1783 had invaded and annexed the Crimea and the northern coasts of the Black Sea; and lastly the Ottoman Empire was, in 1787, involved in a war against both the Austrian Habsburgs and the Russians. These events may have created a 'siege' mentality among some Ottomans, especially those garrisoned or living on the European marches.

Tiryaki Hasan Pasha: a contested hero

Tiryaki Hasan Pasha is the hero of this narrative. He is the ideal Ottoman commander: religious, just, competent, not personally avaricious for power or material possessions and considerate of his men. He is a wise and learned councillor, a competent administrator of affairs; he has an honoured place in the court and advises the grand vizier and sultan. Through the employment of select mnemonic frameworks of definition, and intertextual references to *menakibname* [accounts of heroic and miraculous deeds] and *kesik-baş* [severed-head] literature, he is depicted as a warrior-saint, a doer of exemplary

90 *The* gazavatnames: *rewriting the exemplar*

or miraculous deeds: he communes and intercedes with God and the Prophet on behalf of his men, he performs miracles, and he is portrayed as the epitome of the janissaries' *Bektaşi* saints. So why then is he also described as "a worn out old, dilapidated, drug addict and scoundrel" with "snot running down one nostril, very black, watery eyes with speckled irises . . . limbs . . . like mint stalks" who "if he sat he couldn't get up and if he was up he couldn't sit down, perhaps [without even] the strength to tie up his trouser cord"?[66] His mental capacity and character are also frequently doubted by both the enemy and his own men, who frequently describe him as a scoundrel or senile.[67] Moreover, both the enemy and his own loyal retainers who have fought with him for years frequently comment upon his opium addiction, and the latter often query his commands, assuming him to be intoxicated.[68] Tiryaki Hasan Pasha is full of contradictions: he is part of the central military-bureaucratic officialdom yet outside of it; he is religious, yet heterodox references overshadow his orthodoxy; he is a military hero yet is slyly mocked for his physical and mental weaknesses. Although Tiryaki Hasan Pasha's physical and mental imperfections provide a source of amusement for the audience, this dissonance in his person can most coherently be explained if he is read as a site of contestation for 'popular' audiences' competing attitudes and emotions towards heroes and members of the ruling elite.[69]

Indo-European heroes often occupy a liminal and contradictory position for audiences. Frequently they are depicted as the saviours and champions of the oppressed, but their very success also means they are members of the political and military elite, who are often seen as potential oppressors. Moreover, the violence and force that the hero uses in defence of society can so easily be turned against it, all of which results in audiences adopting an often ambivalent and antithetical attitude towards heroes. The tension and contradictory attitudes that audiences feel towards heroes are thus often reified as, and ameliorated by, the hero being characterised with particular physical or character flaws.[70] The depiction of Tiryaki Hasan Pasha in this scriptum reveals similar multiple tensions that can perhaps best be interpreted as arising from the implied audiences' plural and ambiguous attitudes towards authority figures and heroes.[71]

At the beginning of the scriptum, Tiryaki Hasan Pasha is spatially and politically situated within the heart of the central elite: he is located in the council chamber in the second court, offering advice to the grand vizier before being summoned to the throne room for an audience with the sultan himself. He is offered the position of grand vizier and the governorship of Egypt, both of which he refuses. He then requests, and is given, the governorship of the province of Buda on the Habsburg-Ottoman marches.[72] Outwardly, Tiryaki Hasan Pasha appears the obedient and devoted servant of the sultan and state; he shows suitable obeisance, kisses the floor and declares himself to be the slave of the sultan. However, it is his negotiation with the sultan and his refusal of official positions which first signals the tensions in the narrative and his distance from the official military-administrative system,

The gazavatnames: *rewriting the exemplar* 91

into which he is never fully incorporated. Unlike O.216 (1716) where, when he is ordered by the sultan to accept a number of appointments, he kisses the document bearing the command; in O.R.12961 (1789) he is not commanded to take up a military-administrative post but rather selects his own.[73] By refusing the sultan's appointments, he positions himself outside the military-administrative hierarchy and illustrates that he is not subject to the sultan's power.

This distance from hierarchical structures of dependency is reinforced through his reluctance, as in O.R.700 (1773–1774), to accept praise and gifts: at the end of the siege he is not rewarded in any way by the sultan; he does not receive any robes of honour, swords or horses, and more significantly, he is not made a vizier.[74] In addition, unlike in some of the other scripta, he does not request positions for his men from the sultan or central administration, rather he bestows upon them grants from his own possessions.[75] This distance from the centre is reflected in his naming: in contrast to other scripta, he is never referred to as vizier; he is Hasan Pasha or occasionally Tiryaki Hasan Pasha or Gazi Hasan Pasha. He is therefore both within and without the central administration, simultaneously a member of the imperial elite and outside of it.

There are other tensions apparent in the character of Tiryaki Hasan Pasha as portrayed in O.R.12961 (1789). Although he is generally depicted as an ideal, fair commander who encourages his men through financial incentives and inspiring words, he also intimidates his soldiers and threatens to twist off the head of Arab Oğlu and to kill his men if they flee the battlefield.[76] Likewise, despite being depicted as a paragon of frugality and as not desirous of high office, at the beginning of the narrative, Tiryaki Hasan Pasha comments rather bitterly that his ability was not previously recognised, and he is angry that his worldly goods were sold.[77] This tension again reflects his liminal position and the ambiguous feelings of the implied audience about him. Tiryaki Hasan Pasha is not an imperially sanctioned hero; rather, he is a hero for those who have a distrust of rulers. He cannot thus be depicted unproblematically as a hero, as this entails that he be recognised and rewarded within the military-administrative structure. This incorporation into the state structure would, as Dumézil has argued, result in his eventual distancing from the people for whom he was originally a hero. So he is subverted and left, to some extent, outside the centre. It is worth noting that Tiryaki Hasan Pasha is only depicted in such an ambiguous manner in this particular scriptum. The other *gazavatname* scripta essentially present him as an exemplar of either a successful military border commander, or as a competent, professional member of the imperial military-administrative elite. In all accounts he is figured as a good Muslim, albeit one who exhibits more or less miraculous or spiritual qualities.

In O.R.12961 (1789) Tiryaki Hasan Pasha is portrayed as very religious. He prays at every opportunity: at the five prayer times, when meeting the sultan, when giving his standard to his men, when dispatching his men on

92 The gazavatnames: *rewriting the exemplar*

missions and before engaging the enemy. However, rather than unproblematically representing an orthodox and state-sanctioned Islam, the narrative suggests, through numerous intertextual references and asides, that the Islam of Tiryaki Hasan Pasha is more akin to that of the dervish warrior-saints who populate *menakibname* literature. All of the *gazavatname* manuscripts contain intertextual references to *menakibname* and *kesik-baş* literature and thus offer a potential framing of Tiryaki Hasan Pasha as a warrior-saint. For example, Tiryaki Hasan Pasha is described as possessing miraculous skills and abilities similar to those of the *menakibname* warrior-saints: he predicts the future from natural omens; can discern an individual's true intent; manages to cross unpassable rivers by locating fords previously known to no one but God; finds his way with ease and speed through uncharted mountains; and it is suggested that he indirectly conjures up spirit warriors who help in the final sortie from the castle.[78] He also experiences a number of prophetic visions, most notably his witness and interpretation of a strange bird phenomenon while encamped on his way to take up command of the newly conquered Nagykanizsa castle, at Görösgál near Szigetvár, which he interprets as presaging the sieges of Nagykanizsa.[79] The mention of Görösgál not only references a physical, geographical cartography but also maps a heterodox spiritual and cultural world in that it recalls the scene of a previous *kesik-baş*, or severed-head event. İbrahim Peçevi describes this particular event in his history and says that he took it directly from the account written by the *kadı* who witnessed the event.[80] It thus creates a further intertextual link to *kesik-baş* stories, which are found most usually in *destan* [epic poem], *efsane* [legend] and *evliya menakib* [the heroic or exemplary deeds of Muslim saints] narratives that describe heroic exploits, wars and conquests. As I noted earlier, while a depiction of Tiryaki Hasan Pasha as a *menakibname* inspired warrior-saint can, to some extent, be erased through the presence of more orthodox framings and re-inscriptions, it can also be foregrounded through textual re-inscription, vocabulary choices, the narration of additional miracles and the inclusion of other *menakibname* narratives.[81] O.R.12961 (1789) not only contains nearly all the references to the miraculous abilities of Tiryaki Hasan Pasha present in the other manuscripts but also a number of others. Most notably while attacking an enemy settlement before the siege of Nagykanizsa, Tiryaki Hasan Pasha is involved with three miracles: he locates two previously unknown routes through the mountains, and when he and his men assume their positions around the settlement in readiness for their attack, suddenly fire appears on three sides which aids them in their assault.[82]

His miraculous abilities are also commented upon by the enemy soldiers who fleeing ahead of him burn a bridge they have just crossed only to see Tiryaki Hasan Pasha and his men cross the river by a previously unknown ford. When the enemy witness this, they believe that he has cast a spell and frozen the river, enabling himself and his men to cross.[83] His mystical abilities are further highlighted with his being interpretatively named as a *cadu*

The gazavatnames: *rewriting the exemplar* 93

or sorcerer by the enemy. This word also has, in Turkic folk literature, the connotation of a shamanistic rainmaker or weathermonger.[84] This latter reference is re-invoked with the causal conjunction in the narrative of Tiryaki Hasan Pasha praying and weeping in a state of mystical ecstasy one night and the appearance of a severe snowstorm that decimates the enemy and contributes to the raising of the siege, thereby implying that the prayers of Tiryaki Hasan Pasha, the weathermonger, resulted in the storm.[85]

Self and other

O.R.12961 (1789), like many of the other *gazavatname* scripta, while outwardly affirming imperial Ottoman rhetorics which posit a religiously dominated cartography of difference and violence, implicitly offers alternative and often contradictory systems of conceptualisation and ontology that include an imagination of self which encompasses a diverse range of people from the border region. However, unlike the other scripta, O.R.12961 (1789) implicitly constructs an idea of self that incorporates Turkish-speaking Muslims and a comprehensive spectrum of Hungarian society, including Christians, Muslim converts, peasants, soldiers, commanders and local notables. In O.R.12961 (1789), when Tiryaki Hasan Pasha gives instructions to Kara Ömer Ağa concerning the captured enemy prisoners, he says: "Put the peasants who brought the provisions which came to us from Bubofça castle in soldiers' uniforms and also put some of the people of Islam in Hungarian clothing and let them speak Hungarian together. Pass this infidel amongst them and bring him to your place."[86] Later in the narrative the narrator comments: "and in truth those from the Hungarian soldiers who previously brought the provisions and munitions from the castles of Bubofça, Berzince and Sigetwar were commanders and *ayan* [notables]. The pasha had not given them permission to go and they were dwelling in the castle."[87] These two extracts provide evidence of a degree of interconnection and synthesis between ostensibly different communities: Hungarian-speaking soldiers (of all ranks), as well as civilians, converts to Islam and Christian peasants, are presented as offering support to, or being part of, the Ottoman garrison. Moreover, Hungarians or local Balkan peoples are also included among Tiryaki Hasan Pasha's immediate retinue as his deputies. In O.R.12961 (1789) there is an additional character not present in any other manuscript inscription, Arab Oğlu, who is presented as a very accomplished spy. He infiltrates the parliament or *torvin* held by the enemy Habsburg commanders, insinuates himself into the Habsburg army, persuades an enemy notable entrusted with delivering a letter from the king that he is a local Balkan guide and causes enemy soldiers to declare, "You are not a Turk, you don't look like satan."[88] This suggests that he was a native of the region, despite his name which means son of an Arab.

Commensurate with this redefinition of self to include Hungarians and Christians is a redefinition of the other. In this narrative the mapping of antagonism is superficially in religious terms with the enemy named as infidels. However, this definition is supplanted by alternative readings and ultimately breaks down. While all the other scripta (with the exception of O.R.700 (1773–1774), which also emphasises the polytheistic rather than the Christian nature of the infidels), associate the term *infidel* explicitly with Christianity, here the term is intra-textually equated with polytheist paganism rather than explicitly with Christianity. Throughout the narrative the infidel enemy repeatedly have recourse to, and request aid from not the Christian God but from both the pre-Islamic pagan idol *Lat* and also *Melas*, which here translates as 'a great Lord who is a protector and refuge to others'.[89] While Ottoman narratives occasionally describe Christians as polytheists because of the perceived idolatry of the Christian trinity, they usually use the term *müşrikin* to do so.[90] The absence of this term and the general religiously heterodox nature of O.R.12961 suggests that the frequent association of infidel and the terms *Lat* and *Melas* would not have necessarily connoted to audiences the trinity of Christianity but rather an unspecified polytheistic paganism. This naming practice, in conjunction with other evidence from the manuscript, suggests that the scribe consciously did not want to explicitly and exclusively associate the infidel enemy other with Christians. By intra-textually associating the term *infidel* with pagan polytheists, not only are Christians not automatically included in the definition of other, but more importantly they are not simultaneously excluded from a conception of self. This reconception of the identity of the other is more inclusive and may indicate that the implied audience of this manuscript was more diverse, consisting perhaps of Christians, recent converts, or those with close associations to, and relations with Christians, for whom a simple conflation of enemy and Christian would not be realistic or appropriate.[91] Moreover, throughout the narrative there are a number of references to Christian practices which could suggest that the implied audience was familiar with Christianity and may indicate interaction between the two religious communities.[92]

Rather than map the self-other dichotomy exclusively in terms of religion or ethnicity, in O.R.12961 (1789), despite the often comic and very colourful derogatory language used to describe the enemy, there is an undercurrent of considerable sympathy and respect expressed for the common enemy soldier and a concomitant disrespect and suppressed hostility for the commanders of both sides which is not found in the other scripta in the corpus.[93] The exaggerated nature of the derogatory language suggests that it mainly functioned as entertainment: the enemy are often referred to as accursed swine who "talk shit", frequently howl like dogs and on occasion thrust their heads into their rear ends like bitches and snort and snore like swine.[94] Of more interest is the fact that the narrator comments that the enemy soldiers fought well, displayed the utmost courage in the face of terrible odds and did not voluntarily attack the Ottomans but were coerced into it on pain of death.⁹⁵ This alternative mapping of self and other is coterminous with a shift in the cartography of legitimised violence. Despite the often rather graphic violence, much more mercy and leniency is shown towards ordinary enemy soldiers and civilians. Unlike in the other scripta, Kara Ömer Ağa commands his men to spare the enemy who beg for quarter, and this command is later echoed by Tiryaki Hasan Pasha, who despite arguing that it is too dangerous to incarcerate all 26,000 enemy prisoners in the castle, does not command that they all be put to the sword but grants them a reprieve, arguing that those capable of ransoming themselves should be allowed to do so, whilst those without means will have to earn their freedom as galley slaves.⁹⁶ Thus we have a tension in the narrative between depictions of excessive violence and compassion. The unreality of the violence provides a clue to resolving this contradiction as it suggests that the violence was read and understood as entertainment much as it is in contemporary 'action' films. The compassionate treatment of soldiers and civilians might indicate that the implied audience considered the granting of quarter, the fair treatment of one's opponent and the plight of the common soldier as important issues.

Conversely, through various narrative tensions and evidence of suppressed hostility, both the enemy and Ottoman commanders are figured as the other. The narrative constantly negotiates the implied audience's ambiguous expectations of, and reactions to, authority figures. The enemy commanders, and especially the king, are held responsible for the attack against the Ottomans and the massive defeat and destruction of their army. They are portrayed not only as bad commanders but generally as extremely unpleasant, bloodthirsty murderers. The enemy soldiers frequently fear being killed by their own king and commanders, and this is actualised on three occasions when they are skewered on their commanders' swords while trying to retreat from the Ottomans.⁹⁷ The king's contempt for his soldiers is expressed again when, seeing that the Ottomans have slaughtered many of his men, he comments that this has saved him a job.⁹⁸ He is also depicted as being extremely insensitive to his subjects. After Tiryaki Hasan Pasha's attack on the enemy settlement near the capital of Zirinoğlu, the king inquires of the people who escaped from there whether the livestock he requested for the forthcoming campaign were saved. The people chide him, crying that they have not seen their own families and children, yet he asks about livestock.⁹⁹ This hostility towards elites is also made manifest through humour: the enemy commanders, just like Tiryaki Hasan Pasha and other Ottoman elites, are objects of physical ridicule: "a cannon ball came and struck the canonically unclean [filthy] head of the pope and it even had an effect on the nose of the filthy face of the king and the king turned into a dog that had eaten blood in a slaughterhouse."¹⁰⁰ The audience is also invited to laugh at and mock the grand vizier, İbrahim Pasha, who is subjected to crude treatment when he is made to strip off his clothes in front of the sultan, revealing his black horse-hair underwear.¹⁰¹

96 *The* gazavatnames: *rewriting the exemplar*

Audience and function

In terms of the possible reception of this scriptum, there are a number of vocality cues which may suggest that it was intended to be read aloud to a listening audience. These include repetition of plot events and key phrases,[102] considerable use of direct speech, direct addresses to the audience[103] and the use of interjections by the narrator rather than subheadings to organise or manage the narrative.[104] None of these conclusively proves that the work was intended to be received in vocality, but they do place it further along the vocality axis and situate it within an 'oral storytelling' frame. The episodic narration of this scriptum, which is increased by the presence of the 'prequel' section, also signals an 'oral storytelling' frame. Similar to O.R.700 (1773–1774), which also includes interjections by an implied narrator in a managerial role, there is no use of direct enunciation by the implied author of the work as an authorising device. However, the implied author or scribe does intervene in the narrative on one occasion to express some doubt over the veracity of the narrative he is inscribing.[105]

More than the other scripta, O.R.12961 (1789) provides considerable military information concerning weapons, tactics, ransom protocols and espionage practices.[106] There is also a perhaps exaggerated concern for booty, financial inducements and rewards: Tiryaki Hasan Pasha distributes far more financial largesse throughout the tale, and carriages overflow with gold, thousands of slaves, animals and other valuable items.[107] The fair distribution of this booty is also stressed with both Tiryaki Hasan Pasha and the grand vizier declaring that whatever the soldiers find is theirs to keep.[108] The language of this scriptum is equally unusual and interesting. It is often extremely crude and colourful, especially when describing the gruesome details of battles and insulting the enemy; there are numerous common and unusual proverbs and popular phrases.[109]

> God is the Greatest, those oily balls of rags burning with a *khar-khar* sound were poured onto those pine boats the boats caught fire in the places where they kissed and started to burn with a fierce crackling sound. The infidels who were inside willy-nilly threw themselves into the water and drowned and their souls went to hell. The other infidels saw this situation and were conquered and ruined. And some tongues were captured. But the *gazis* of Islam, like tigers and leopards roaring amorously entered into battle and they caused to rain cannons and muskets and bomb-shells on the heads of the infidels like rain. They fought from dawn until noon. There was confusion and that day Kanije castle wore a shirt made from fire and like a dragon scattered fire at the infidels. That day they fought such that the angels in the sky and the fish in the sea admired [them]. The community of Muhammad were victorious and successful and the infidels were routed and they turned their faces. That day fourteen thousand of the infidels died and one of

The gazavatnames: *rewriting the exemplar* 97

the *gazi*s struck the brother of the pope with a musket and that day the execrable one died.[110]

In addition to the comic descriptions of the enemy and Ottoman commanders, alcohol and drugs also offer the opportunity for humour: there are two comic interludes involving drunken enemy soldiers and Arab Oğlu.[111]

While it is impossible to determine the various audiences of the work during the past two hundred and fifty years, the unusual proverbs and expressions, Ottomanised foreign phrases, references to Christianity, the extensive military and local border knowledge, intertextual references to *menakibname* literature, an implicit imagining of self which includes Christians and Hungarians and a conception of the other as polytheistic infidels rather than as specifically Christian suggest an implied audience familiar with the borderland between the Ottomans and the Habsburgs, whose cartography of conflict was less mapped on a Christian-Muslim dichotomy but was situated in a more general border culture and network of local, rather than imperial, allegiances and alliances. I would, therefore, tentatively speculate that the implied or intended audience of this particular scriptum would have consisted of people of mixed religious, ethnic and linguistic backgrounds located on or around the border area.[112] Furthermore, the colourful language, the tension felt for the state elites and commanders, the sympathy expressed for the enemy soldiers and the concern for booty, monetary reward and its fair distribution indicate that the audience may have consisted of soldiers or those closely involved with active military communities. This would therefore explain the manifest sympathy for the common soldier, military concerns and the greater degree of expressed tolerance for non-Muslim communities.

In Chapter 3 I outlined three frameworks or approaches for analysing Ottoman manuscripts that do not implicitly rely on the typographic model which presumes and privileges the idea of an original, singular, authorial text that is subsequently copied more or less accurately by scribes who possess varying degrees of literacy. In this chapter I demonstrated through a detailed discussion of three scripta in the *gazavat-i Tiryaki Hasan Paşa* corpus how the employment of these models allows for a nuanced reading of the narratives and the subtle differences among them. If the individual scripta are read within a performative instead of a typographic paradigm, then the differences, rather than signal scribal incompetence, become meaningful and provide information about how different scribes read, interpreted and reinscribed the tale for different implied audiences. Similarly, the use of the idea of ethical reading makes sense of supposed narrative 'incoherence' without recourse to the vocabulary of degeneration and incompetence. It also highlights the different reading strategies and literacy practices that various Ottoman textual communities employed. Lastly, the use of the ocularity-vocality continuum in conjunction with an analysis of marginalia and scribal rewriting provides an insight into the reception of Ottoman texts that is more

98 The gazavatnames: *rewriting the exemplar*

multilayered and useful than simply condemning the scripta as inscribed by semiliterate scribes or a product of a culture that had not fully interiorised literacy. Importantly, employing a theory of meaning in which meaning is located in the audience or interpretative community rather than found in the text or the intentions of the author allows us to glimpse how narratives evolved and were rewritten to meet the expectations of different audiences. It also provides an explanation of genre fluidity and how the 'same' text can be rubricated as history and story: as treatise and *menakibname*.

Notes

1 See Deborah Tannen, "What's in a Frame? Surface Evidence for Underlying Expectations," in *Framing in Discourse*, ed. Deborah Tannen (Oxford: Oxford University Press, 1993), 20, quoting the research of J.D. Bransford and J. J. Franks, "The Abstraction of Linguistic Ideas," *Cognitive Psychology* 2 (1971), and J. D. Bransford and M. Johnson, "Consideration of Some Problems in Comprehension," in *Visual Information Processing*, ed. W. G. Chase (New York: Academic Press, 1973). See also D. Jarrett, "Pragmatic Coherence in an Oral Formulaic Tradition," in *Coherence in Spoken and Written Discourse*, ed. Deborah Tannen (Norwood, NJ: Ablex, 1984), 160, and Thomas L. Berger, "'Opening Titles Miscreate': Some Observations on the Titling of Shakespeare's Works," in *The Margins of the Text*, ed. D. C. Greetham (Ann Arbor: The University of Michigan Press, 1997), 155.
2 Of the twenty Nagykanizsa manuscripts that have titles, only three describe the work with the word *gazavat*, and one with the word *muharebe* [battle] – BBU: Bub.3459 (1668–1669); PBN: Sup.Turc.170 (1760); Vienna: Nationalbibliothek, H.O.71b (undated) (henceforth referred to as VNB: H.O.71b); and Vienna: Staatsarchiv, Nr.508 (undated) (henceforth referred to as VSA: Nr.508). LBL: O.R.33 (undated) uses the word *gaza* [campaign] but also describes it as a *hikaye* [story]. Five describe it as *hikaye*, five as *tarih* [history], two as a *menakib* [narrative of exemplary deeds] and one as a *risale* [treatise]. The manuscripts that describe it as a *hikaye* are LBL: O.R.12961 (1789), PBN: Nr.525 (undated), LBL: O.R.33 (undated), Istanbul: Arkeoloji Müzesi, No.374 (1803) (henceforth referred to as IAM: No.374) and BPN: A.Oct.34 (undated). Those that describe it as a *tarih* are IMK: A.E.Tar.187 (undated), IMK: A.E.Tar.188 (1810), IMK: A.E.Tar.189 (1715), MBS: O.R.393 (undated), Berlin: Preußische National-Bibliothek, Oct.3442 (1616) (henceforth referred to as BPN: Oct.3442) and CUL: O.R.700 (1773–1774). The contents page of O.R.700, which was probably added later, describes the work as history [*tarih*]. A.R.Tar.189 includes a number of different titles, most of which use the term *tarih*. It is possible that the classification of A.E.Tar.187, A.E.Tar.188 and A.E.Tar.189 as 'histories' through rubrication occurred after their inscription and may have been undertaken when they were incorporated into Ali Emri's library collection. The manuscripts rubricated as narratives of exemplary deeds are MIHK: No.5070 (1757) and VNB: H.O.71d (1754). BMTAK: O.216 (1716) is rubricated as a treatise. Many of the manuscripts have a number of titles added at various times. Here, with the possible exception of A.E.Tar.187, A.E.Tar.188 and A.E.Tar.189, I am only referring to titles or incipits which appear to have been written by the scribe at the time the manuscript was written. Some of these titles, although spatially or visually delineated as titles, are more descriptive rubrics or addresses, for example, O.R.33 fol.1b *This Is the Story of the Conquest of Kanije and the Campaign of Tiryaki Gazi Hasan Pasha*.

The gazavatnames: *rewriting the exemplar* 99

3 In his catalogue, A. Hilmi, *Fihrist al-kutub al-Turkiyah al-mawjudah fi al-Kutubkhanah al-Khidiwiyah* (al-Qahirah: al-Matba'ah al-'Uthmaniyah, 1306) entry 231, describes CDK: No.235 (undated) as having the title *The Gazavat of Hasan Pasha* despite there being a title coterminous with the inscription of the actual manuscript on fol.1b, which reads *The Recounting of the Gaza and Cihad of the Deceased Hasan Pasha which Occurred During the Siege of Kanije Castle*. Pal Fodor also notes in a personal email dated 25 June 2001 that he was informed by a colleague that BMTAK: O.216 was probably erroneously rubricated as *Hatha Risale-i Divan Efendisi ya Tiru Gazi Hasan Pasha* despite this being the actual title written above the text.
4 Even for printed works it is not always possible to assign a single title. For example, Jim McLaverty, "Questions of Entitlement: Some Eighteenth-Century Title Pages," in *The Margins of the Text*, ed. D. C. Greetham (Ann Arbor: The University of Michigan Press, 1997), 191, argued that an attempt to determine a single title for Pope's works is doomed to failure largely because Pope used different arrangements of his works to serve different literary purposes.
5 P. N. Boratav, "Hikaye," in *Encyclopaedia of Islam*, ed. P. J. Bearman Th. Bianquis, C. E. Bosworth, E. van Donzel and W. P. Heinrichs, 2nd ed. (Leiden: Brill, 1960–2000).
6 Although, this too does not preclude the introduction of more imaginative elements if required to convey the desired message or moral. The Ottoman historian Naima, in describing the seven key requisites for writing history, notes that authors should limit themselves to "strictly appropriate embellishments", quoted in Lewis Victor Thomas, *A Study of Naima*, ed. Norman Itzkowitz (New York: New York University Press, 1972), 116.
7 See Christine Woodhead, "Tarikh," in *Encyclopaedia of Islam*, ed. P. J. Bearman, Th. Bianquis, C. E. Bosworth, E. van Donzel and W.P. Heinrichs, 2nd ed. (Leiden: Brill, 1960–2000), for mention of *tarih, menakib* and *gazavatnames*.
8 Group one consists of BPN: A.Oct.34 (undated), BPN: Oct.3442 (1616), BU: T.F.46 (1689), CDK: No.235 (undated), IAM: No.374 (1803), IMK: A.E.Tar.187 (undated), LBL: O.R.33 (undated), PBN: Sup.Turc.170 (1760), VNB: A.F.234 (1720), VNB: H.O.71a (undated), VNB: H.O.71b (undated), VNB: H.O.71c (1671) and VSA: Nr.508 (undated).
9 I do not want to suggest that there is a necessary correlation among works written for an audience with a more orthodox political or religious outlook and the inscription of these works within a discourse of fixity and authority but rather that there appears to be, with regard to these examples, at least a contingent correlation. Group two scripta include MBS: O.R.393 (undated), PBN: Nr.525 (undated), BBU: Bub.3459 (1668–1669), MIHK: No.5070 (1757), VNB: H.O.71d (1754), BMTAK: O.216 (1716), PBN: Sup.Turc.170 (1760) and IMK: A.E.Tar.189 (1715).
10 Group three scripta include CUL: O.R.700 (1773–1774), IMK: A.E.Tar.188 (1810), LBL: O.R.6442 (1815), London: British Library, O.R.12961 (1789), Paris: Bibliothèque Nationale and Sup.Turc.873 (1734) (henceforth referred to as PBN: Sup.Turc.873). BU: T.F.46 (1689) has no introduction and commences with the Nagykanizsa narrative but can essentially be classified with the group 1 scripta.
11 For example, the birds witnessed by Tiryaki Hasan Pasha at Göröşgál vary among the scripta: in IAM: No.374 there are rooks and falcons followed by eagles; in BPN: Oct.3442 they are rooks and ravens followed by eagles; whereas in VNB: H.O.71b the first group consists of rooks and ravens and the second, crows.
12 The Qur'anic passage from which the quotation is taken is as follows: "When Saul led his armies, he said: 'God will test you by a stream. Whoever drinks its

water will not be of me; but those who do not drink shall be on my side. The only exception will be, those who scoop up a palmful of water with their hands.' And but for a few they all drank of its water. When they had crossed it, and those who believed with him, they said: 'We have no strength to combat Goliath and his forces today. But those who believed they have to face their Lord, said: 'Many a time has a small band defeated a large horde by the will of God. God is with those who are patient (and persevere).' And when they were facing Goliath and his hordes they prayed: 'O Lord, give us endurance and steady our steps, and help us against the deniers of truth.' By the will of God they defeated them, and David killed Goliath, and God gave him kingship and wisdom, and taught him whatsoever he pleased." Qur'an, 2:249–251.

13 Interestingly, in CDK: No.235 there is no Qur'anic quotation, just the gloss.
14 Qur'an, 51:56 and 3:28, respectively.
15 BBU: Bub.3459 (1668–1669).
16 BU: T.F.46 (1689), CDK: No.235 (undated), IMK: A.E.Tar.187 (undated), IMK: A.E.Tar.188 (1810), LBL: O.R.33 (undated), MBS: O.R.393 (undated), PBN: Sup.Turc.170 (1760), PBN: Nr.525 (undated), VNB: H.O.71a (undated) and H.O.71c (1671). Six of the scripta do not include this digression on obedience at all: O.R.700 (1773–1774), LBL: O.R.6442 (1815), LBL: O.R.12961 (1789), VNB: A.F.234 (1720), Oct.3442 (1616) and PBN: Sup.Turc.873 (1734).
17 VNB: H.O.71a (undated) fol.25a. The Qur'anic quotation is from 4:59.
18 See n.12.
19 See Chapter 3.
20 BBU: Bub.3459 (1668–1669). BPN: A.Oct.34 (undated), IAM: No.374 (1803), IMK: A.E.Tar.189 (1715) and PBN: Sup.Turc.170 (1760). PBN: Sup.Turc.170 (1760) has two endings, this one and the first already discussed. Quotation comes from BPN: A.Oct.34 fols 63b–64a.
21 This discussion exemplifies two distinct political philosophies: the first stresses political absolutism and the God-given right of the ruler as the only legitimate source of power to exert ultimate authority and sovereignty. The second emphasises the preeminence of justice and the right of people to remove an unjust ruler. This debate was also prevalent throughout Europe in the early modern period. Kant exemplifies the view that one must be in obedience to authority and not rebel against tyrannical or corrupt regimes. Immanuel Kant, *The Metaphysics of Morals*, trans. Mary Gregor (Cambridge: Cambridge University Press, 1991). In contrast, John Locke, *Two Treatises of Government*, ed. Peter Laslett (Cambridge: Cambridge University Press, 1988), argues that as part of the social contract people have a right to rebel against a tyrannical government. See Cesare Cuttica, "Anti-Jesuit Patriotic Absolutism: Robert Filmer and French Ideas (c. 1580–1630)," *Renaissance Studies* 25/4 (2012), for one example of the debate.
22 IMK: A.E.Tar.187 fol.52b.
23 Ibid., fol.53a.
24 Individual unusual or foreign words are often short vowelled in Ottoman manuscripts to assist the reader.
25 BPN: A.Oct.34 fols 63b-64a.
26 VNB: H.O.71d (1754), BMTAK: O.216 (1716) and MIHK: No.5070 (1757).
27 VNB: H.O.71d (1754) fol.67a.
28 BMTAK: O.216 fol.2b.
29 Other group two manuscripts, PBN: Nr.525 (undated) and MBS: O.R.393 (undated) also interpretively name Hasan Pasha in more orthodox terminology. PBN: Nr.525 fols.5b and 6a describe him as "the vizier of most high renown the exalted Gazi Hasan Pasha" or "the vizier of manifest consciousness [shining heart] Gazi Hasan Pasha". IMK: A.E.Tar.188 shows evidence of significant scribal re-inscription and cannot be classified as either belonging to group one

The gazavatnames: rewriting the exemplar 101

or two. However, in this work Hasan Pasha is also securely located among the official military-administrative framework by being named as "from among the great viziers in the imperial campaign" and "an unequalled vizier endowed with Platonic wisdom, and a man of the sword and of valour unparalleled in his time for both his courage and insight and good judgement in public affairs and one of the most wise and good councillors" (fol.1b).

30 This work is found in four manuscripts – BMTAK: O.216 (1716), PBN: Sup. Turc.170 (1760), VNB: H.O.71d (1754) and MIHK: No.5070 (1757) – all of which are group two.
31 BMTAK: O.216 fol.72a.
32 CDK: No.235 contains a number of other works, including the story of his exalted personage Murad Pasha, who was the grand vizier and commander in the year 1016 [*Hikaye-i Vezir-i Azam Serdar olan Murad Paşa Hazretleri Bin On Altı Senesinde*], which is the account of Grand Vizier Kuyucu Murad Pasha's campaign in Anatolia against the *celali* rebels in which Tiryaki Hasan Pasha also played a prominent role.
33 Julia Boffey defines an anthology as a number of items brought together under some determining principle and miscellanies as more random collections, "Short Texts in Manuscript Anthologies: The Minor Poems of John Lydgate in Two Fifteenth-Century Collections," in *The Whole Book: Cultural Perspectives on the Medieval Miscellany*, ed. S. Nichols and S. Wenzel (Ann Arbor: The University of Michigan Press, 1996), 73.
34 BMTAK: O.216 fol.97b and 99a. The sultan, when appointing him *beylerbeyi* of Buda, also attaches a plume to his head, thereby marking him with a sign which denotes incorporation.
35 A few lines later he says something similar when describing the implied reception of his narrative: "when it is read to *gazis* and our religious friends in the *meclis*" BMTAK: O.216 fol.3b. See Philippe Carrard, "Theory of a Practice: Historical Enunciation and the Annales School," in *A New Philosophy of History*, ed. Frank Ankersmit and Hans Kellner (London: Reaktion Books, 1995), 117, for a more detailed discussion on the use of the first-person plural.
36 VNB: H.O.71d fol.23b.
37 Ibid., fol.76b.
38 On CUL: O.R.700 fol.107b the scribe-author has identified themself "on Saturday in the month of the sacred *Muharrem* in the year one thousand one hundred and eighty seven, from the hand of the humble and contaminated Mehmed Said Rahmzade ibn al-hac Mustafa Efendi ibn al-hac Ahmed ibn al-şeyh veli-allah ibn al-molatı."
39 Ibid., fol.76b.
40 Ibid., fols.83a and 99b. For other examples see fols 82b, 102a and 103a and b.
41 Ibid., fol.76b.
42 Ibid., (1773–1774) fol.77b.
43 Ibid., fol.78a. This contrasts with the other scripta in which the grand vizier issues the command to his steward. He also issues commands to the *beylerbeyi* of Rumeli to capture various castles (O.R.700 fol.78b). All of the *gazavatname* inscriptions include ostensibly verbatim quotations in the form of direct speech of various campaign discussions. Rhoads Murphey, "Ottoman Historical Writing in the Seventeenth Century: A Survey of the General Development of the Genre after the Reign of Ahmed I (1603–1617)," in *Essays on Ottoman Historians and Historiography*, ed. Rhoads Murphey (Istanbul: Eren, 2009), 91, has argued that this use of a rapportage style in everyday language provides a sense of immediacy and dramatic enhancement and indicates a potentially broader audience than that commonly associated with histories that circulated primarily among the elite.

102 The gazavatnames: rewriting the exemplar

44 Stanley Fish, "How To Do Things with Austin and Searle: Speech-Act Theory and Literary Criticism," in *Is There a Text in This Class? The Authority of Interpretive Communities*, ed. Stanley Fish (Cambridge, MA and London: Harvard University Press, 1980), 213.
45 Ann Rosalind Jones and Peter Stallybrass, *Renaissance Clothing and the Materials of Memory* (Cambridge: Cambridge University Press, 2000), 3.
46 Ibid., 2.
47 Ibid., 11.
48 For more on the role of Ottoman robes of honour, see Jennifer Wearden, "Siegmund von Herberstein: An Italian Velvet in the Ottoman Court," *Costume* 19 (1985), and Veronika Gervers, *The Influence of Ottoman Turkish Textiles and Costume in Eastern Europe* (Toronto, Canada: Royal Ontario Museum, 1982).
49 In IMK: A.E.Tar.188 (1810) the incorporation of Tiryaki Hasan Pasha into the imperial elite and his personal subordinate association with the sultan is more pronounced because the sultan bestows on Tiryaki Hasan Pasha robes of honour from among his own clothes and equipment from his own equipment; see fol.54a.
50 For example IMK: A.E.Tar.187 fols.58b–59a. In IMK: A.E.Tar.188 fol.54a the sultan bestows upon him robes of honour from his own clothes and three sets of equipment from his own equipment. See IMK: A.E.Tar.189 fol.18a and IAM: No.374 fol.55a–b for Tiryaki Hasan Pasha making direct requests.
51 He does, however, receive three fur robes, one on top of the other, from the grand vizier when he meets him at Osijek at the beginning of the narrative (CUL: O.R.700 fol.77b). However, given the manner in which the personal and political relationship between them is depicted, I would suggest that this gift giving is more the result of friendship than that between a superior and subordinate. Indeed the grand vizier addresses Tiryaki Hasan Pasha as his brother. Again in the last few sentences we are told that the grand vizier sent Tiryaki Hasan Pasha a fur and a sword shortly before recommending to the sultan that he be given his position as grand vizier as he is the better man (CUL: O.R.700 fol.107b).
52 CUL: O.R.700 fol.107a.
53 The correspondence by letter in which Zirinoğlu rebukes Hasan Pasha for all the death and asks what he will do when face-to-face with Jesus is here transposed to correspondence between Archduke Matthias and Tiryaki Hasan Pasha.
54 Peter Sugar, "The Ottoman 'Professional Prisoner' on the Western Borders of the Empire in the Sixteenth and Seventeenth Centuries," *Études Balkaniques* 7 (1971): 82, and Lajos Fekete, *Türkische Schriften aus dem Archive des Palatins Nikolaus Esterhazy 1606–1645* (Budapest, 1932), 21.
55 CUL: O.R.700 fol.107a.
56 LBL:O.R.33 also describes it as the capital of the Hungarian king.
57 Géza Pálffy, "The Origins and Developments of the Border Defence System against the Ottoman Empire in Hungary (Up to the Early Eighteenth Century)," in *Ottomans, Hungarians, and Habsburgs in Central Europe: The Military Confines in the Era of Ottoman Conquest*, ed. Géza Dávid and Pál Fodor (Leiden, Boston and Köln: Brill, 2000), 38 and 46. The referent for Zirinoğlu is probably György Zrínyi, captain-general of the border fortresses around Nagykanizsa in the late sixteenth century.
58 LBL: O.R.6442 fol.60b. The literal translation is: "he laughed from under his moustache."
59 Ibid., fol.94a. VNB: H.O.71d fol.66b اینکلیس; BPN: A.Oct.34 fol.63a انکولس; PBN: No.525 fol.62a انکلیس; BBU: Bub.3459 fol.108a انکولوس. For a more

detailed discussion of the king of the Lutherans' episode in the manuscript corpus see Claire Norton, "'The Lutheran Is the Turks' Luck': Imagining Religious Identity, Alliance and Conflict on the Habsburg-Ottoman Marches in an Account of the Sieges of Nagykanizsa 1600 and 1601," in *Das Osmanische Reich und die Habsburgermonarchie in der Neuzeit. Akten des internationalen Kongresses zum 150-jährigen Bestehen des Instituts für Österreichische Geschichtsforschung, Wien, 22.-25. September 2004*, ed. Marlene Kurz, Martin Scheutz, Karl Vocelka and Thomas Winkelbauer (Wien: Mitteilungen des Instituts für Österreichische Geschichtsforschung, 2005), 77–79.

60   CUL: O.R.700 fol.106b.
61   Ibid., fol.84a.
62   Ibid., fols 84a, 92a and 106a, respectively.
63   There are also a number of missing folios in LBL: O.R.12961. The first gap occurs after folio 1 and occurred before the work was paginated and is of an unknown quantity. The other three omissions occur after fols.49, 58 and 60. In these cases the loss occurred after the inscription of Arabic script pagination because these numerals jump from 49 to 51, 59 to 61 and from 62 to 67, respectively.
64   Ibid., fols.89b and 90b–92b.
65   Ibid., fol.87a–b.
66   Ibid., fol.7b. The grand vizier describes him as an old, senile, addict and rascal (fol.3b), and both the enemy and his own loyal retainers who have fought with him for years frequently comment upon his opium addiction, and the latter often query his commands, assuming him to be intoxicated (fols.7b, 39a-b and fol.60a). On fol.2b Tiryaki Hasan Pasha himself makes a self-deprecating remark playing on his name and alleged opium addiction.
67   Ibid., fols 12b–13a, 39a–b, 40b and 59b.
68   The enemy refer to him thus on ibid., fol.7b, his own men on fol.39a–b and fol.60a. The grand vizier calls him an addict on fol.3b, and on fol.2b Tiryaki Hasan Pasha himself makes a self-deprecating remark playing on his name and alleged opium addiction.
69   J. M. Stitt, "Ambiguity in the Battle of Şórr and Hrungnir," in *Telling Tales: Medieval Narratives and the Folk Tradition*, ed. Francesca Canadé Sautman, Diana Conchado and Giuseppe C. Di Scipio (Basingstoke: Macmillan, 1998), 132.
70   Tiryaki Hasan Pasha's physical infirmities could be read as a sign of the warrior, as 'the stigmata of valor'; see Georges Dumézil, *The Destiny of the Warrior*, trans. Alf Hiltebeitel (Chicago, London: University of Chicago Press, 1970), 162 and 106–107. See also Dumézil, *The Stakes of the Warrior* (Berkeley: University of California Press, 1992). I discuss this topic in more depth in Claire Norton, "Smack-Head Hasan: Why Are All Turkic Superheroes Intemperate, Treacherous, or Stupid?" in *Super/Heroes: From Hercules to Superman*, ed. Angela Ndalianis, Chris Mackie and Wendy Haslem (Washington: New Academia Press, 2007).
71   It should be noted that in this manuscript, Tiryaki Hasan Pasha is depicted in a similar manner to other contested Turkic heroes, such as the gluttonous and slothful Jolio and the greedy, dishonourable Köroğlu. See Norton, "Smack-Head Hasan" for more on this.
72   See LBL: O.R.12961 fol.2b for the grand vizier's request for advice, fols 3b–5a for the conversation between Hasan Pasha and the sultan and fol.4b for his request for the governorship of Buda.
73   BMTAK: O.216 fols 97a–b and 99a; in LBL: O.R.12961 fol.5a he requests Buda and then Nagykanizsa.
74   The grand vizier, however, sends him a fur, a kaftan and a bejewelled sword when he hears that Nagykanizsa is safe (LBL: O.R.12961 fol.84b).

104 *The* gazavatnames: *rewriting the exemplar*

75 Ibid., fol.87b.
76 Ibid., fols 10b–11a and 17a: "and you should be aware that if any of you remain behind or turn back then even if the ox grows horns I will find you and as the severest punishment for Allah I will kill you. Even if you were my children."
77 Ibid., fol.2b.
78 Ahmet Yaşar Ocak, *Türk Folklorunda Kesik Baş* (Ankara: Türk Kültürünü Araştırma Enstitüsü, 1989); and Ocak, *Bektâşî Menâkıbnâmelerinde Islam Öncesi Inanç Motifleri* (Istanbul: Enderun Kitabevi, 1983). The abilities and skills of *menakibname* warrior-saints are described in the third section of Ocak, *Kültür Tarihi Kaynağı Olarak Menâkıbnâmeler (Metodolojik Bir Yaklaşım)* (Ankara: Türk Tarih Kurumu Basımevi, 1992), 70–95. For crossing a previous unknown ford, see IMK: A.E.Tar.187 fol.2b; for discerning an individual's true intent fol.42a-b and for spirit warriors, see fol.52a–b.
79 IMK: A.E.Tar.187 fols 5a–b. See Norton, "Sacred Sites, Severed Heads," for a more detailed analysis of the *menakibname* and *kesik-baş* elements in LBL: O.R.12961.
80 Peçevi, *Tarih-i Peçevi*, 355. Peçevi writes it in rhymed couplets with the *kadı* as the narrator and gives it the title *ve min kerâmâti'l-guzât*.
81 Five manuscripts in the corpus contain other works that could be categorised as *menakibnames*: MIHK: No.5070 (1757), VNB: H.O.71d (1754) and VNB: A.F.234 (1720) contain versions of the *Menakib-i Mahmud Paşa-i Veli* or *Mahmudname*; see Chapter 3 n.26, for more information on this work. CUL: O.R.700 (1773–1774) is bound with a number of other works including two *menakibnames*: the *Menakib-i Şamsu'd-Din* and the *Menakib-i Başir Çelebi Tabib*. CDK: No.235 (undated) contains a number of other works, including the *Risale fi Menakib al-Şeyh Mehmed Ak Şamsu'd-Din*.
82 LBL: O.R.12961 fols.16b, 17b and 19a, respectively.
83 Ibid., fol.32b.
84 See Nora K. Chadwick and Victor Zhirmunsky, *Oral Epics of Central Asia* (Cambridge: Cambridge at the University Press, 1969), 163.
85 O.R.12961 fols 66b–67a.
86 Ibid., fol.46b.
87 Ibid., fol.56b.
88 Ibid., fols 9b–10b, 11b, 13a, 21a and 22b.
89 Ibid., fols.16a, 22b, 23a, 42a, 46a and 79a On occasion *Lat* is combined not with *Melas* but with *Mümelat* (fol.31a).
90 Katib Çelebi in his account of the sieges of Nagykanizsa describes the enemy as *müşrikin* on two occasions, Katib Çelebi, *Fezleke*, 139 and 160. Lubomyr Andrij Hajda, "Two Ottoman Gazanames Concerning the Chyhyryn Campaign of 1678," (PhD diss., Harvard University, Cambridge, MA,1984), 24, states that in the *gazaname* of the *Chyhyryn* campaign, the Christian enemy are generally given the epithet *müşrikin*.
91 It is always possible that audiences would have interpreted the *Lat* and *Melas* references as signifying Catholicism in particular as opposed to Christianity in general and would then have identified the enemy other as Catholics rather than Christians or Protestants.
92 Such references include the enemy plan to capture Ottoman settlements and convert the mosques to churches by hanging bells from the minarets and lighting candles inside (fol.8a); an oblique reference to baptism (fol.8a); details of Christians burning candles and camphor in the churches and giving alms and making sacrifices when they hear that Hasan Pasha has left Buda (fol.31a); and a reference to the enemy soldiers shouting *kyrie eleison*, part of the Roman Catholic prayer of the mass, when in battle (fol.84b).

93 The enemy are described as "fucked ducks"; shrivelled up like hedgehogs; with their noses up each other's bottoms; and as human *şiş* kebabs on their commanders' swords; see ibid., fols.64a–b, 66a, 17a–b, 65a, 71a and 80a, respectively.
94 Ibid., fols.64a, 8a, 11b, 17b, 21b, 34a, 79a and 85b for some more examples.
95 Ibid., fols.80b–81a and fol.65a. On three occasions they are forced at sword point to continue fighting the Ottomans; see fols.25b, 71a and 80a. The enemy soldiers also mention that they are afraid to flee because of what their king will do to them when he catches them (fol.65b).
96 Ibid., fol.82a and fols.83b–84a; see also fols.83b–84a. All prisoners are slaughtered by the walls of the castle in the other scripta, and the river runs red with their blood. When Tiryaki Hasan Pasha attacks the enemy settlement near to Zirinoğlu's capital, women and young boys were not slaughtered but were taken prisoner (fol.19b).
97 Ibid., fol.65a, fol.71a and fol.80a.
98 Ibid., fol.80a–b.
99 Ibid., fol.20a–b.
100 Ibid., fol.94b.
101 Ibid., fols.6b–7a.
102 When Tiryaki Hasan Pasha commands Kara Ömer Ağa to march captured enemy prisoners through groups of Hungarians and feed them misinformation before releasing them the audience is essentially told this three times: once when Tiryaki Hasan Pasha gives Kara Ömer Ağa his instructions, again when Kara Ömer Ağa actually does it and lastly when the prisoners report their experiences back to their commanders (ibid., fols.55b–58b). Other repetition occurs through events being recounted a second time through the literary device of incorporation in a letter; see, for example, fols .3b and 84a.
103 Such addresses to the audience usually occur at the end of digression or when the implied narrator makes a section break and shifts scene: see LBL: O.R.12961 (1789) fol.6a: "Meanwhile let our story come to Hasan Pasha"; fol.5a: "while the treasurer was diligently arranging Hasan Pasha's retinue, our story meanwhile returns to Buda and comes to İbrahim Pasha and to Buda"; fols.27b–28a. "But meanwhile, my life has become senile and is not joyous. Let's go to our story and the grand vizier, Ibrahim Pasha." See also fols.31a, 52a, 87b, 78b, 77b and so on.
104 Changes in scene are facilitated through the use of *ez-in-canib* [from this side] and comments by the narrator already cited. In contrast, Katib Çelebi, *Fezleke*, and Naima, *Tarih-i Naima*, use section headings. Câfer Iyânî *Cihadname* IMK: A.E.Tar.190 uses headings written in the margins of the manuscript in the same scribal hand which provide a brief summary of events. Examples of such headings include: "the battle of Berzence" (fol.3a) and "the battle of Kozma" (fol.6b). Some are slightly longer, such as fol.17b: "after the aforementioned Hasan Bey had been appointed to the sancak of Pozsega, Şahsuvar Pasha was defeated in Szigetvár and again the sancak of Szigetvár was given to Hasan Bey." These marginal headings are generally written at an angle to the main text, but the last example cited is upside down.
105 Ibid., fol.75a: "After that he issued a *ferman* and all of the people of the castle in a great procession left the castle and advanced straight towards the camp. The responsibility is on the narrator." This conveys the idea that the scribe cannot answer for the truth of a particular section. Perhaps the idea that everyone vacated the castle, leaving it empty and vulnerable to attack, created this doubt.
106 Ibid., fols.44a, 49a and 51a; fols.71a, 74a and 80a–b; fols.9a and 82a; and fols.9a, 11b–12a and 13a.
107 Ibid., fols.9a, 11b, 23b 43b and 53b. Money is also given out to those of other ranks accordingly. For booty, see fols.18a and 82a.

108 Ibid., fols.76b and 28a.
109 For example, fols.17b–18a: "The soldiers grabbed the handles of their swords in their hands and gathering some of them up in groups they cut them in two and cutting and lacerating others they, with a single swipe, cut off their heads and the blood started to sweep away the bodies. That morning the sun of the world power rose bright red like a copper cup from the steam of the blood" – see also fols.71b and 73b. The metaphor of the wolf and the sheep is also used extensively, for example, in fol.33a and fol.81a. Lastly, the phrase *kuskununa kuvvet kamçıya bereket demek* occurs frequently in this scriptum, see fols.18a, 26a, 33a and 94b. On three occasions there are references to the enemy king becoming Jewish or being the ruler of a Jewish country (fol.50b). "And because they were fired upon much pain was suffered and when they explained this situation to the accursed Makaş Hersek, while the swine was [already] an infidel he became Jewish"; see also fols.59a and 65a. There are also frequent references to waking a sleeping snake (fol.32b): "the infidels turned into those who had found a snake in a bag and their souls leapt into their heads"; see also fols.20a, 89b and 92b.
110 Ibid., fol.53a.
111 Ibid., fols 9b–10a and fols.22b–23b
112 As outlined by Mark L. Stein, *Guarding the Frontier: Ottoman Border Forts and Garrisons in Europe* (London: Tauris Academic Studies, 2007), Finkel, "French Mercenaries," and Claire Norton, "Liminal Space in the Early Modern Ottoman-Habsburg Borderlands: Historiography, Ontology, and Politics," in *The Uses of Space in Early Modern History 1500–1850*, ed. Paul Stock (New York: Palgrave Macmillan, 2015), while the Ottoman Empire was in general a polyethnic, multifaith, rather cosmopolitan Islamic empire, the Ottoman-Habsburg borderlands were a space of particular ontological fluidity where multiple communities and peoples coexisted and clashed but perhaps more importantly constituted a 'shared community' in which differences were at times elided or glossed. In particular, Stein and Finkel have both demonstrated the religiously diverse nature of Ottoman garrisons and armies along this border.

5 Writers reading
Reading the *Gazavat-i Tiryaki Hasan Paşa* with Katib Çelebi and Naima

This chapter will focus on how two seventeenth- and eighteenth-century Ottoman historians, Katib Çelebi and Naima, read, interpreted and rewrote narratives of the sieges of Nagykanizsa.[1] These two re-inscriptions provide evidence of how both authors read their source narratives and how they expected their implied or intended readers to read the event. Their readings are particularly significant because Naima's inscription of events was, and is, received by both Ottoman and modern audiences as constituting *the* official Ottoman version of the past. However, because Naima incorporated Katib Çelebi's *Fezleke* virtually in toto into his history, it is the latter which essentially operated as "a decisive interpretative junction in seventeenth-century Ottoman historiography", and therefore it was Katib Çelebi's selection, reading and interpretation of sources which ultimately become accepted as the 'true' version of events.[2]

Katib Çelebi's account of the sieges of Nagykanizsa makes clear that he had access to a number of alternative source texts for his narrative. His text evinces a familiarity with the versions present in the histories of İbrahim Peçevi, Abdülkadir Topçularkatibi and Hasan Beyzade, and it is more than likely that he had also read Câfer Iyânî's *Cihadname-i Tiryaki Hasan Paşa*.[3] However, despite his familiarity with these other sources, Katib Çelebi, for his description of the 1601 defence of Nagykanizsa, mainly relied on an account originally sourced from an unidentified scriptum in the *gazavatname* corpus. Indeed, he incorporated large sections of the *gazavatname* account verbatim into his narrative.[4] Despite this virtual in toto inclusion, the small, yet not insignificant, alterations occasioned by his rewriting demonstrate that he read and understood the *gazavatname* narrative in a quite distinct manner from that of some other reinscribers. Through an analysis of the small vocabulary changes, textual additions and omissions and the different intertextual, framing and paratextual structures of the narrative, it is possible to analyse, indirectly, how he read, interpreted and responded to his source narrative and also how he expected his intended audience to read it.[5]

In this chapter I will demonstrate how Katib Çelebi's rewritings not only situate his narrative in a more politically and religiously orthodox framework but also how they work to control the reception of the narrative as factual history. In doing so, I will foreground the manner in which audiences recognise and construct the dichotomies of fiction/non-fiction and story/history. In particular I will consider the role that framing, rubrication and intertextuality play in determining the received status of a narrative. Through such a discussion, a number of the problems inherent in traditional, representationalist explanations of fiction and genre classifications will be exemplified. I will then briefly outline a less problematic explanatory model which accounts for how audiences actually construct and recognise the genre and fictional status of a work. Specifically, I will argue that although the term *fiction* is generally understood as meaning, something akin to 'invented story', the decision to apply the term to a particular text is not made by audiences in terms of external referentiality but is rather determined by reference to specific community-defined protocols and interpretative strategies employed and understood by both the author and audience.

Orthodoxing the text

Katib Çelebi's re-inscription of the *gazavatname* source suggests that he reacted to it in a far more conservative manner than some of the other scribe authors. His use of intertextual references, the framing of the work, depiction of characters and the language used all intersect to present the work in a more religiously, socially and politically orthodox framework. Unlike some of the *gazavatname* re-inscriptions, it is hard to read Katib Çelebi's account as critical of the administration or as a manifesto for heterodox, dervish-inspired Islam.[6] Tiryaki Hasan Pasha is not figured as a heroic, heterodox border warrior or as a representative of the distant and mistrusted military-bureaucratic centre but as an ideal statesman and orthodox Muslim.

Katib Çelebi situates the text within an orthodox mapping of Islam through his use of a network of intertextual references more often associated with orthodoxy and a simultaneous elision or over-coding of the potentially more heterodox *menakibname* references present in the *gazavatname* versions. This repositions Tiryaki Hasan Pasha as a devout, orthodox, competent commander rather than as a heterodox warrior-saint endowed with mystical powers. It is not necessary to postulate that Katib Çelebi consciously erased the *menakibname* references. Their omission or over-coding can be explained as a result of his reading the text from within an interpretative community that possessed a more orthodox outlook, and as such some of the more heterodox references may not have made sense or seemed inappropriate, so they were unconsciously ignored, omitted or rewritten to make the narrative more coherent. For example, in Katib Çelebi, the ford crossed by Tiryaki Hasan Pasha is not described as "previously unknown by anyone save Allah" as it is in the *gazavatnames* but as previously known by Tiryaki Hasan Pasha.[7] He is, therefore, credited with local, not mystical, knowledge. Similarly, while Tiryaki Hasan Pasha is interpretatively named as a *cadu*, or sorcerer in the *gazavatnames*, Katib Çelebi renames him *sahır*, also often translated as sorcerer. Although, initially this appears to be a rather insignificant semantic difference, in effect it situates the narrative in a different network of intertextual relations and equates Tiryaki Hasan Pasha, not with a heterodox shamanistic rainmaker but with a Qur'anic Moses.[8] This comparison is reinforced through a series of oblique and more direct Qur'anic references. When describing the assault on Nagykanizsa by the enemy, Katib Çelebi employs a Qur'anic analogy and states that: "The cannons, which were fired from the castle poured out fire on the enemy like the staff of Ibn Imran [Moses] against the pharaoh marked by terror and Haman."[9] This directly refers to the incident in which Moses [Ibn Imran] uses his staff to demonstrate that he is a prophet of God after having been called a sorcerer, or *sahır*, by the infidels.[10] The implication is that both Moses and Tiryaki Hasan Pasha are named as *sahır* by the enemy infidels and subsequently demonstrate, through miraculous acts, the real power of God. In the same way that Moses wished to free his people from the slavery of the Egyptians and was given the power to do so by God through the medium of his staff, so the analogy implies that Tiryaki Hasan Pasha wants to free the besieged Nagykanizsa garrison and is enabled to do so by the power of God. The snowstorm that decimates the Habsburg enemy and leads to their abandonment of the siege can also be interpreted within this analogy: it can be read as a parallel of the hailstorm that issued from the staff of Moses.[11] Thus, this analogy works to situate events and Tiryaki Hasan Pasha's apparently magical abilities in a far more orthodox Islamic context.

Katib Çelebi's choice of vocabulary also encourages audiences to make Qur'anic intertextual links. For example, when describing the battle that resulted from the enemy's attempt to cross the river moat surrounding Nagykanizsa, he describes the enemy as *ahzab* – [troops, cohorts, bands, combined forces and confederates] which allows audiences to draw a parallel between the Arabian tribes, described by the same term in the Qur'an, who went against Medina and Muhammad at the Battle of the Trench (5/627) and were met and stopped by 'the moat' and between the enemy and Tiryaki Hasan Pasha.[12] Qur'anic intertextuality is also present in the insults the enemy hurl at Tiryaki Hasan Pasha. After the enemy has executed the two servants who flee the besieged castle, it parades their severed heads below the walls of Nagykanizsa and cries out to Hasan Pasha, naming him as *Azazel*.[13] As is made clear in the *hadith* of Ibn Abbas, quoted by al-Tabari in his *Tafsir*, in Islamic tradition *Azazel* is another name for *Iblis* or Satan, the *jinn* who was cast out from heaven for refusing to worship Adam.[14] In the Judaic and Christian traditions, there is also an element of incarceration associated with the name. *The Book of Enoch of the Apocrypha* describes *Azazel* as one of the angels who went from heaven to mate with women and who taught men various skills which ultimately led them into sin. He was punished by God by being bound and thrown into a ravine in the desert.[15] Thus the naming of Tiryaki Hasan Pasha as *Azazel* both presents him as Satan, the enemy of God, but also allows a potential comparison to be drawn between his imprisonment in a castle on a rock amidst swamp and water and *Azazel* imprisoned in the desert. One reader at least was doubtful that future readers would be familiar with the term *Azazel*, so he provided a gloss in the margin of manuscript Sale60, stating, "Azazel means Satan."[16]

Katib Çelebi's reinterpretation of Tiryaki Hasan Pasha in a politically more orthodox frame is illustrated in his depiction of him as a loyal member of the central military-administrative bureaucracy and as a role model for other soldiers, commanders and officials. This is achieved through eliding and rewriting certain sections in the *gazavatnames* which could be read as challenging central authority or which present Tiryaki Hasan Pasha as somehow removed from, or external to, the military-administrative hierarchy. For example, unlike in the *gazavatnames*, in the *Fezleke* Tiryaki Hasan Pasha is not presented as the equal of the grand vizier, and when they meet it is not as a brother or friend. Although his opinion is sought concerning the direction of the campaign before the capture of Nagykanizsa, the grand vizier is presented as making the final decision.[17] However, the clearest indicator of Tiryaki Hasan Pasha's inclusion in the state elite and his consequent submission to and dependency upon the power and authority of the sultan is evident in the sultan's dispatch to him of a *hatt-i hümayun* [imperial rescript] copied onto a tablet to which the keys of the castle are affixed by a golden chain with the instruction that he "read it out to the *gazis*".[18]

Katib Çelebi's reimagining of Tiryaki Hasan Pasha as an ideal Ottoman commander – well-respected, pious, beloved by his men and loyal to the centre – results in his reinterpretation of the 'cannon' event described in Chapter 3. According to Katib Çelebi's re-inscription, Tiryaki Hasan Pasha issues the same command that his men should not fire the cannons at the besieging Habsburg army.[19] However, on the Friday when the second enemy scouting party beg that a cannon be fired, Katib Çelebi writes that the Ottoman soldiers immediately, on the instructions of Tiryaki Hasan Pasha, answered that they did not have any cannons in the castle, and if they had have had, they would have definitely fired them and not refrained from killing the enemy. He therefore omits two important aspects of the passage as presented in the *gazavatnames*: the challenge to Tiryaki Hasan Pasha's authority and the incoherence of the linear narrative. The elision of the challenge to Tiryaki Hasan Pasha's authority by his own men functions as an example of interpretative omission and can be understood as a consequence of a different frame of interpretation employed by the author when reading the event. In Katib Çelebi's narrative, Tiryaki Hasan Pasha stands metaphorically for the ideal Ottoman commander who would therefore necessarily be respected and obeyed by his men. Within such a framing, a challenge to his authority appears incoherent and incongruous, so it is disregarded. The omission of the challenge might also result from a preference for different reading strategies, in particular a preference for linear reading rather than ethical reading practices: as noted, omitting the challenge makes the narrative far more coherent from a linear perspective. If Katib Çelebi was not familiar with the emic systems and rhetorical conventions required to read the text ethically and therefore make sense of it, he may have rewritten it to make it coherent from the perspective of linear reading practices.[20]

Making fiction fact: framing the siege of Nagykanizsa as history

Despite the almost verbatim incorporation of the *gazavatname* narrative into the *Fezleke*, and in contrast with the *gazavatname* accounts, which are today read as story or folk literature, the *Fezleke* has been received since the seventeenth century as non-fictional history, that is, as comprising true, factual knowledge. It is the concomitant bestowal of authority occasioned by this reclassification as non-fiction that has positioned the *Fezleke* as history and has permitted its use as a potential historical source by present-day historians.[21] However, because the *Fezleke* is essentially a re-inscription of the *gazavatname* accounts, there are no extra 'facts' present which could account for a different epistemological status. Thus it provides an edifying example of the argument that the distinction between fact and fiction, history and story, is not epistemological in nature but conventional. In other words, genre and fictional status are determined by adherence to communally agreed-upon protocols and conventions and not because of some special correspondence between the past and the narrative.[22] Katib Çelebi, by reframing the *gazavatname* narrative in accordance with the genre protocols commonly associated with history, in effect creates a particular horizon of expectations among audiences. The framing, rubrication, vocabulary, intertextual references and the status of the author all intersect in the *Fezleke* and label or signal the account as non-fictional history. Or to paraphrase Margreta de Grazia, the apparatus of the text predisposes the reader to specific modes of reading and understanding, which in turn determine the text's identity and genre, which then impacts upon the ascription of the terms *fiction/non-fiction* and *literature/history*.[23]

Among such indicators of the genre 'history' is the inclusion of a copy of the *hatt-i hümayun* [imperial rescript] sent by the sultan to Tiryaki Hasan Pasha, conferring upon him the position of vizier. The reproduction of such an official document, in effect a primary source, confirms and authorises the narrative and legitimises the work as history and Katib Çelebi as a historian. Similarly, the inclusion of two different narrative versions of the flight of the servants suggests that Katib Çelebi had access to, and researched, a number of different sources, which again positions the work as history, not fiction.[24] This is reinforced by his incorporation of direct and indirect references to the works of other historians such as İbrahim Peçevi, Hasan Beyzade and Abdülkadir Topçularkatibi.[25] Likewise, the explicit identification of the narrator with the author together with an erasure of all evidence of enunciation and subjective presence, with the exception of 'I' as historian, organiser of the text, and arbitrator of alternative narratives helps to position the work as history. This contrasts with the *gazavatname* narratives where there is no such conflation and 'I' is often figured as an eyewitness or a transmitter of the tale but never as a historian and manager of the narrative. The dating practices of the *Fezleke* also work to indicate its 'factual' status. While the *gazavatnames* occasionally refer to the day of the week on which key moments of the siege occurred, Katib Çelebi gives the calendar dates.[26] This use of the calendar locates and fixes events in a known world and time and asserts the realism of history not fiction.

Katib Çelebi's use of more complex grammatical forms and Persian and Arabic vocabulary, together with a decontextualised discourse, also signals academic or historical writing particularly to a modern academic audience.[27] Katib Çelebi decontextualises the narrative through an increased use of subordinative rather than additive grammatical structures, relative clauses and intensifiers and through the inclusion of linguistic features such as chronograms. This decontextualisation is particularly pertinent for modern audiences whose horizon of expectations surrounding academic scholarship, and specifically the distinction between 'factual' history and 'fictional' historical literature, is intimately associated with the presence of expository prose, possibly the most decontextualised type of discourse. Lastly, the subheadings are in Persian, which as a language of *authoritas*, refinement and high culture for the Ottomans, imbues the work with gravity and also positions it intertextually with the great classical histories of Islamic civilisations and empires.

The structuring of the narrative also conveys the genre of history to audiences. It is broken into discrete sections by headings that are distinguished from the body of the text, either spatially or graphically. While the section titles in manuscript Rawl.or.20 are marked in red ink, in the nineteenth-century printed version, they are spatially distinct.[28] These headings summarise the following paragraph and thus not only act as explanatory introductions and construct each event as a discrete phenomenon, but they also delineate the work as history through their chronological arrangement. The narration of the Nagykanizsa sieges does not form a discrete narrative unit but is interspersed with descriptions of other events happening simultaneously in the Ottoman Empire. It is therefore read diachronically, as part of a continuous unfolding history, as one event among many in a war. In contrast, the *gazavatnames* are structurally subdivided, and events are managed, by the use of narratorial interjections such as the phrase *ez-in-canib*, which literally translates as 'from this side' but is used in a similar manner to 'meanwhile'. These interjections do not identify specific events such as "the capture of the castle" or the "flight of the servants" as do the headings in the *Fezleke*, but they indicate scene changes when the action shifts from one person or place to another. The *gazavatname* narratives are therefore treated more synchronically, which to modern audiences positions them more as fictional stories than as histories.

One of the manuscript copies of the *Fezleke*, Sale60, exhibits a structural characteristic that reinforces the potential reception of this particular

Writers reading: with Katib Çelebi and Naima 113

edition of the work as history: a contents page.²⁹ This occupies the first ten folios of the manuscript and consists of a grid-like structure in which the year headings and subheadings of events are noted with their corresponding folio numbers. Furthermore, each new year is indicated numerically on the outside edge of this grid, which makes it much easier to search through the contents. Whereas most of the titles are in black ink, the page numbers, headings for new calendar years and key words and expression are given in red. This further enables one to scan the index and locate with ease incidents such as deaths, meetings, appointments and events involving the sultan. The presence of such a contents page suggests reading practices different from those implied by some of the *gazavatname* accounts: that the work was not necessarily intended to be read through in a linear fashion but rather could be consulted much like a contemporary reference book. It also reflects the different cultural-intellectual background of the author: the establishing and drawing up of calendars was very much a skill practised by bureaucrats, not soldiers.

The contents page also represents an ocularity cue: it is of no use to a listening audience; its sole function is to aid an individual reader. Sale60 is suffused with ocularity cues of varying types, including the presence of marginalia, the liberal use of red ink, and other graphic non-linguistic semiotic practices such as overlining, all of which suggest that it was not only intended by the scribe to be read but that it was *actually* read by readers.³⁰ There are examples of marginalia in at least two different hands throughout the manuscript, indicating that at least two people read it. That these apparently anonymous readers read it as factual history and not as fictional story is suggested by the content of the marginalia. The marginal notations, sourced from İbrahim Peçevi, Abdülkadir Topçularkatibi and the *gazavatname* narratives, in effect constitute a dialogue between these works and the *Fezleke* because they contain additional information not present in Katib Çelebi's account. At least one Ottoman reader therefore read this account within a greater intertextual network of other historical accounts. I will return to the question of this reader in the second half of this chapter.

Manuscript Sale60 contains two pagination systems. The first utilises Eastern Arabic numerical notional signs written in ink and was inscribed during, or soon after, the production of the manuscript. It commences after the contents table at the beginning of the manuscript. However, superimposed over this pagination system, commencing on the first folio of the actual physical manuscript, not the text, is another pagination system written in pencil in Arabic numerals, which was probably added to the manuscript in the nineteenth or twentieth century. The original pagination system conceives of the text itself as the object, and together with the contents page, functionally serves to facilitate the location of particular passages from the *Fezleke*. In contrast, the more traditional Western academic pagination system treats the manuscript, *not* the work, as the object of pagination. It nullifies the purpose of the contents page and changes the function to which the text can be put. The manuscript ceases to be a history carefully paginated and indexed for the ease of a scholar wanting to read the work and becomes instead an extant scholarly object from the past to be classified and studied akin to a museum exhibit. The object of study has shifted from the *Fezleke* as a text to the manuscript itself. This highlights a different function of the text: audiences today do not read this manuscript as a copy of the *Fezleke*; for that they tend to use the much more accessible printed version: rather they read this manuscript because it is a particular copy of the *Fezleke*; it is *this* copy of the *Fezleke*. Within the purview of this shift in function, the contents page ceases to be an aid to facilitate the location of particular events in the *Fezleke* and becomes instead evidence of ocularity or Ottoman reading practices.

The power of the reframing of the *Fezleke* as non-fiction is illustrated in the subsequent acceptance as fact, by Ottoman and modern historians, of Katib Çelebi's 'fictional' additions. His uncorroborated description of the Nagykanizsa garrison's successful attempt to manufacture more gunpowder during the siege is likely to be a fictional addition as it occurs in no earlier description of the siege.[31] Similarly, he has embellished certain other incidents quite dramatically, most notably the gunpowder explosion in one of the towers which ostensibly occurred during the first siege. Of the three Ottoman historians who were present at the first siege of Nagykanizsa in 1600, only Peçevi and Topçularkatibi refer to an accidental explosion of gunpowder in the Habsburg-held castle, and they disagree as to when it occurred. Peçevi states that it occurred before the enemy relief army appeared, whereas Topçularkatibi argues that it happened after the defeat and flight of the enemy army.[32] Hasan Beyzade, who was present at the siege and composed the *fethnames* [victory missives] celebrating the capture does not mention any explosion, nor do any other European sources.[33] In the *Fezleke*, however, these vague allusions to an accident have become a deliberate act of sabotage and heroic sacrifice by an Ottoman prisoner who, by throwing a lighted fuse into the gunpowder store, blew up the tower in which he and his fellow prisoners, including "women, youths and especially virgins", were imprisoned.[34]

What can these examples of the effect of framing on the fictional status and genre of the Nagykanizsa narratives tell us about the fiction/non-fiction, story/history dichotomies? Conventionally it is argued that non-fiction is distinguished from fiction by the presence of facts expressed as propositions, which are made true by their correspondence to, or accurate representation of, a mind-independent reality. Similarly, many historians have claimed that history is epistemologically distinct from story or fiction; it constitutes justifiable true belief because it *represents* the 'actual' through the inclusion of verifiable facts, facts made true by their direct correspondence to the past. This model of historical knowledge implies a reliance on empiricist epistemologies, realist ontologies and the correspondence theory of truth.[35] It presupposes an appearance-reality distinction. That is, it assumes the existence of an unmediated reality which exists independently from our subjective value judgements, interests and interpretative practices and acts as a foundation for our knowledge claims, claims that we can substantiate as true because of their correspondence with, or representation of, this reality. The most obvious problem with this representationalist explanatory model of knowledge is its reliance on representation, correspondence and the appearance-reality distinction that ultimately causes it to collapse into extreme scepticism. From where can we distinguish appearance from reality, the scheme of our perceptions from the content, the subjective from the objective, the noumenal from the phenomenal? How can we verify the accuracy of the correspondence between reality and our perception of it to guarantee the truth of our facts or propositions? Moreover, as outlined in the introduction developments in language-based modes of criticism in the twentieth century have made explicit "the fictions of factual representation" and led to an understanding that fiction and non-fiction, story and history, share modes of narrativity and representation.[36] As verbal artefacts they are essentially indistinguishable from one another, something that further complicates the representationalist claim that history constitutes a special type of knowledge. In addition to these theoretical problems, there are more practical concerns. The representationalist explanation of genre and fictional status does not describe tangible praxis; it does not delineate how audiences actually construct and recognise these categories. It also forces changes in fictional status and genre to be explained using the vocabulary of error: if there is one true picture of the world, then past or alternative classifications must be incorrect or false.

I want to elucidate an alternative explanatory model to explain how and why the Nagykanizsa narratives have been variously received as fiction or non-fiction, story or history, one which abandons the vocabulary of metaphysics and correspondence theories of truth and meaning for a pragmatist theory of justification (or a Rortian conversationalist view of knowledge) based upon our practice.[37] Therefore, rather than utilise an epistemic model which relies on an always unavailable external referent to justify our beliefs or provide authority for our truth claims, it is more heuristically beneficial and coherent to employ a model in which we conceive of our relationship with reality in causal rather than representational terms. That is, the world causes our perceptions, but as they are framed, processed and filtered through our subjective interpretative frameworks, it is futile to attempt to speculate as to what the world, or reality, is really like in itself – all we have access to is our subjective perception of the world. Rorty argues that knowledge claims are not justified by correspondence to an ontologically grounded extra-social authority, but rather they are authorised in terms of a justificatory responsibility tied indexically to our community and social practices. In other words, it is the protocols or standards of warranted assertibility determined by the community – our sociocultural practices – that validate and justify our beliefs and knowledge and thus distinguish fact from fiction.[38] Such an approach would mean that rather than correspondence, with an always-inaccessible reality guaranteeing the truth, validity or usefulness of our beliefs, communally agreed-upon patterns of praxis or justification would provide the guarantee. When we describe something as true, factual or non-fictional, we are not commenting upon its representational relationship to a non-linguistic, unmediated reality; rather, we are endorsing it within a particular framework for a specific audience and function.

In the context of historical knowledge, the protocols of writing history, the precepts implicit in the historical method, constitute the communally agreed-upon practices that guarantee the knowledge claims of particular propositions or texts and therefore signal to audiences that a text is trustworthy, not in terms of its correspondence to the past as it is in-itself but in terms of its coherence with the functional expectations of particular audiences. The distinction between historical fiction and literary history therefore rests on the expectations of the audience and the interpretative operations performed rather than on an epistemological difference.[39] It is the narrative's adherence to the particular set of protocols or desiderata stipulated by current academic historical praxis that allows audiences to distinguish between history and story, fact and fiction, and also to critically evaluate particular histories as good or bad. It is this semiotic scaffold established and maintained by "communities of the competent," not correspondence to a mind-independent past, that therefore signals the genre, fictional status, textual intentions and truth claims of a work to audiences.[40] These practices constitute a readable code that states that sentences susceptible to verification can be verified according to the norms of historical practice and that interpretative sentences have been constructed following generally accepted rules of reasoning.[41] Historical truth is therefore essentially synonymous with integrity of method – but a method that is contingent and closely bound up with particular contexts and sociopolitical interests.

The importance of these protocols in determining fictional or factual status is evident from Partner's argument that despite many historians acknowledging and accepting the challenge of postmodernism and non-representationalist epistemologies to traditional conceptions of historical knowledge, they continue to adhere to the integrity of method manifested through the disciplinary protocols, not because it ensures correspondence with a real past but because this is what writing academic history in the twenty and twenty-first centuries consists of – non-adherence to these protocols can open historians to charges of fraud or shoddiness and may even exclude their work from being considered part of the genre of history.[42] For non-representationalists the historical method does not therefore facilitate, or enable, any correspondence between the past and historians' narratives; it is simply a contingent and socially determined praxis or set of genre conventions – a set of genre conventions that are, moreover, subject to change as and when the community deems it necessary. However, if historians want their texts to be recognised by audiences as history, then they must, to some degree, produce readings of texts and write narratives that align with audience expectations. While they can modify or discard a few of the practices or protocols of history writing, they cannot abandon them all simultaneously and still have their work judged to be history.

The epistemic status of a narrative, its status as fact or fiction, true or false, is not therefore inalienable and fixed forever. Rather it shifts with situational, disciplinary and other contextually variable factors: criteria internal to interpretative communities and their needs, not external to them. It is precisely the fluidity of these protocols that can explain the impact of framing on the shifting status of the Nagykanizsa narratives from fiction to non-fiction and vice versa. Katib Çelebi's account of the sieges is judged to be non-fictional history because it looks like non-fictional history. The acknowledgement that the 'fictional' *gazavatname* account was incorporated into the *Fezleke* does not necessarily cause a reclassification of the latter as legendary narrative or bad history. Indeed such is the reputation of Katib Çelebi as a forerunner of modern historians among current Ottomanists that this observation is more likely to result in a recategorisation of the *gazavatname* narratives as history. Similarly, the identification of a number of 'fictional' or uncorroborated elements in Katib Çelebi's narrative does not, in effect, alter present-day categorisations of his work as history because the majority of the work continues to abide by modern history-writing protocols and standards. Indeed the slight variation in norms and protocols signalled by the presence of these 'fictional' additions instead simply foregrounds the fluidity of the genre 'history' and makes explicit the differences between Ottoman and modern academic conceptions of the term. For many Ottoman interpretative communities, an essential criteria of history was not an isomorphic correspondence to a mind-independent past reality but was rather that it conveyed the appropriate message. This will be clearly illustrated in the discussion of Naima and his re-inscription of the sieges of Nagykanizsa below.

Naima: reading Katib Çelebi reading a *gazavatname*

Naima (1655–1716) was a career bureaucrat born into the Ottoman military-administrative system; his father was janissary commander of Aleppo. In his youth he took up a palace apprenticeship before embarking on a *kalemiye* [civil service] career. He held various posts in the financial administration and was appointed *vakanüvis* [official historian] for a time. Naima's main work, generally known as the *Tarih-i Naima* [*The History of Naima*] and completed in 1704, is a chronological history covering the years 1591–1660 in the *Tarih-i al-i Osman* genre. Like many other Ottoman histories, it is a critical compilation of the work of his predecessors in conjunction with sections authored by Naima himself. He dedicated two volumes of his history to two former grand viziers, Hüseyin Köprülü Pasha and Moralı Hasan Pasha, with whom he was connected by ties of patronage.[43]

When writing his history Naima utilised the works of a number of earlier Ottoman historians, most notably Hasan Beyzade and Katib Çelebi.

However, his account of the defence of Nagykanizsa in 1601 is virtually an in toto integration of the latter's narrative. There are, though, a few noteworthy variations between the two texts. In particular, Naima has, at times, divided up the narrative in a slightly different manner and rewritten the subheadings, all of which work to affect a subtle shift in emphasis. For example, he has divided the section in Katib Çelebi's work titled "Recounting the Grace of Allah and the Kindnesses of God" into two parts. The second section, given the new title "Recounting the Giving [of Rewards] and the Return", includes details of the various appointments, salary changes and rewards bestowed as a consequence of that year's activities.[44] This division has the effect of foregrounding both official administrative practices and the role of key personnel in networks of state patronage, perhaps reflecting the sociopolitical context Naima wrote within. He also changed some of the title headings to reflect his reading and understanding of a particular event. Specifically, he changed the title of the section narrating the defeat of Mihal Vitealzul [Michael the Brave] from "the defeat of the army of the enemy Mihal" to "the reason for the dismissal of Kaymakam Hafiz Pasha".[45] This reframes the events in terms of shifts in internal appointments and personal fortunes and allows one to read the Mihal incident as arising from bad administrative decisions, which subsequently led to the downfall of Hafiz Pasha. Lastly, Naima re-edits the account of the events surrounding the death of Ibrahim Pasha and in particular includes in a separate section titled "A Strange Sign", the bird omen that Tiryaki Hasan Pasha witnessed at Görösgàl.[46] The foregrounding of this omen may reflect Naima's increased interest in astrological matters and his perception of their usefulness in foretelling the future. Such an interest is also evident in the very rare changes he made to Katib Çelebi's account of the *Haile-i Osmaniye*, most notably his more elaborate and scholarly exposition of the astrological inauspiciousness of Sultan Osman and his reign.[47]

Naima also intersperses a couple of short sections of his own composition into his re-inscription of Katib Çelebi's text. The first of these is a short poem on the nature of history. Immediately after the section in which Katib Çelebi has noted that there are two different accounts of how Tiryaki Hasan Pasha was able to manipulate King Ferdinand into executing the two servants who had fled Nagykanizsa, Naima adds the following verse:

> Certainly some call the lover cypress and some *elif*
> The aim of all of them is one, but the telling differs.[48]

This short diptych has explanatory force on two distinct levels. Firstly, Naima argues that although the two signifiers, the cypress tree and the sign *elif*, have different referents they can both be used to signify the beloved. Thus they both serve the same function: to refer to the uprightness, straightness and gracefulness, both figuratively and morally, of the beloved.[49] The placing of the poem immediately after the two different versions of events permits audiences to draw an analogy with the practice of history writing: there may exist two distinct narratives which appear to possess different referents, but these, like the cypress and the *elif*, in certain contexts can both signify the same thing and thus serve the same function historically. In other words, although the two tales of the servants differ in the details, the function of them both is identical: they highlight how Tiryaki Hasan Pasha was clever enough to turn the treachery and gullibility of the enemy against them. However, the word chosen by Naima for cypress, *ar'ar*, enables the analogy to be taken a stage further. *Ar'ar* has two different meanings with two distinct referents.[50] It is frequently used to describe the juniper tree in Ottoman but can also be used, especially in Persian, to refer to the cypress tree. Here again, while the signifier can be understood as possessing two distinct referents, the function is the same; both refer to a tall, straight tree. This reading is only available to a reader with a knowledge of both Ottoman and Persian. One could therefore reasonably speculate that its purpose was to suggest that while two superficially different narratives purportedly describing the same event may seem to contradict each other, to the educated reader, who can see the true purpose of history, their identical functions will become clear, and apparent differences will be erased. The poem can thus be read as providing evidence of an Ottoman perception of the function of history: that it is not necessarily, or solely, about accurately representing the past or telling *the* truth about what *really* happened but that it also has a didactic, exemplary or moral function. From this perspective, therefore, two apparently different tales may serve the same function and so both be 'true': both tales highlight the cunning of Tiryaki Hasan Pasha and stress the importance of such a characteristic for a military commander.

Naima also includes two pieces of *nasihat* or advice not present in Katib Çelebi's account.[51] The first occurs after the besieged Ottoman *gazis* defeat the enemy's planned assault against the castle in reinforced pine boats. The second occupies a separate section titled "Words of Warning of the End" and occurs after the Ottomans have finally defeated the besieging army. The first interjection essentially praises the bravery, obedience and steadfastness of the soldiers and the experience and leadership of Tiryaki Hasan Pasha and suggests that because Tiryaki Hasan Pasha was a respected leader, his men trusted and believed in him even when the situation appeared hopeless, and as a result of their firmness of stance, the enemy were defeated. Similarly, the second stresses the importance of possessing rectitude, obedience and bravery. It praises both the men for not rushing into the enemy camp to grab the available booty but instead waiting until there were sufficient soldiers to safely collect it and Tiryaki Hasan Pasha for giving this command and ensuring fair distribution. The addition of these two sections foregrounds the framework within which Naima read Katib Çelebi's narrative: as a model of how commanders and their soldiers should behave, stressing the importance of obedience and bravery.[52] While for Katib Çelebi, Tiryaki Hasan Pasha is an exemplary Muslim administrator, for Naima he is figured more as an exemplary military leader.

In his narrative of the 1600–1601 sieges of Nagykanizsa, Naima also includes a few extracts from other works. Some of these are verbatim incorporations, whereas others are paraphrases of information from other sources. As argued in Chapter 1, the unreferenced inclusion of extracts from other historical accounts in the works of Ottoman historians fulfilled the same role as citation practices do in contemporary academic writings, that is it, in effect, diachronically situated the work into an existing system or network of knowledge. On a number of occasions, though, Naima directly references his source. This should not, however, be interpreted as evidence of proto-twentieth-century academic historical protocols or praxis. In the context of the *Haile-i Osmaniye*, Piterberg argues that Naima's citation of Hasan Beyzade was employed as a "concise summation" of what the cited author "had intended to convey" – by explicitly citing Hasan Beyzade, Naima is acknowledging that he is aware of why and how Katib Çelebi himself used Hasan Beyzade, and he wishes to emphasise this use.[53] Citation for Ottoman historians could, therefore, have had an emphatic function rather than a locative or authorising one. In the context of the sieges of Nagykanizsa Naima includes a direct reference to Hasan Beyzade:

> and the one who transcribes events, the historian, Hasan Beyzade said, 'a robe of honour and sword was also bestowed upon this insignificant one in reciprocation for the service of composing and writing the *fethname* of the gaza.'[54]

This reference occurs at the end of a long paragraph which has been directly taken from Hasan Beyzade's history by Naima and is not found in Katib Çelebi. The direct citation may have been intended to emphasise that this section is not included in Katib Çelebi but is from an eyewitness account.

Naima also included extracts sourced directly from Peçevi, Topçularkatibi and a *gazavatname* narrative in his re-inscription of Katib Çelebi's *Fezleke*.[55] For example, Naima initially includes verbatim Katib Çelebi's version of the cannon event. However, in his narration of the enemy's plea on the Saturday for the Ottomans to fire a cannon at them, he additionally introduces a few lines taken directly from the *gazavatnames*:

> But when Hasan Pasha instructed them with this plan and said, "say we have no cannons" the ağas objected and when they said, "it is not good to say these words to the enemy. If it wasn't their intention to come against us they will fall to covetousness and it will be the cause of their coming." "Obey my words. There is a place that you don't know about and I hid the cannons in that place."[56]

Writers reading: with Katib Çelebi and Naima 121

Naima's insertion here of a section derived from the *gazavatname* corpus has the effect of reinterpreting the cannon event. The inclusion effectively recaptures the possibility of an ethical reading of the event and thus Tiryaki Hasan Pasha's claim to mystical knowledge.[57] Such a reading may have accorded more with his imagination of Tiryaki Hasan Pasha as an exemplary military leader and his emphasis on the importance of obedience regardless of the order given.

Tarih-i Naima, Fezleke and the mystery of the anonymous reader

A manuscript copy of Katib Çelebi's *Fezleke*, Sale60 includes a large number of marginal notations, many of which are accompanied by the stylised Ottoman phrase "it was recorded or "it is not included". The section which describes the 1600–1601 sieges of Nagykanizsa includes six such marginal comments, five of which provide additional information sourced from other works, and one offers a gloss on the word *Azazel*. Four are accompanied by the phrase "it was recorded" and one with "it is not included". Of the four marginal comments accompanied by "it was recorded", the first provides extra information concerning the capture of Kopar and Szöcsén castles by Lala Mehmed Pasha on his journey from Buda to join the first siege of Nagykanizsa in 1600.[58] The only other sources that mention the capture of these two *palankas* are a number of the *gazavatnames*, most notably BPN:Oct.3442, thus presumably the writer had read a *gazavatname* account.[59] The second provides more details about the river Berk, which surrounded Nagykanizsa castle. I have been unable to find this particular phrase in any source other than in the *Tarih-i Naima*.[60] The third relates to Katib Çelebi's description of the cannon event. The marginal comment appears to be a 'quotation' from a *gazavatname* account, which reads:

> Then Hasan Pasha said, "say these words". When the *ağas* said, "it is not good to say these words to the enemy if it was not their intention to come against us they will come [now]", he said, "obey my words there is something you do not know. I have hidden the cannons in a place."[61]

It therefore reasserts both the challenge to Hasan Pasha's authority and its resolution through his claim to secret knowledge, which is elided in Katib Çelebi's account. The reader-writer is not trying to re-create the *gazavatname* manuscript; rather he is providing evidence of how he read this event and also how they expected other readers to read it. For this reader Katib Çelebi's rewriting of the cannon event within a framework privileging linear narrative coherency does not make sense and destroys part of the meaning that they read in the *gazavatname* account. It is this 'meaning' that they attempt to reinsert or reinscribe through the marginal note. The comment also potentially changes future readings of this manuscript. Readers not familiar with the *gazavatname* corpus or those who read privileging narrative coherency may find the marginal note incomprehensible and dismiss it, but for those familiar with the *gazavatnames* or with different reading strategies such as ethical reading, the marginal note becomes meaningful. The last example, positioned next to a description of how Sefer Ağa helped to defend the castle from attack, provides more information on his career and is almost certainly originally derived from Peçevi.[62] The marginal comment accompanied by the phrase "it is not included" is probably originally derived from Topçularkatibi and concerns the sending of the *bey* of Semendire to Osijek and the building of a *palanka* there.[63]

All of these marginal notes, with the exception of that concerning the capture of Kopar and Szöcsén, have been included verbatim in Naima's re-inscription of the *Fezleke* in his *Tarih-i Naima*. It is highly unlikely that this link is coincidental and that both the writer of this marginalia and Naima happened to have access to the same primary sources and subsequently chose to include these pieces of information in exactly the same place. In particular, Sefer Ağa is mentioned three times in the *Fezleke*, and yet both Naima and the marginalia writer chose to add information about his future career, taken from Peçevi, to exactly the same reference.[64] What, therefore, is the relationship between these marginal comments in the *Fezleke* and Naima's *Tarih-i Naima*? Before considering three possible explanations for this relationship, I will summarise what can be established about the inscriber of the marginalia. The manuscript itself is not dated, so it is impossible to establish an earliest date for the inscription of the marginalia.[65] However, the writer of the marginalia was not the inscriber of the text as written in the same hand as the marginalia, on folio 1a in the position of a title, is "the history Fezleke is in the writing of the deceased Molla Isazade." The writer of the marginalia has also written comments, terminated with the same stylised phases, in another manuscript: a copy of Katib Çelebi's *Cihannüma*, Oxford: Bodlein Library, Sale67. Therefore it appears that the mysterious annotator had not only an interest in the works of Katib Çelebi but also had either access to, or possession of, at least two of them.

The first explanation of the link between the marginalia and the *Tarih-i Naima* postulates the annotator as a reader with access both to Sale60 and a copy of *Tarih-i Naima*. This reader has then painstakingly compared both works and has noted in the margins of Sale60 the additions incorporated by Naima into his re-inscription of the *Fezleke*. This explanation despite appearing superficially the most convincing is beset with a number of flaws. Firstly, there is the issue of why anyone, with the exception of an Ottoman scholar writing a book on the subject, would bother to minutely compare the two texts and then note down Naima's additions in the margins of the *Fezleke*. The additions are not that significant in terms of size and content that they can be easily noticed or remembered from a casual reading of both works. More problematically, however, is the fact that this reader-writer has omitted perhaps the largest and most significant addition Naima made to his inscription of the *Fezleke*'s narrative of the sieges of Nagykanizsa: the passage derived from Hasan Beyzade, which includes details concerning the end of the first siege and the issuing of the *fethnames*. Similarly, the marginal comment about Kopar and Szöcsén castles found on folio 43a is not found in Naima. If the writer of the Sale60 marginalia did have access to the *Tarih-i Naima* and copied into the margins all Naima's additions, they must also have had independent access to a copy of the *gazavatname* accounts, which provide the only other source for this information.[66] Although this is perfectly plausible, the principle of economy, or Ockham's razor, requires one to consider any simpler and less convoluted explanations.

The second explanation assumes that an unknown reader inscribed these marginal additions into Sale60. Subsequently Naima acquired a copy of the manuscript and then incorporated both Katib Çelebi's text and some of these marginal comments into his history. This assertion explains more economically and coherently both the omission of the Szöcsén and Kopar note and the inclusion of the *fethname* paragraph from Hasan Beyzade in Naima. It is known that Naima had himself read the history of Hasan Beyzade, and so he could have copied the marginal comments and independently incorporated this paragraph.[67] His omission of the Szöcsén and Kopar note can be explained as a result of him choosing not to include it in his history, perhaps because it did not accord with the other sources that he had access to.

The final explanation assumes that the marginal comments were made by Naima himself in the process of preparing his own history. Such a view assumes both Sale60 and Sale67 to have been Naima's personal copies of Katib Çelebi's works that he annotated while researching his own history. Having written in the margins of the *Fezleke* additional pieces of information gleaned from other sources and histories, he later incorporated many of them into his own history, but some, such as the Kopar and Szöcsén note, he did not. Such a view explains the presence of the *fethname* addition sourced from Hasan Beyzade in the *Tarih-i Naima*, but not written in the margin of Sale60, as a later addition or afterthought added by Naima into his history. I find the latter explanation, that Naima had access to and annotated Sale60 and Sale67, to be the most persuasive and coherent, but I feel that a more in-depth comparison and study of the marginalia in Sale60, Sale67 and Naima's history is necessary. Such a study would be extremely worthwhile and would, depending on its conclusion, provide a greater insight into either the literary practices of an Ottoman historian or the reception strategies of Ottoman readers.

If we abandon a model of historical knowledge predicated on a representationalist epistemology as argued for in the introduction and instead conceive of history as another type of literary writing that is past focused and bound by particular generic protocols, then we can more coherently understand how the more 'fictional' *gazavatnames* become 'factual' when framed in a particular way by Katib Çelebi. We conventionally classify literary genres as factual or fictional not only on the basis of their correspondence to reality but on the basis of their accordance with cultural norms and expectations. By analysing how two Ottoman historians read and rewrote narratives of the sieges, we gain an insight into Ottoman literacy practices and the frameworks in which individuals read particular texts. I also suggest that a preliminary analysis of the marginalia in Sale60 initially points to it being Naima's personal, annotated copy of Katib Çelebi's *Fezleke* that he used when writing his own history. Further analysis could provide an interesting contribution to our knowledge of the writing of one of the most notable eighteenth-century Ottoman histories.

Notes

1 Katib Çelebi's account is included in his *Fezleke al-tevarih* [*The Summary of History*], which is a continuation in Ottoman Turkish of his earlier Arabic work *Fazlaka akval al-ahvar fi 'ilm al-tarih va'l-ahbar*. It is a history written within the conventions of Ottoman chronicle writing at the time and begins with events in 1592. Lacunae towards the end of the work suggest that it remained unfinished at the time of Katib Çelebi's death in 1657. See Gottfried Hagen, "Katib Çelebi," in *Historians of the Ottoman Empire*, ed. Cemal Kafadar, Hakan Karateke and Cornell Fleischer (2007), https://ottomanhistorians.uchicago.edu/en/historian/katib-celebi (accessed 25/09/12). I have used two manuscript version of this work; OBL: Rawl.or.20, also known as olim Bodl.Or.70, and OBL: Sale60; numbers [20] 2058 and [21] 2059 in H. Ethé, *Catalogue of the Persian Mss. in the Bodleian Library Part II Turkish, Hindustani, Pushtu and Additional Persian MSS* (Oxford: Clarendon Press MCMXXX, 1930), col.1167, and a nineteenth-century printed edition, Katib Çelebi, *Fezleke*. All references, unless otherwise stated will be to the printed version as it is the most widely available. Naima's account of the sieges is included in his history *Ravat al-husayn fi khulāsat-i akhbar al-khāfikayn*, more usually known as known as *Tarih-i Naima* [*The History of Naima*]. I have used the nineteenth-century edition published in Istanbul by Matbaa-i Âmire, in 1281–1283/1864–1866.
2 Gabriel Piterberg, "A Study in Ottoman Historiography in the Seventeenth Century," (PhD diss., Oxford University, 1992), 231; see 91 and 269 for his reiteration that inclusion into the *Tarih-i Naima* seals or names an account as the de facto official version.
3 Katib Çelebi, *Fezleke*, 170, directly cites Peçevi, but he also indirectly incorporates material from Peçevi on a number of occasions. For example, see references to the capture of the Lave/Lak fort and the killing of the brigands, 137–138. For direct incorporation of sections from Hasan Beyzade, compare Hasan Beyzade, *Telhis-i Tacü't-tevarih*, fols.467a-b and Katib Çelebi, *Fezleke*, 140. For similarities in content between Katib Çelebi, *Fezleke*, and Topçularkatibi, *Tevarih*, compare the description of cannons in Topçularkatibi, fol.131a and Katib Çelebi, 136–137, and a reference to camels Topçularkatibi, fol.139a and Katib Çelebi, 141. Katib Çelebî, *Fezleke*, and Câfer Iyânî, *Cihadname*, both mention that the enemy commenced their siege on the Prophet Muhammad's birthday (Monday, 12 *Rebiülevvel*) and link this fact to the ultimate success of Tiryaki Hasan Pasha in defending the castle; compare the *Fezleke*, 157, and *Cihadname*, fol.27b.
4 The existence of BPN: Oct.3442, inscribed in 1616, demonstrates that it was a *gazavatname* that was the source for Katib Çelebi rather than the other way round.
5 Such non-linguistic semiotic structures include indexes, folio numbers, red ink, overlining and the stability of the text.

6 See for example the analysis of LBL: O.R.12961 and CUL: O.R.700 in Chapter 4.
7 Katib Çelebi, *Fezleke*, 136.
8 In Turkic folk literature *cadu* has the connotation of a shamanistic rainmaker or weathermonger. See Nora K. Chadwick and Victor Zhirmunsky, *Oral Epics of Central Asia* (Cambridge: Cambridge at the University Press, 1969), 163.
9 Katib Çelebi, *Fezleke*, 160.
10 Qur'an, 29:39; 7:107 and 117; 26: 32 and 63; 28:31; 40:22.
11 Bible, Exodus ch.9 v.23.
12 Katib Çelebi, *Fezleke*, 160. Qur'an, Sura 33 (al-Ahzab). The Battle of the Trench is also known as the Battle of the Confederates – *gazavat al-ahzab*).
13 "Look, Azazel Hasan Pasha at the heads of Your Sons Kenan and Handan," Katib Çelebi, *Fezleke*, 163. In the printed version of *Fezleke* the word is اردك, which probably represents a variation in the orthographic register by the typesetter. In the two manuscript editions it reads اززل.
14 For descriptions of Iblis refusing to worship Adam and being cast out, see Qur'an 7:11–18; 15:31–44; 17:61–65; 18:50; 20:116–123; and 38:71–85. The relevant hadith is quoted in F. Rosenthal, trans., *The History of al-Tabari [Ta'rikh al-rusul wa'l-muluk]* vol. 1, *General Introduction and from the Creation to the Flood* (Albany: State University of New York Press, 1989), 254. Rosenthal mentions that this tradition is also quoted in Tabari, *Jami'al-bayan'an ta'wil ayal-Qur'an*, vol. 1 178 (edition by Bulaq, 1323–1329), also known as the *Tafsir*.
15 Roger H. Charles, trans., *The Apocrypha and Pseudepigrapha of the Old Testament* (Oxford: The Clarendon Press, 1913), see 8:1–3; 9:6; 10:4–9. This theme is echoed in Jewish tradition where *Azazel* is variously described as the name given to the goat, which is sent into the desert or wilderness on the Day of Atonement, the place where it is sent to, or the name of an evil demon.
16 OBL: Sale60 fol.51a. All references in Sale60 are to the Eastern Arabic script pagination and not to the later Arabic numeral system.
17 "When he said [this] all of the *beys* and pashas approved of this idea. The capture of Kanije had taken up place in the commander's heart. Hasan Pasha fell into agreement . . ." Katib Çelebi, *Fezleke*, 136.
18 Ibid., 171–172.
19 Ibid., 151.
20 For the reference to emic systems see Dennis Jarrett, "Pragmatic Coherence in an Oral Formulaic Tradition," in *Coherence in Spoken and Written Discourse*, ed. Deborah Tannen (Norwood, NJ: Ablex, 1984), 170–171.
21 For example, Suraiya Faroqhi, *Approaching Ottoman History: An Introduction to the Sources* (Cambridge: Cambridge University Press, 1999), 152–153, argues that in the *Fezleke* Katib Çelebi exemplifies the writing of history as a branch of scholarship rather than as a literary genre.
22 For a more in-depth discussion on the classification of texts as fiction or non-fiction see Claire Norton and Mark Donnelly, "The Siege, the Book and the Film: *Welcome to Sarajevo* (1997)," in *The Fiction of History*, ed. A. L. MacFie (London: Routledge, 2014).
23 Margreta de Grazia, *Shakespeare Verbatim: The Reproduction of Authenticity and the 1790 Apparatus* (Oxford: Clarendon Press, 1991), 11.
24 Katib Çelebi, *Fezleke*, 163.
25 See n.3.
26 Katib Çelebi, *Fezleke*, 151–152, for example.
27 See Deborah Tannen, "Relative Focus on Involvement in Oral and Written Discourse," in *Literacy, Language and Learning: The Nature and Consequences of Reading and Writing*, ed. David Olson, Nancy Torrance and Angela Hildyard (Cambridge: Cambridge University Press, 1985), 137–138, for a discussion of the decontextualised nature of expository prose and its use in academic scholarship.

28 Compare OBL: Rawl.or.20 and Katib Çelebi, *Fezleke*.
29 OBL: Sale60.
30 OBL: Rawl.or.20 also displays particular ocularity cues including the use of red ink, overlining and the later addition of points. That these points were a later addition can be adduced from the fact that a gap has not always been left for them in the text, and they have been squashed in. Paul Saenger, "The Separation of Words and the Physiology of Reading," in *Literacy and Orality*, ed. David Olson and Nancy Torrance (Cambridge: Cambridge University Press, 1991), 206, has argued that points and spaces, by providing a clear indication of conceptual or phrasing breaks, can facilitate silent or individual reading of texts which do not indicate vowels. These points do not indicate breaks equivalent to sentence breaks in modern English or Turkish, nor breaks for breath; rather, they seem to delineate discrete thought units.
31 Katib Çelebi, *Fezleke*, 161.
32 Peçevi, *Tarih-i Peçevi*, 233, and Topçularkatibi, *Tevarih-i al-i Osman*, fol.138a.
33 Hasan Beyzade, *Telhis-i Tacü't-tevarih*; cf. Richard Knolles, *Generall Historie of the Turks*, 3rd ed. (London: printed by Adam Islip, 1621); Nikolaus Istvanffy, *Historiarum de rebus vngaricis* (Cologne: Hierat, Anton, 1622); and W. P. Zimmerman, *Eikonographia aller deren ungarischer Statt Vostunge Castellen und Hauser welche von Anfang der Regierung Rudolphi des anderen Romischen Keyser biss auffdas 1603* ... (Augsburg, 1603).
34 Katib Çelebi, *Fezleke*, 138. Katib Çelebi also attributes indirectly the surrender of the castle to this explosion and concomitant destruction of the garrison's gunpowder (Katib Çelebi, *Fezleke*, 138 and 140–141).
35 See Mark Donnelly and Claire Norton, *Doing History* (London: Routledge, 2011), especially Chapter 6 for a more detailed discussion of representationalist and non-representationalist theories of knowledge in the context of history.
36 Hayden White, "The Fictions of Factual Representation," in *Tropics of Discourse: Essays in Cultural Criticism*, ed. Hayden White (Baltimore: The John Hopkins University Press, 1978), 121–122. See also Nancy Partner, "Historicity in an Age of Reality-Fictions," in *A New Philosophy of History*, ed. Frank Ankersmit and Hans Kellner (London: Reaktion Books, 1995), 24 and Kalle Pihlainen, "Narrative Objectivity Versus Fiction: On the Ontology of Historical Narratives," *Rethinking History: The Journal of Theory and Practice* 2/1 (1998).
37 Bjørn Ramberg, "Richard Rorty," in *The Stanford Encyclopedia of Philosophy*, ed. Edward N. Zalta (Spring, 2009 Edition). http://plato.stanford.edu/archives/spr2009/entries/rorty/ (accessed 24/8/16).
38 See also Stacie Friend, "Fictive Utterance and Imagining II," *Proceedings of the Aristotelian Society* 85 (2011); and Friend, "Fiction as Genre," *Proceedings of the Aristotelian Society* 11/2 (2012).
39 See Robert F. Berkhofer, *Beyond the Great Story: History as Text and Discourse* (Cambridge, MA: The Belknap Press of Harvard University Press, 1995), 69.
40 Phrase is from Thomas Haskell, following Francis Abbot, cited in Richard Rorty, *Truth and Progress: Philosophical Papers*, vol. 3 (Cambridge: Cambridge University Press, 1998), 74 n.11.
41 Nancy Partner, "Reality-Fictions," 23. Such protocols for twenty-first-century academic history writing include the use of standard models for the ascription of cause, effect and contingency; the physical framing of the work as history through the employment of a critical apparatus, or the icons of scholarship, such as the acknowledgements, explanatory introduction, footnotes, bibliographical references, appendices and indexes; invocations of authority such as the identification of the narratorial voice with the known author and the attribution of information to cited sources; coherence, both intra- and intertextually, including intersubjective agreement among historians; inclusiveness – the narrative should explain coherently all the evidence available; a decontextualised

tone achieved generally through the use of expository prose; and an explicit explanatory purpose or function. See Partner, "Reality-Fictions," 22–23 and 26; Paul Armstrong, *Conflicting Readings: Variety and Validity in Interpretation* (London: North Carolina Press, 1990), 13–16; Matt F. Oja, "Fictional History and Historical Fiction: Solzhenitsyn and Kis as Exemplars," *History and Theory* 27/2 (1988): 119–121; Michal Zellermayer, "An Analysis of Oral and Literate Texts: Two Types of Reader-Writer Relationship in Hebrew and English," in *The Social Construction of Written Communication*, ed. B. Raforth and D. Rubin (Norwood, NJ: Ablex, 1988), 299–300; Tannen, "Relative Focus," 137–138; and Berkhofer, *Beyond the Great Story*, 51–52.

42 Partner, "Reality-Fictions," 22. It could, however, also be viewed as evidence of the conservative power of the history profession to reproduce its own disciplinary norms.

43 Gabriel Piterberg, *An Ottoman Tragedy: History and Historiography at Play* (Berkeley: University of California Press, 2003), 47; Lewis Victor Thomas, *A Study of Naima*, ed. Norman Itzkowitz (New York: New York University Press, 1972), 5. Thomas's work provides considerable detail on Naima's life and the connections between Naima's history and the sources that he used.

44 cf. Katib Çelebi, *Fezleke*, 141–142, and Naima, *Tarih*, 245.

45 cf. Ibid., 144, and ibid., 247–248.

46 cf. Ibid., 148, and ibid., 254–255.

47 See Piterberg, "A Study of Ottoman Historiography," 270.

48 cf. Katib Çelebi, *Fezleke*, 163 and Naima, *Tarih*, 277.

49 "Servi" and "Elif" in *Türk dili ve Edebiyatı Ansiklopidisi*, vol. 7, 537, and vol. 3, 24.

50 cf. Francis Joseph Steingass, *A Comprehensive Persian-English Dictionary: Including the Arabic Words and Phrases to Be Met with in Persian Literature*, 9th ed. (London and New York: Routledge, 1995), 844, and James W. Redhouse, *A Turkish and English Lexicon* (Beirut: Librairie de Liban, 1974), 1294.

51 Naima, *Tarih*, 273 and 286.

52 Thomas, *A Study of Naima*, 90–91.

53 Piterberg "A Study of Ottoman Historiography," 270.

54 Naima, *Tarih*, 244 cf. Hasan Beyzade, *Telhis-i Tacü't-tevarih*, fol.468a.

55 For example, there is a section derived from Peçevi providing more information about the career of Sefer Ağa, Naima, *Tarih*, 272, and Peçevi, *Tarih-i Peçevi*, 239, and a longer section originating from Topçularkatibi about Mehmed Kethüda, the *bey* of Semendre, and his rebuilding of Osijek bridge and *palanka* with a thousand musketeers and some Frenks; see Naima, *Tarih*, 251, and Topçularkatibi, *Tevarih*, fol.142b.

56 Naima, *Tarih*, 260. Compare IMK: A.E.Tar.187 fol.8b: "After that the *ağas* came altogether. They spoke to Hasan Pasha. 'Woe is me my Lord. Let's not say bad news such as this to the infidels because if their aim was not to come, when they hear this news they will surely come against us' they said. Gazi Hasan Pasha, (may god grant heavenly bliss on him) said, 'obey my words because there is something that you don't know. I have hidden the cannons in a place.'"

57 See Chapter 4 for a discussion of ethical reading and the cannon event.

58 It reads "to these castles they also took Kopar and Szöcsén *palankas* and they wrote this" in OBL: Sale60 fol.43a next to lines 29–30.

59 BPN: Oct.3442 fol.3b. While this manuscript specifically mentions Szöcsén and Kopar, many of the other *gazavatnames*, for example, IMK: A.E.Tar.187, IMK: A.E.Tar.188 and IAM: no.374, mention Szöcsén and 'Kopan' – now known as Koppány. This shift from n to r suggests a variation in the orthographic register.

60 "[T]he aforementioned river leaves Lake Balaton and flows to the Dirava" (OBL: Sale60 fol.43b. Naima, *Tarih*, 238).

128   *Writers reading: with Katib Çelebi and Naima*

61 OBL: Sale60 fol.48a next to lines 2–4. A close variation is also present in Naima, *Tarih*, 260.
62 OBL: Sale60 fol.50a next to the last two lines of the folio: "[T]he aforementioned Sefer Ağa was sekban başı. Later he became a pasha and found fame" (c.f. Peçevi, *Tarih-i Peçevi*, 239). It is also found in Naima. The same marginal comment is also found on fol.24b of VNB: Mxt.200. This undated manuscript appears to be a rather confused collection of fragments from both a *gazavatname* account and also Katib Çelebi's account of the defence of Nagykanizsa.
63 OBL: Sale60 fol.46a. Topçularkatibi, *Tevarih*, fol.142b.
64 Katib Çelebi, *Fezleke*, 142, 153 and 160.
65 I have only really examined the marginalia relating to the sieges of Nagykanizsa, and it is possible that elsewhere in the manuscript, the anonymous annotator provides more information about themselves.
66 An alternative explanation presents itself at this juncture. I have only had access to the printed edition of the *Tarih-i Naima*, and it is entirely possible that this marginal comment is included in manuscript copies of Naima's history but was subsequently edited out by the typesetter of the printed edition.
67 Evidence that Naima had read Hasan Beyzade is provided by the inclusion of the *fethname* paragraph and Naima's comment that he consulted Hasan Beyzade's account of the *Haile-i Osmaniye*. See Piterberg, "A Study of Ottoman Historiography," 270.

6 Nationalism and the reinvention of early modern identities

"For History is the raw material for nationalist or ethnic or fundamentalist ideologies. [. . .] The Past is an essential element, perhaps the essential element, in these ideologies."[1]

Historical narratives are not neutral and impartial in their depiction of geopolitical space; they reflect, and help constitute, particular views of sovereignty. At a time when the nation-state and nationalism are the predominant means of delineating geopolitical space and articulating identity, historical narratives can and do, often unconsciously and without explicit acknowledgement, articulate and reproduce primordialist or essentialist explanations of nationalism and employ models that conceive of identity as inherent and unitary.[2] That is to say, historians frequently assume that national communities have always existed *sui generis* and that national identity is coextensive with a distinct immutable and enduring ethnic identity or community 'essence' that while dormant during periods of external oppression, will always struggle towards political and territorial autonomy and self-realisation.[3]

The modernist or constructivist understanding of national identity as contingent, invented, flexible and constantly being renegotiated in response to environmental and contextual factors is not widely accepted. This, in conjunction with the predilection in historical writing for teleology, results in evidence often being narrowly interpreted as establishing enduring, constant identities and thus the uncritical and anachronistic retrospective projection of current national identities onto early modern communities.[4] Such a practice is further exacerbated at times of fervent nation building when historians and accounts of the 'before now' are drafted to help establish a national identity and to legitimise claims for nation-state status through the establishment or invention of a suitable past that exemplifies the longevity and enduring nature of the nation. Earlier identities not congruent with the new vision are forgotten or reinterpreted, and history becomes a tool to serve new, contemporary agendas. While we cannot free ourselves from presentist, geopolitical perspectives, uncritically projecting nation-state-influenced conceptions of identity onto earlier communities is, at best, not particularly

130 Nationalism and reinvention

useful and, at worst, can lead to history being used to justify or legitimise extremist political or separatist aims that can, and have, led to 'ethnic cleansing' and violence.[5]

In this chapter, working with a constructivist model of national identity as contingent and constantly being reinvented, I will explore how nation-state cartographies and the possible ethno-geographic imaginaries they permitted not only shaped the remembering and inscription of nineteenth- and twentieth-century Ottoman and Turkish accounts of the 1600–1601 sieges of Nagykanizsa but facilitated the performance and thus reification of ethnocultural and national identities. Although I will mainly focus on Namık Kemal, *Kanije*, and Cavid Baysun, *Tiryaki Hasan Paşa ve Kanije Savaşı*, as representative of nineteenth- and twentieth-century Ottoman and Turkish narratives of the 1600–1601 sieges of Nagykanizsa, I will also make mention of a number of other accounts.[6]

Nineteenth-century accounts

By the end of the nineteenth century when Namık Kemal wrote his account of the sieges of Nagykanizsa, both the reality of the Ottoman-Habsburg border and the dominant frameworks available for the conception of space and identity had changed, resulting in significantly different narrative accounts of the Nagykanizsa sieges and concomitant imaginations of identity. The Ottomans had lost their Hungarian territories at the end of the seventeenth century, and the nineteenth century witnessed numerous wars and uprisings in the Balkans as various groups attempted to secede from the Ottoman Empire and establish new states. Ideologically, discourses centred upon notions of constitutionalism and nationalism within a framework of Ottomanism were becoming more dominant among Ottoman intellectuals and were providing a scaffold for the reinvention of Ottoman identities in response to the challenge from Europe and the gradual fragmentation of the empire.[7] History writing was extremely important in the search for a new Ottoman identity and in reshaping Ottoman legitimising ideology. Through the reframing and reconstruction of the past in historical works, a new self-identity was defined, current problems were addressed and guides were provided for future action.[8] Of these intellectuals and reformers, Namık Kemal attempted to construct a new common Ottoman identity and sense of self for the changed times through his writing. He rewrote the tale of the siege of Nagykanizsa castle at the end of the nineteenth century, and his very popular version was published in a number of different editions.[9] Namık Kemal was attracted to charismatic historical figures that he could use to galvanise people into action and inspire patriotism.[10] His historical work *Kanije*, similar to the *Silistre Muhasarası* [*The Siege of Silistre*] and the incomplete *Osmanlı Tarih-i* [*Ottoman History*], emphasised the heroic, military nature of the Ottomans and exemplified bravery, self-sacrifice and virtue through a description of historical events in an attempt to provide new models of identity and interpretations of the past for a nineteenth-century, proto-nationalist Ottoman middle class and elite.[11] The didactic nature of *Kanije* is apparent in the preface, where he states, "[O]ur main aim in the treatise is to humbly serve and increase the patriotism and zealous public spirit of the Muslims by remembering and reminding the soldiers of the imperial army of some of the glorious deeds of the Ottoman army."[12] The fact that his work became standard reading for school children demonstrates that *Kanije* not only reflected Ottoman proto-nation-state cartographies but was also instrumental in their imagination.[13]

Geography is a primary constituent of the ontology of a collective: the practice of how and where we locate ourselves in the world enables us to give meaning to self and other. Space is not just given; it is socially constructed into discrete territories by institutions, organisations, social movements and armed forces. Concomitant with changes in spatial imaginaries are changes in the moral or political space and in the juridico-political power associated with it.[14] While the sovereignty articulated by nation-state-dominated imaginings is considered operative over all of a legally demarcated territory within a linear fixed border, the spatial and political imaginings of empire implicit in earlier narratives such as the *gazavatnames* define communities in terms of centres of radiating influence and power with more porous and indistinct borders.[15] Whereas the early modern *gazavatnames* described the enemy besieging Ottoman-held Nagykanizsa castle according to geographical or political identity labels such as Austrians, Hungarians, Bohemians, Poles, *Frenks*, Croatians, Slovenes, Herzegovinians and "Zirinoğlu and his men", in Namık Kemal's *Kanije* the enemy are named in nation-state terms as Germany, France, Italy and Russia.[16] The reinterpretation of the term *Frenk*, which essentially signified to early modern Ottoman audiences western European Christendom in general, as France within Namık Kemal's (and Ahmed Refik's) nation-state dominated framework, has the unintentional and erroneous consequences of implying that France was part of the Habsburg coalition besieging Nagykanizsa, when in fact France was allied with the Ottomans at this time.[17] Similarly, Namık Kemal's insertion of Russia into the seventeenth-century, anti-Ottoman Habsburg coalition reflects a shift in the mapping of antagonisms. Namık Kemal, writing just after the Crimean War and a century of frequent Russo-Ottoman conflict, has the Russians firmly located in his cartography of warfare and correspondingly names them as the enemy.

The nation-state paradigm also affects the imagination of cartographies of enmity and depictions of self and other. The Habsburg adversaries of the Ottomans in Namık Kemal and Ahmed Refik's accounts are no longer drunken, accursed infidels [*kafir/kuffar*] but are renamed as the enemy [*düşman*]; the Ottoman army is no longer the divinely favoured army of Islam [*asakir-i Islam*] but the Ottoman army [*asakir-i Osmaniye*].[18] This shift can also be seen in nineteenth-century printed editions of earlier manuscript works such as the *Fezleke* by Katib Çelebi. Although the printed edition generally remains faithful to the text given in the manuscripts, each occurrence of the word *infidels* [*kuffar*] has been substituted with the word *enemy* [*âda*] in the printed edition.[19]

The shift away from a religious basis for imagining alterity allows an ethnic or linguistic component to be introduced. Late nineteenth- and twentieth-century nationalisms were often accompanied by a redefinition of self and other in ethnic or linguistic terms, and although many Ottoman intellectuals such as Namık Kemal were somewhat inconsistent on this point in their definition of self, their articulation of the other does reflect an ethnic and linguistic component in contrast to that of earlier narratives.[20] In both Namık Kemal and Ahmed Refik's narratives, it is no longer appropriate or coherent to conceive of or imply a sense of self that includes Hungarian speakers. Therefore the Hungarian soldiers, peasants and notables present in Nagykanizsa castle in the early modern *gazavatname* accounts are here transformed into prisoners, despite a loss of narrative coherency.[21] Similarly, the locals of the border area, here implicitly imagined as non-Muslim, non-Turkish speakers, are transformed from individuals with whom various early audiences did, or could, empathise and identify with into the enemy other. Namık Kemal has Tiryaki Hasan Pasha declare, "[M]y sons! We are on the border. In our midst there are so many infidels, both prisoners and locals and hey, you can't stuff up their ears. Won't they hear the discussion I have with you? If they hear, won't they give news to the enemy?"[22] Namık Kemal also redescribes in his account the two young men who in the *gazavatname* accounts, motivated by fear, flee the castle and escape to the besieging Habsburg army. He presents them as Hungarians and ascribes their motivation for flight to a desire to apostatise and abandon Islam. The border therefore is no longer a middle ground, a place of interaction, communication and synthesis, a space in which the forging of different, shared identities based upon local concerns occurs. Instead it is a place of hostility, fear and separation, a place inscribing the differences among communities.

Authorising texts: making fiction fact

Although one of the key source texts for Namık Kemal's *Kanije* appears to have been Katib Çelebi's *Fezleke*, he also claims that much of it was derived from a now-lost manuscript, the *Hasenat-i Hasan* by Fa'izi, who was ostensibly an eyewitness participant in the siege and a close friend of the commander, Tiryaki Hasan Pasha: "in the heart of the treatise many things have been taken from the book of Fa'izi which has the title *Hasenat-i Hasan*."[23] Despite the fact that all other extant references to Fa'izi and his manuscript post-date the publication of Namik Kemal's *Kanije*, they have become reified to such an extent that the *Hasenat-i Hasan* is frequently cited as a primary source for the siege.[24] The existence of both the author and manuscript has been uncritically accepted as fact, not fiction, by scholars and cataloguers such as Levend, Bursali Mehmed Tahir, Babinger, Çabuk and Ersever.[25]

Nationalism and reinvention 133

However, I argue that Fa'izi is in fact a fictionalised narrative construct and thus offers an instructive paradigmatic case of the influence of framing on genre classification and fictional status discussed earlier in Chapter 5. Later audiences' reification of Fa'izi and his manuscript has occurred not because of any isomorphic correspondence to reality (no additional facts have come to light proving his existence), but it has occurred because Fa'izi and his role in Namik Kemal's *Kanije*, make the same pattern that non-fiction makes; that is, he looks real or factual.

There is, however no corroborative source for the existence of Fa'izi and his work. Although some scholars – Levend, Babinger and Bursalı Mehmed Tahir – have tentatively identified him as Kafzade Fa'izi, records show that Kafzade Fa'izi would only have been twelve at the time of the siege, and none of the contemporaneous Ottoman writers who discuss Kafzade Fa'izi's life and works mention that he was present at the siege of Nagykanizsa or that he later wrote about it.[26] There are also no extant manuscripts of the *Hasenat-i Hasan* and no mention of it in Ottoman bibliographical works of the seventeenth century, such as Katib Çelebi, *Kashf al-zunūn 'an asāmī al-kutu wa-al-funūn* [*The Removal of Doubt from the Names of Books and the Arts*].[27]

A consideration of the possible narrative functions of Fa'izi further strengthens the argument that he was a literary device employed by Namik Kemal to frame his work as non-fictional history. Firstly, the character of Fa'izi works to frame *Kanije* as history through his portrayal as an extraordinary eyewitness and author of a primary source narrative of events. Secondly, potentially controversial assertions and the introduction of fictive characters, events and interpretations not found in any other source are presented as quotations from Fa'izi.[28] In this manner their reception as indicators of fictionality is contained and limited to the work of Fa'izi, allowing Namik Kemal's *Kanije* to still be read as non-fictional history. In addition, while the inclusion of direct speech contextualises and brings a sense of immediacy to a narrative by permitting a greater degree of identification with the participants through the use of the first person, it simultaneously tends to shift the perceived genre from that of history to literature.[29] To control this fictionalising tendency of direct speech, Namık Kemal frames the various speeches as quotations from Fa'izi. Analogously, references to Tiryaki Hasan Pasha's superhuman feats of strength and endurance are presented as quotes from Fa'izi.[30] In this manner Namık Kemal does not transgress the conventions inherent in the secular enlightenment-influenced approaches to history prevalent at that time and thus ensures the continued reception of his work as non-fiction.

Namık Kemal uses the citation of earlier Ottoman historians and primary sources to further legitimise his work and diachronically situate it within the genre of history. Unlike earlier Ottoman histories, where the author would utilise large quotations from the work of previous historians without specifically citing the source, Namık Kemal not only directly cites the author but also places the passage in quotation marks. However, the paramount concern of Namık Kemal when citing Naima does not appear to have been to facilitate historical scholarship and enable readers to locate the origin of particular passages in the manner of twentieth- and twenty-first-century academic praxis because many of his references are in fact inaccurate. Rather, the quotations constitute an authorising tool; they provide a framework within which his history can be read as diachronically linked to earlier Ottoman histories, such as those by Naima, İbrahim Peçevi and Mustafa Ali, all of which help to establish his work as an example of Ottoman 'factual' history writing.[31] For example, when Namık Kemal first cites Naima, he does so in a manner reminiscent of the protocols of modern academic scholarship which therefore works to situate *Kanije* firmly within the genre of modern western European history writing; "[t]he tale is on page 229 of the first volume of the book which was printed in six volumes in the imperial printing office in Istanbul as Naima's History. Those who are curious should investigate."[32] However, on three subsequent occasions Namık Kemal uses references to Naima's history to corroborate supposed details from Fa'izi but only the last citation to the enemy's vision of the green-turbaned soldiers can actually be found in Naima.[33] Moreover, he also gives Peçevi as a reference for the green-turbaned soldiers, but again this is inaccurate.[34] Therefore it appears that Namık Kemal is using the citation of Naima and Peçevi to authorise his own imaginative fabrications.

Twentieth-century Turkish nationalism

> "[T]he Ottomans had usurped the sovereignty of the Turkish nation. And they continued this usurpation for six hundred years. Now the Turkish nation has put an end to this and taken back its sovereignty".[35]

The importance of history in creating the imaginary spaces that define a people and influence their interpretations of self and other was evident to the founders of the Turkish Republic. In Turkish twentieth-century histories of Nagykanizsa a preexisting popular tale has been co-opted and reinterpreted as a tool to forge a national identity, inculcate audiences with a particular sense of self and Turkishness and to justify the existence of the Turkish state. The cartographies implicit in these accounts reflect and perpetuate a nation-state-orientated geopolitical map within which ethnicity and language play a determining role.[36] The accounts by Baysun, Ersever and Savaşkurt are all didactic in nature and were all published by state institutions: the military and the ministry of education.[37]

While Turkey inherited a centralised administration and standing army from the Ottoman Empire, the fragmentation of the empire resulting from the twentieth-century Balkan wars and the First World War meant that unlike nations such as France, it did not have preexisting, well-established frontiers and a long history as a stable and fixed collective entity that could be easily reimagined into a Turkish nation. It had to, therefore, essentially invent itself in linguistic and ethnic terms. However, the pluralistic and polyglottal nature of the Ottoman Empire made the establishment of a historical continuity in ethnic or linguistic terms between the former empire and the new republic difficult. Consequently, an earlier Turkish history was sought and found in the past of the central Asian Turks.[38] The state, through the commissioning of histories and control of academia, promoted the 'official history thesis' – the core of which was a teleological presupposition that the present Turkish nation-state was a natural evolution from earlier Turkish communities.[39] These twentieth-century accounts of the sieges of Nagykanizsa all reinterpret Ottoman history in accordance with a Turkish nation-state, ethnolinguistic-dominated cartography, and map physical, moral and political space accordingly. They reimagine the Ottoman Empire as the penultimate in a long succession of Turkish states, and the deeds of earlier military heroes are invested with a new significance, that of serving the new nation and glorifying its name.[40]

Gövsa, in his *Encyclopaedia of Famous Turks: The Works and Lives of Turks Who Won Fame in Literature, Art, Knowledge, War, Politics and Every Field*, which includes a section on Nagykanizsa and Tiryaki Hasan Pasha, explicitly states that he is involved in imagining a Turkish national community: "I worked to gather together in one volume the men that I thought necessary that they know from the point of view of Turkish culture."[41] Furthermore he continues, "[I]t is necessary to register that the 'Famous Turks' were not chosen from the point of view of race, only that they were chosen from the point of view of their suitability to the country and national culture." Similarly, Vahit Çabuk's *Tiryaki Hasan Paşa'nın gazaları ve Kanije Savunması* is published in the *Tercüman 1001 Temel Eser* series, which frames the works published as those representing a thousand years of Turkish culture and history and "which add meaning to our history and strength to our national identity".[42] Kemal Ilıcak, the owner of the *Tercüman* newspaper, wants to communicate these forgotten works to a younger generation because "they form the basis and essence of more than a thousand years of our history."[43]

Turkish nationalism developed in a historical space structured by European imperialism and within which the Ottoman state and other nationalisms had to compete for the same cultural, geographical and ideological space. There was, therefore, a perceived need to provide legitimisation for a Turkish sovereign state in Asia Minor, and it thus became a key feature of Turkish history written in a nationalist frame.[44] Savaşkurt's stated intention in writing his history was to demonstrate that Turkish soldiers developed particular military strategies before European commanders such as Napoleon, Frederick the Great and Hitler and that therefore they were at least the equal of their European contemporaries.[45] His contention that the tactics of Timur and Sultan Selim were used as exemplars by Western military leaders has two functions: first, by identifying Timur as a Turkish commander, Savaşkurt references both a non-Ottoman Turkish past and the longevity of the Turks as a people and (proto)-nation and thus stresses their right to national status; second, by stressing that Turkish commanders were at least the equal of their European contemporaries, he is attempting to rebut the claim that Turkish rule automatically results in a decline in prosperity and culture, which again emphasises the Turkish right to nation status.[46]

Imaginations of self and other

The self implicit in the twentieth-century narratives of the sieges of Nagykanizsa is imagined as Turkish and not Ottoman.[47] The campaign is redefined as the Turkish-Austrian war fought by the Turkish army with Turkish soldiers for Turkish land.[48] Nagykanizsa is remembered and commemorated as another heroic Turkish, not Ottoman, defence. Tiryaki Hasan Pasha is given a new identity as a Turkish hero fighting to preserve national territory. This appropriation of the Ottoman state as Turkish is further emphasised in Baysun through his use of the first-person plural, which further enables modern Turkish audiences to identify with their 'Turkish' ancestors: it is always *our* soldiers who defend *our* land.[49] Ersever does sometimes use the term *Ottoman* but almost exclusively in negative contexts: "thus the Ottoman state lost to the enemy through weakness which was born from tyranny." This contrasts with his use of the term *Turk*: "the Turkish army was victorious" and "despite the mistakes of the commander [...] the great victory that was won at Kanije brought a smile to the face of the Turkish nation."[50] This latter quotation reflects the peasantist ideology popular in many Turkish historical narratives at the time which contrasts the pure unspoiled noble Turkish warrior or peasant with the corrupt and ineffectual Ottoman elite, thereby providing evidence for the necessity of a revolution.[51]

The concept of Turkishness as a language and ethnicity also remaps cartographies of antagonism so that all non-Turks within the empire are viewed with mistrust and become a symbol of alterity. Consequently, ideas of self, and the referent for 'Ottoman', are changed. Kara Ömer Ağa, who was depicted as a local of Hungary and a native speaker of Balkan languages in the *gazavatnames*, is transformed into an ethnic Turk in Baysun's account, and his ability to speak Balkan languages is forgotten. Hungarians here, as in Namık Kemal's *Kanije*, are depicted exclusively as the enemy, with the Hungarians in the castle being redefined as prisoners, not soldiers, and the two fleeing servants also being described as Hungarian.[52] This shift in the depiction of Ottoman non-Turks and non-Muslims from self to other is also reflected in other historical works of this period: Danişmend not only argued in the *Izahlı Osmanlı Tarih-i Kronolojisi* that the *devşirme* were potential traitors, but he also concluded that Christian *sekbans* [temporary infantry recruits] were not as trustworthy as Muslim ones.[53]

This shift from religion to ethnicity as the determinant of otherness is exemplified in the description of the enemy character, Kozma. Câfer Iyânî, in his seventeenth-century account of the siege *Cihadname-i Hasan Paşa*, portrays Kozma as an infidel in accordance with his religiously dominated cartography of violence, but in Baysun it is ethnicity which divides self from other, and Kozma is redescribed as a Hungarian.[54] This is echoed in Çabuk's transcription and Turkification of Câfer Iyânî's *Cihadname*, where he describes Kozma in the index as a "rebellious Hungarian *Bey*" despite there being no indication of his ethnicity in the manuscript.[55] Çabuk also erases the religious framework of the original text by redescribing Kozma as "accursed" rather than as a "base infidel" as Câfer Iyânî does.[56]

This example demonstrates the effacement of a religiously dominated cartography by the secularising discourse of the new republic. Although religion had been an important element in the construction of a self-identity in the early days of the Turkish Republic, by the mid-twentieth century the state officially espoused an imagining of community within a secular framework.[57] Earlier accounts of the sieges of Nagykanizsa were very much written and received within a religious framework, for example, the heterodox Islam of some of the *gazavatnames* and the more orthodox Qur'anic intertextuality of Katib Çelebi's *Fezleke*. Likewise, although Namık Kemal adopted a political cartography predicated upon the nation-state, his moral framework was still largely Islamic as is evidenced in his use of religious phrases, Qur'anic quotations and in his construction of Tiryaki Hasan Pasha as an exemplum of not only a good soldier and commander but also of a good Muslim.

Conversely, the twentieth-century accounts exhibit an erasure of religion evident in the relative absence of religious phrases, prayers and blessings. There are no Qur'anic quotations, and all references to jihad have been removed. The *Gülbang-i Muhammadî* is not cried before assaults and battles, and neither is the chant "Allah, Allah". Although Baysun writes that "*gazis* in Kanije Castle cried out three times with one voice", what they cried is carefully not specified.[58] Similarly, while the impetus of the besieged in the *gazavatnames* and the *Fezleke* is generally expressed in terms of religion, in the twentieth-century accounts it is articulated within the structure of the nation: in the *gazavatnames* Tiryaki Hasan Pasha and his men are prepared to sacrifice their souls for Allah, but in Baysun they sacrifice them for the fatherland and the nation; in the *gazavatnames* Tiryaki Hasan Pasha shouts "long live the padişah", but in Baysun he shouts "long live the nation".[59] The depiction of Tiryaki Hasan Pasha as a mystical warrior-saint or heterodox dervish is also effaced with the removal of the *menakibname* intertextual elements and references to his mystical powers and divine influence. This shift reflects the state's attempt to replace the role that the *tarikat* or heterodox dervish movement played in providing guidance with that of secular knowledge and science as exemplified in Atatürk's dictum: "the truest guide for everything in the world, for civilisation, for life, for success is

138 *Nationalism and reinvention*

knowledge and science."[60] Religion is present, but it is a nationalised, contained, delimitated religion.

Historical forgetfulness

Further evidence of the impact of nation-state-dominated cartographies is evident in the focus of the various narratives. In contrast with accounts coterminous with the events, all of the twentieth-century accounts concentrate upon the defence of Nagykanizsa by Tiryaki Hasan Pasha and barely even mention the capture in the previous year.[61] This shift is exemplified in Gövsa, *Encyclopaedia of Famous Turks*, where although there is an entry for Tiryaki Hasan Pasha, the grand vizier, Ibrahim Pasha who captured the castle in 1600, is noticeably absent. This realignment of priorities is continued in possibly the most widely distributed and received account of the sieges, the film *Kanije Kalesi*, which focuses exclusively on the defence.[62]

This forgetfulness is less a matter of oversight or apathy than the employment of a historically structured viewpoint reflecting the shift in moral and juridico-political imaginaries accompanying the nation-state orientated cartography. As noted, the imagining of imperial sovereignty, for example, depicts influence diffusing outwards from a centre into fluid and amorphous border zones.[63] In such areas, low-level border raids and attacks were viewed as normal and semi-legitimate military operations.[64] However, the linear boundaries of the nation-state enclose territory over which the state is deemed to have exclusive dominion, and this affects the legitimate praxis of violence with the unauthorised crossing of the boundary providing a clear *casus belli* for war. Consequently, in a nation-state-dominated world the only legitimate military action is defensive, and the exaltation of previous victories by 'ancestors' outside the boundaries of the current nation-state is problematic.[65] Therefore the celebration of the capture of Nagykanizsa is not accordant with contemporary moral military cartography.

This shift in juridico-political cartographies towards an acceptance of the legal integrity of the nation-state and a concomitant emphasis on the defence is evidenced in the twentieth-century narratives in a number of ways. For example, Baysun narrates events from the viewpoint that the Ottomans legitimately controlled the territory under their dominion and were aggressed against by their enemies: "the Austrians with the Hungarians who were affiliated to them, together with the help of other nations attacked our land, burnt our villages and crushed our *palangas* [small forts]."[66] The Ottomans are depicted as only wanting to protect their land and not as desiring to capture enemy territory: "our soldiers, who were protecting our land, with their commanders at their head raided the enemy countries, took revenge and returned back."[67] In this manner, the capture of Nagykanizsa is positioned by Baysun as an instance of preemptive defence against continuous enemy incursions into Ottoman territory, occurring within the framework of a larger defensive campaign. This contrasts with the *gazavatname* accounts which describe numerous Ottoman raids into enemy territory, the razing of settlements and capture of livestock, booty and civilians without any concern for the illegality of such 'aggressive' actions.

Similarly, the *gazavatnames* and Katib Çelebi's *Fezleke* frame the initial siege of Nagykanizsa by the Ottomans within the greater narrative of the capture of the capital and surrounding lands of the Habsburg King by arguing that its seizure will put the city [Vienna] and "the lands of the infidel" within three day's march of the army of Islam.[68] In Baysun, however, Nagykanizsa is presented only as "the key to Mekomorya", a region on the Hungarian and Slovenian borders.[69] This reflects the effacement of the Ottoman aim to capture Vienna. It is no longer appropriate within the nation-state discourse to situate the capture of Nagykanizsa within a narrative culminating in the intended conquest of Vienna, the capital of another nation-state.

Twentieth-century Turkish accounts may emphasise the Ottoman defence of Nagykanizsa rather than the capture for two additional reasons: firstly, because their nation-state imaginary is largely premised on a rejection of the Ottoman state, especially their much-criticised 'aggressive expansion policy', and secondly as a consequence of the role the Turkish War of Independence [*kurtuluş savaşı*] occupies in the Turkish cartography of conflict.[70] This war in the 1920s is generally configured in Turkey as a war of defence against foreign attack, and in the twentieth-century accounts, the defence of Nagykanizsa appears to be used as a synecdoche for this war.[71] I argue that by framing his account in terms of an attack upon "our lands by our neighbours", using the first person plural and addressing the audience with such rhetorical questions as "would we have remained opposite as wretched spectators as the *çeteler* [brigands] oppressed our country?", Baysun is indirectly referencing the War of Independence.[72] He is, in effect, positioning the defence of Nagykanizsa as an allegory of this war and of the defence of the newly formed Republic of Turkey.[73]

A reading of nineteenth- and twentieth-century accounts of the sieges of Nagykanizsa demonstrates not only the influence that nation-state cartographies have on our mapping of self and other but the degree to which past-focused literary writing, including histories, are integral components of the performance and imagination of national (and proto-national) identities – a point reinforced by the fact that many of the accounts were published by state ministries. The way we remember and the things we forget both play a fundamental role in our creation or imagination of the present; narratives reflect but also fashion our world. Through the discussion of the uncorroborated author Fa'izi and his *Hasenat-i Hasan*, I returned to the question of how genre distinctions and boundaries are negotiated and why authors might want to frame their texts in particular ways. This discussion of the authorisation of texts raises the question of the current preeminent, sociocultural and epistemological status that histories enjoy when compared to other past-focused literary writing. In the conclusion I ask what obligations such a status places on historians.

Notes

1 Eric Hobsbawm, *On History* (London: Abacus, 1998), 6.
2 Umit Özkırımlı, *Theories of Nationalism: A Critical Introduction* (Basingstoke: Palgrave, 2000), summarises and critiques the three main approaches to the study of nationalism: primordialism, modernist and ethno-symbolism.
3 In the context of histories of the Ottoman-Habsburg marches, I give some examples of historians who do this in my article: Claire Norton, "Narrating the 'Yoke of Oppression': Twentieth-Century Hungarian Scholarship of the Ottoman-Hungarian Borderlands," in *Nationalism, Historiography and the (Re) Construction of the Past*, ed. Claire Norton (Washington: New Academia Press, 2007).
4 I use Fine's conception of ethnicity here which is based on the idea that one belongs to a community with others who share a common language, territory and history: John V. A. Fine, *When Ethnicity Did Not Matter in the Balkans: A Study of Identity in Pre-Nationalist Croatia, Dalmatia, and Slavonia in the Medieval and Early-Modern Periods* (Ann Arbor: The University of Michigan Press, 2006), 2.
5 For a more detailed account of nationalism, identity and historical narratives of the south-east Balkans under Ottoman rule, see Claire Norton, "Nationalism and the Re-Invention of Early-Modern Identities in the Ottoman-Habsburg Borderlands," *Ethnologia Balkanica* 11 (2008).
6 Namık Kemal, *Kanije* (Istanbul: Matbaa-i Ebüzziya, 1311/1893–1894), was first published in 1290/1873 under the pseudonym of Ahmed Nafiz by the Hayal Matbaası. It was republished in 1303/1886 and in 1311/1893 under Namık Kemal's own name by the Matbaa-i Ebüzziya and again in 1335/1917 by the Matbaa-ı Amire. All references are to the 1311/1893 edition. It has also been translated into Turkish: Namık Kemal, *Kanije*, trans. Hakki Tarik (Istanbul: Vakit Basımevi, 1941); Cavid Baysun, *Tiryaki Hasan Paşa ve Kanije Savaşı* (Istanbul: Milli Eğitim Bakanlığı Köy Kitaplığı no.15, Milli Eğitim Basımevi, 1950).
7 Eric Zürcher, *Turkey: A Modern History* (London and New York: I. B. Tauris and Co. Ltd., 1997), 7–72; Christoph Neumann, "Bad Times and Better Self: Definitions of Identity and Strategies for Development in Late Ottoman Historiography, 1850–1900," in *The Ottomans and the Balkans: A Discussion of Historiography*, ed. Fikret Adanir and Suraiya Faroqhi (Leiden, Boston and Köln: Brill, 2002), 57–78 and 59–60; Selim Deringil, *The Well-Protected Domains: Ideology and the Legitimation of Power in the Ottoman Empire 1876–1909* (London, NY: I. B. Tauris, 1998), 108; and David Kushner, *The Rise of Turkish Nationalism 1876–1908* (London: Frank Cass, 1977), 98.
8 Neumann, "Bad Times and Better Self," 62–63.
9 See n.6.
10 Şerif Mardin, *The Genesis of Young Ottoman Thought: A Study in the Modernization of Turkey* (New York: Syracuse University Press, 2000), 335. In this regard the aims of Namık Kemal were very similar to those of Ahmed Refik, who in his work titled *Meşhur Osmanlı Komandanlar*, [*Famous Ottoman Commanders*] (Istanbul: Kitaphane-i Islam ve Askeri Ibrahim Hilmi, 1318/1900–1901), sought to reinvent an Ottoman past through stirring historical vignettes to provide a new sense of identity for an audience living through transformative geopolitical times. As part of this work Ahmed Refik includes a description of the 1600 and 1601 sieges of Nagykanizsa castle.
11 Neumann, "Bad Times and Better Self," 70; Mustafa Kutlu, "Namık Kemal," in *Türk Dili ve Edebiyatı Ansiklopedisi* (Istanbul: Dergah Yayımları, 1985–1986), vol. 6, 519; Ömer Faruk Akün, "Namık Kemal," in *İslam Ansiklopedisi: İslam*

Alemi Tarih, Cografya, Etnograf ve Biyografya Lugatı (Istanbul: Maarif Matbaası, 1940–1988), vol. 9, 70; Namık Kemal, *Silistre Muhasarası* (Istanbul: Teodor Kasap Matbaası, 1290); Namık Kemal, *Osmanlı Tarih-i* (Istanbul: Mahmud Bey Matbaası, 1326/1908). Namık Kemal also wrote histories of Saladin and Mehmed II.

12 Namık Kemal, *Kanije*, 3–4.
13 Deringil, *The Well-Protected Domains*, 109, mentions that his work became standard reading for Ottoman school children. See Mark Donnelly and Claire Norton, *Doing History* (London: Routledge, 2011), 125–129, for an introductory analysis of the intersection of nationalism and school curricula.
14 Michel Foucault, "Questions on Geography," in *Michel Foucault: Power/Knowledge*, ed. Colin Gordon (New York: Pantheon, 1980), 68, notes that "territory is no doubt a geographical notion, but it is first of all a juridico-political one: the area controlled by a certain kind of power," quoted in Michael J. Shapiro, *Violent Cartographies: Mapping Cultures of War* (Minneapolis, MN and London: University of Minnesota Press, 1997), 15.
15 Benedict Anderson, *Imagined Communities: Reflections on the Origin and Spread of Nationalism* (London: Verso Press, 1991), 19.
16 IMK: A.E.Tar.187, fol.6b and Namık Kemal, *Kanije*, 47–48, 65 and 98.
17 Ahmed Refik, *Meşhur Osmanlı Komandanları* (İstanbul: İbrahim Hilmi Matbaası, 1318/1900–1901), 322.
18 Namık Kemal, *Kanije*, 99. Ahmed Refik, *Meşhur Osmanlı Komandanları*, 314 and 318, also refers to the enemy as *düşman*. However, he describes the Ottoman army as *Osmanlı ordusu*, employing Turkish grammar rather than the Persian, and replacing the Arabic *asakir* with the Turkish word *ordu*. This may reflect the growing significance of the Ottoman language reform and simplification movement which had begun with the efforts of Şinasi in the mid-nineteenth century to replace the excessively ornate official Ottoman with its heavy reliance on Persian and Arabic grammar and vocabulary with a clear, concise, vernacular Turkish accessible to all.
19 Katib Çelebi, *Fezleke*, 135 line 14, and OBL: Rawl.or.20 fol.103a; cf. also 137 line 20 and fol.104a.
20 Eric Hobsbawm, *Nations and Nationalism since 1780: Programme, Myth and Reality* (Cambridge: Cambridge University Press, 1990), 102.
21 Namık Kemal, *Kanije*, 79; Ahmed Refik, *Meşhur Osmanlı Komandanları*, 340.
22 Ibid., 52.
23 Ibid., 3–4. For the suggestion that Fa'izi was an eyewitness and colleague of Tiryaki Hasan Pasha see such phrases as "the famous poet Fa'izi concerning his memoirs in the book that he wrote, mentioned from his conversations and friendly chat which he had had that [. . .]", 11, and "although the commander in chief lost Hasan Pasha from his side the rare peers, Kuyucu Murad Pasha and Lala Mehmed Pasha came to the world. The bodies of the two heroes apparently said to the late Fa'izi that they were sure that with the help and favour of God the imperial army would be successful. The tale is from the book of Fa'izi", 19–20.
24 See Vahit Çabuk, *Tiryaki Hasan Paşa'nın Gazaları ve Kanije Savunması* (Istanbul: Tercüman 1001 Temel Eser No.129, 1978), 7, and H. Z. Ersever, *Kanije Savunması ve Tiryaki Hasan Paşa* (Ankara: Türk Asker Büyükleri ve Türk Zaferleri Seri no.12, Genelkurmay Askeri Tarih ve Stratejik Etüt Baskanlığı Yayınları Gnkur. Basımevi, 1986), 78.
25 A. S. Levend, *Gazavat-nameler ve Mihaloğlu Ali Bey'in Gazavat-namesi* (Ankara: Türk Tarih Kurumu Yayınlarından / XI. Seri, No. 8, Türk Tarih Kurumu Basımevi, 1956), 101–102; Bursalı Mehmed Tahir, *Osmanlı Müellifleri*, 2 vols. (Istanbul: Matbaa-i Amise, 1333/1914–1915), 386; Franz Babinger, *Die Geschichtsschreiber der Osmanen und ihre Werke* (Leipzig: Otto Harrassowitz,

1927), 155–156; Çabuk, *Tiryaki Hasan Paşa*, 7; Baysun, *Tiryaki Hasan Paşa*, 12; and Ersever, *Kanije Savunması*, 78. Ersever Turkifies the title of the apparently lost work, renaming it as *Kanije Muhasarası* and describes Namık Kemal as the person who simplified Fa'izi's work.

26 Levend, *Gazavat-Nameler*, 102.

27 For a printed version of the work including the Arabic text with a Latin translation and indexes, see Gustav Flügel, *Lexicon bibliographicum et encyclopaedicum* [...], 7 vols. (Leipzig and London, 1835–1858) available via Googlebooks https://books.google.co.uk/books?id=CSlTAAAAcAAJ&lpg=PA9&ots=L9tHvRk6Nf&dq=G.%20Fl%C3%BCgel%2C%20Lexicon%20bibliographicum%20et%20encyclopaedicum&pg=PP1#v=onepage&q=G.%20Fl%C3%BCgel,%20Lexicon%20bibliographicum%20et%20encyclopaedicum&f=false (accessed 30/6/16).

28 For example, the 18,000 heads brought in front of Tiryaki Hasan Pasha and the enemy's vision of the green-headed Turks: Namık Kemal, *Kanije*, 118 and 127. For imaginative characters and events, see the nameless man whose impassioned speech is the cause of the commander Ibrahim Pasha's decision to attack, 30; the character of Abdulrahim who questions the wisdom of Grand Vizier Ibrahim Pasha, 34; Sokullu Hasan, the soldier who criticised Hasan Pasha for lying under oath, 56–57; and the incident in which Hasan Pasha is found weeping from despair, 70.

29 Deborah Tannen, "Oral and Literate Strategies in Spoken and Written Narratives," *Language* 58 (1982): 1–21; E. Ochs, "Planned and Unplanned Discourse," in *Discourse and Syntax*, ed. T. Givon (New York: New York Academic Press, 1979); and William Labov, *Language in the Inner City* (Philadelphia: University of Pennsylvania Press, 1972), argue that narration is more vivid when speech is presented as first-person dialogue rather than as third-person reported speech. The use of direct speech also tends to shift the apparent function of the work from a didactic, pedagogical function to one of entertainment.

30 Namık Kemal, *Kanije*, 61–63 and 67–68, for his descriptions of the eighty-seven-year-old Tiryaki Hasan Pasha being tied onto his horse, then leading the attack against the enemy, leaping into the trenches, personally filling in breaches in the castle walls and sustaining numerous sword wounds as a result of the raging battle.

31 Ibid., 41, for a reference to Mustafa Ali and 127 for a reference to Peçevi. The citation practices of twenty-first century historians are designed to both facilitate historical scholarship and to legitimise the works through placement in an intertextual network of other authorised histories.

32 Ibid., 21.

33 Ibid., 34, concerning the character Abdulrahim; 38 on the soldiers becoming angry with Ibrahim Pasha because they were prevented from chasing the fleeing enemy relief force; and 127 on the enemy's vision of the green-turbanned Turks. See also 41 for Namık Kemal's inaccurate claim that Naima wrote that the besieged Habsburg forces capitulated in the 1600 siege because of a lack of provisions.

34 Ibid., 127, "In the narration of this tale there is agreement of the pens of Fa'izi, Naima and Peçevi." A second reference to Peçevi is, however, accurate. Ahmed Refik, *Meşhur Osmanlı Komandanları*, also references the work of previous historians, but he does so in a manner more in keeping with twenty- and twenty-first-century academic history protocols, using footnotes, giving page numbers and occasionally quoting from the cited works. In particular, he quotes, Naima, *Tarih-i Naima*, Katib Çelebi, *Fezleke*, Peçevi, *Tarih-i Peçevi* and Namık Kemal, *Kanije*; see 318, 327, 341. Although he cites the authors of all the other works, he only gives the name of Namık Kemal's work, *Kanije*. Also of interest is

Ahmed Refik's very modern practice of not only giving the Ottoman version of place names but also the German or Hungarian equivalent, 314 and 322.
35 Atatürk, *Söylev (Nutuk)* (Ankara: Ankara Üniversitesi Basımevi, 1964), vol. 2, 475 and 483, quoted in Büşra Ersanlı, "The Ottoman Empire in the Historiography of the Kemalist Era: A Theory of Fatal Decline," in *The Ottomans and The Balkans: A Discussion of Historiography*, ed. Fikret Adanır and Suraiya Faroqhi (Leiden, Boston and Köln: Brill, 2002), 141.
36 In particular I will concentrate on the account by Baysun, *Tiryaki Hasan Paşa*, but I will also discuss A. Savaşkurt, *Kanije Müdafaası* (İstanbul: Askeri Mecmua 138 sayılı Askeri Matbaası, 1945), Ersever, *Kanije Savunması*, and various encyclopaedia entries.
37 Baysun, *Tiryaki Hasan Paşa*, was published in 1950 by the ministry of education in the village library series, Savaşkurt, *Kanije Müdafaası*, in 1945 by the Istanbul Military Press and Ersever, *Kanije Savunması*, in 1986 by the General Staff Military History and Strategic Studies Ministry Publications as number 12 in the 'Great Turkish Soldiers and Turkish Victories' series.
38 Hobsbawm, *Nations and Nationalism*, 102.
39 Ersanlı, "The Ottoman Empire," 115–116 and 130. The main principles of this thesis were: Ottoman history is insufficient to explain the origins of the Republic; Turkish history stretches back to pre-Ottoman and pre-Islamic times; the Turks created the most ancient civilisation of the world; the Ottoman state was the penultimate political entity in a long line of Turkish states; and post-1600 Ottoman political life was corrupt and defective, and thus a revolutionary break was necessary.
40 See Graham Dawson, *Soldier Heroes: British Adventure, Empire and the Imagining of Masculinities* (London and New York: Routledge, 1994), 1, for a discussion of the role of the hero in imagining the nation.
41 I. A. Gövsa, *Turk Meşhurları Ansiklopedisi: Edebiyatta, Sanatta, ilimde, Harpte, Politikada ve her sahada şöhret kazanmış olan Türklerin Hayatları Eserleri* (Istanbul: Yedigün Neşriyatı, 1946), no page number, under the heading "bitirirken" at the end of the encyclopaedia.
42 Kemal Ilıcak, "Introduction to the *1001 Temel Eser Series*," in Çabuk, *Tiryaki Hasan Paşa*, 5–6. Ilıcak also notes in his introduction that the distribution and publication of these classic Turkish works is so important that he is making no profit from the enterprise besides a feeling of pride and the pleasure of doing his duty.
43 Ibid.
44 Ibid., 101 and 112.
45 Savaşkurt, *Kanije Müdafaası*, 3.
46 See the Allied memorandum of 23 June 1919, addressed to the Sèvres Peace talks, quoted in Halil Berktay, "The 'Other' Feudalism: A Critique of Twentieth Century Turkish Historiography," (PhD diss., University of Birmingham University, 1990), 107: "In no European, Asian or African country has the establishment of Turkish rule not been followed by a decline in material welfare and culture; conversely, in no country has the end of Turkish rule not been followed by a rise in prosperity and by cultural development. Among European Christians as well as the Moslem peoples of Syria, the Arab lands and Africa, the Turk has done nothing but ravage and destroy what he has conquered . . ."
47 Savaşkurt, *Kanije Müdafaası*, does refer to the Ottomans, but by conjoining the term *Osmanlı* with Turk, he ensures that Ottoman is read as a subgroup of Turk.
48 For example, Baysun, *Tiryaki Hasan Paşa*, 4–6, 9 and 11–13. Baysun begins his work, "The Turkish state stretched into the middle of Europe for a long time . . ." therefore clearly framing it as part of Turkish, not Ottoman, history.
49 See also Baysun, *Tiryaki Hasan Paşa*, 3: "[a] large portion of Hungary was found in our hands" and "around the end of the 16th century our borders were a field of head to head fighting."

50 Ersever, *Kanije Savunması*, 5–6 and 76. See also 3, 17 and 21 for further examples.
51 Ersanlı, "The Ottoman Empire," 130 and 135. Such a view is reflected in Baysun, *Tiryaki Hasan Paşa*, 13 and 26, who habitually depicts the viziers as relatively ineffectual; see also Savaşkurt, *Kanije Müdafaası*, 5, where he notes that "even the sultans had been caused to accept bribes".
52 Baysun, *Tiryaki Hasan Paşa*, 31.
53 Ersanlı, "The Ottoman Empire," 138, and I. H. Danişmend, *Izahlı Osmanlı Tarih-I Kronolojisi* 4 vols. (Istanbul: Türkiye Yayınevi, 1947–1955). The *devşirme* was the practice of conscripting Christian boys, usually from the Balkans, into Ottoman state service, often the military, but also the administration. Many of Ottoman grand viziers were products of the *devşirme*.
54 Baysun, *Tiryaki Hasan Paşa*, 6, and Câfer Iyânî *Cihadname* IMK: A.E.Tar.190 fol.6b. The character of Kozma only occurs in Câfer Iyânî and Baysun.
55 Çabuk, *Tiryaki Hasan Paşa*, 196.
56 c.f. Câfer Iyânî, *Cihadname* IMK: A.E.Tar.190 fol.6b and Vahit Çabuk, *Tiryaki Hasan Paşa'nın Gazaları ve Kanije Savunması* (Istanbul: Tercüman 1001 Temel Eser No.129, 1978), 35.
57 The categorisation of the Turkish-speaking Orthodox Christian Karamanlıs of central Anatolia as Greeks and their subsequent expulsion in 1923 demonstrates that Islam was an essential part of the imagining of Turkish nationalism in the 1920s. However, it later became less significant as evidenced in the tendency to blame the failure of the Ottoman Empire upon the conservative religious stance of the elite and the consequent anti-religious polemics found in popular journals in the 1930s. Religion was also blamed for the denigration of women in the empire. Ersanlı ("The Ottoman Empire," 142 and 144). See also Erik Zürcher, "The Vocabulary of Muslim Nationalism," *International Journal of the Sociology of Science* 137 (1999), for a detailed discussion on the Islamic nature of the national independence struggle which culminated in the foundation of the Turkish Republic. He argues that Ottoman Muslim solidarity formed the basis of the conception of the independence movement and the new state, whereas ethnicity and native language played only very minor roles in the thinking of the resistance leaders. However, from the late 1920s onwards, the official ideology was one of secularism and a part-ethnic, part cultural-linguistic Turkish nationalism.
58 Baysun, *Tiryaki Hasan Paşa*, 34.
59 Ibid., 10, 16, 23 and 27 and, for example, IMK: A.E.Tar.187 fols 20a, 20b and 41a.
60 Salih Omurtak, Hasan Ali Yücel, İhsan Süngü, Enver Ziya Karal, Faik Reşat Unat, Enver Sökmen and Uluğ İğdemir, "Atatürk," in *İslam Ansiklopedisi: İslam Alemi Tarih, Coğrafya, Etnografya ve Biyografya Lugatı*, vol. 1 (Istanbul: Milli Eğitim Basımevi, 1965), 780. The key word in the dictum is *mürşid* [guide], which is more commonly used to denote a spiritual guide or head of a religious order, especially a dervish order, but here is linked to knowledge and science.
61 Baysun, *Tiryaki Hasan Paşa*, devotes two pages to the capture and thirty to the defence; Ersever, *Kanije Savunması*, gives less than six pages to the capture and fifty four to the defence. In contrast the eyewitness historians, Hasan Beyzade, *Telhis-i Tacü't-tevarih*, does not mention the defence, and Topçularkatibi, *Tevarih-i âl-i Osman*, dedicates ten folios to the capture but only half a folio to the subsequent defence. Only Peçevi, *Tarih-i Peçevi*, divides his attention equally between the capture and the subsequent defence by the Ottomans.
62 *Kanije Kalesi* (35mm), it was directed by Yılmaz Atadeniz, screenplay by Turgut Özakman, produced by Dadas Film (Kadir Kesemen) and starred Cüneyt Arkın; see A. Özgüç, *Türk Filmleri Sözlüğü: 1980–1983* II (Istanbul: Sıralar Matbaası,

n.d.), 173. For examples of negative reviews, see Evren Burcak, *Milliyet*, 31 December 1982.
63 Anderson, *Imagined Communities*, 19.
64 For descriptions of the virtually continuous, low-level skirmishes and border raids on the *militärgrenze*, even during prolonged periods of official peace, see the correspondence between Ottoman and Habsburg border commanders in which requests are made for the return of prisoners, for example, the letter, dated 1649, between the chief janissary *ağa* of the fortress of Nagykanizsa to Count Adam Batthyany at Körmend Collection No. P1313 Fascicle 249 Document 226a in the Hungarian National Archives, Batthyany Family Archives, transcription in Peter Sugar, "The Ottoman 'Professional Prisoner' on the Western Borders of the Empire in the Sixteenth and Seventeenth Centuries," *Études Balkaniques* 7 (1971): 82.
65 Attacks can however, be legitimised by being framed as defensive: for example, individual attacks in the Second World War are sanctioned because the war itself was framed by the Allies as a defensive war against the Nazis, and it is largely from this perspective that it is narrated today.
66 Baysun, *Tiryaki Hasan Paşa*, 3. See also: "Because the *sancak* of Szigetvár was a region that was frequently raided by enemy raiders the bringing of Tiryaki Hasan Bey to the head [of the region] was very suitable," 3, which again reinforces that it was the Ottomans who were being attacked and thus justifies their subsequent capture of the castle; and "The war stretched on, the enemy trampled underfoot our land from four sides . . ." 10.
67 Ibid., 3.
68 IMK: A.E.Tar.187 fol.3b and Katib Çelebi, *Fezleke*, 137.
69 Baysun, *Tiryaki Hasan Paşa*, 14. Katib Çelebi, *Fezleke*, 137, also uses the phrase "the key to Mekomorya" but adds that the capture of Nagykanizsa will facilitate the conquest of the other enemy castles around Lake Balaton and the enemy lands in general. Mekomorya is referenced in Lajos Fekete, *Die Siyıkat-Schrift in der türkischen Finanzverwaltung*, vol. 1 (Budapest: Akadémiai kiadó, 1955), 419.
70 Berktay, "The 'Other' Feudalism," 101 and 126.
71 From the Turkish viewpoint once the decision to form a new Turkish nation on the territory remaining to the defunct Ottoman Empire after the Mudros armistice (1918) had been taken, the War of Independence became essentially a defensive war to remove the foreign occupiers from Turkish territory.
72 Baysun, *Tiryaki Hasan Paşa*, 3–4.
73 The most resonant echoes of the War of Independence, however, are found in the film version of events, *Kanije Kalesi*. This is the only account to include women, and although their presence reflects contemporary genre and audience expectations, it is also a direct allusion to the War of Independence. Although offered a chance to leave the castle and take refuge in Belgrade before the siege begins, they refuse and assist in the war effort by bringing in supplies in carts, tending to the injured and physically repairing the damaged walls, all of which are recurrent motifs in the many narratives of the War of Independence. P. B. Kinross, *Ataturk: A Biography of Mustafa Kemal Father of Modern Turkey* (New York: Quill, William Morrow, 1964), notes that women "drove the carts over mountain and plateaus [. . .] to the front" during the War of Independence and adds that when the carts the women were driving to the front broke down, they would hoist the loads onto their backs and carry them for miles, 312. Kinross also cites Churchill describing how Mustafa Kemal "called upon the wives and daughters of his soldiers to do the work of the camels and oxen which he lacked", 311, and also the poem by Fazil Hüsnü Dağlarca, *Mustafa Kemal'ın Kağnısı*; see http://

www.anafilya.org/go.php?go=7d492700206c6 (accessed 2/10/12) for a copy of the poem among many others on the Internet. The presence and military actions of the women in the film connote to a Turkish audience nationalism, democracy and secularism and in particular the Kemalist nationalism that helped define a modern Turkish identity. Furthermore, the women's declaration in *Kanije Kalesi* that they will not leave the castle because the blood of their fathers and sons was spilt there, and their subsequent collection of provisions from their nearby houses and farms create the impression that Nagykanizsa was the ancestral and historical home of Turkish peasants rather than a castle captured only a year before. This temporal incongruity not only legitimises and authorises the Ottoman presence in the castle, but it also reinforces the analogy between the War of Independence and the siege of Nagykanizsa: both were defensive battles to protect the fatherland.

Conclusion
Making the sieges of Nagykanizsa morally defensible

Introduction

Throughout this book I have argued that the cartographic spaces of different interpretative communities impacted upon the narration of the 1600–1601 Ottoman-Habsburg sieges of Nagykanizsa in such a way that divergent, plural pasts were constructed or remembered. Audiences reading the same text within different interpretative frameworks for quite diverse functions constructed a variety of distinct, often complimentary or overlapping, but sometimes incompatible, meanings. One of the aims of this book was to deconstruct certain assumptions surrounding particular genres of Ottoman writing, their epistemological status and how audiences have responded to them. In particular, I have tried to demonstrate that neither audiences, genre classifications, nor the factual status of texts were, or are, necessarily stable and homogeneous. Through a study of the various narratives articulated in official documents, correspondence, histories and *gazavatname* accounts, I have tried to make explicit the reading strategies, conceptual schemas and agendas of Ottoman and modern Turkish audiences, but I have also highlighted the role that viewpoint, readers' interpretative frameworks and function play in constructing pasts. Every story is narrated from somewhere; no account unproblematically corresponds, directly or indirectly, to a hypothetically existent, singular, noumenal past.[1]

Writing history within a non-representationalist epistemological framework (in the vocabulary of historical theorists, adopting a postmodern or deconstructionist approach) means that we must abandon a notion of historical narratives as somehow corresponding to what really happened in the past and instead see them as situated, literary narratives which engage with, and provide a subjective interpretation of, a variety of oral, written and material texts. Historians have responded to this conception of historical discourse as perspectival, political and ideological in a variety of ways. Some entrenched empiricist historians have reacted unfavourably to the exposure of historical narratives as politically and ideologically situated texts and have vociferously decried the postmodern challenge while still adhering to the belief that objective, non-ideological accounts of the past are possible.[2]

Others, while acknowledging some of the heuristically beneficial consequences of postmodernism, have ultimately baulked at the loss of a firm, mind-independent foundation for historical knowledge.[3]

In the context of the present work there are a number of scholars who having embraced the subjective, contested, plural nature of history as they understand it, have written narratives, which through their form and blurring of genre boundaries, foreground the ultimately arbitrary and contingent nature of traditional empiricist history as articulated by reconstructionist historians. The work of Jonathan Walker on the early modern Venetian general of spies, Gerolamo Vano, is one such example, but the work of Paul Antick on Bhopal and Palestine is worth noting in this context as well.[4] Other 'postmodern' historians have responded by employing unconventional sources and methods to empower, or give voice to, those marginalised or excluded from mainstream historical discourse and as such have experimented with more unconventional content.[5] In his ethnographic accounts of Saramaka history, Richard Price, experimenting with forms of historical representation, gives voice to people previously silenced by traditional historical and anthropological methodological preferences.[6] In *First-Time* he communicates the Saramaka past through Saramaka forms of knowledge and traditions of scholarship. The pages of the book are divided horizontally with the upper section carrying the Saramaka 'texts' presenting "discrete fragments of Saramaka knowledge" and the lower section Price's 'commentary'. In *Alabi's World* he develops this multivocality a step further and uses four different type faces to represent the voices of the eighteenth-century Saramakas, the German Moravian missionaries and Dutch colonial officials as well as the voices of twentieth-century scholars, including himself. In a similar manner, the articles in Pandey, *Unarchived Histories*, not only foreground and problematise the manner in which unarchived histories have been disenfranchised (or unarchived) by the process and politics of archiving, but in doing so they produce narratives of those who are often silenced or represented in ways which serve dominant interests and forms of knowledge. In particular, they demonstrate that it is only through the concomitant challenge posed to the "inherited grids of legibility and illegibility, knowledge and non-knowledge" that arises from the insurgent political movements of the subaltern and marginalised that the unarchived is translated into an archive and non-histories into history.[7]

In addition to reconceptualising the traditional form and focus of histories, some historians, acknowledging that all histories are politically situated and ideological, have viewed this as providing an opportunity to rethink the possible functions that histories might have. Gumbrecht, rejecting unilinear and totalising history but recognising the desire of people to experience past worlds, explores experientiality as a possible function of historical discourse. Claiming that history no longer has any obvious pragmatic or didactic function and that he never intended his book to contain anything morally or politically edifying nor to be original, witty or stylistically beautiful, he argues that its function is simply to suggest a web of realities that shaped the behaviour and interactions of 1926 and thereby create an immediate and sensual illusion that the reader is "in 1926".[8] His book explores how far a text can provide the illusion of the impossible – a direct experience of the past.[9] Pihlainen, in arguing for post-problematic histories, has envisaged a similar role for history.[10] As briefly mentioned in the introduction to this book, a post-problematic history would not ask questions of, nor seek meaning in, the past; it would not attempt to establish constructionist metanarratives, explanatory processes, patterns or teleologies. It could, instead, serve an antiquarian function, the collection of information on a particular topic but with the acknowledgement that any narrative constructed around such an activity would not in any way correspond to the past but would reflect present issues and concerns. I think Gumbrecht's *In 1926* can be considered to exemplify such a history in that there is no thesis or framing research question: it is, in many ways, an antiquarian collection of information or montage that is "strictly descriptive".[11] Such an approach is reminiscent of that of Walter Benjamin and his claim, "I have nothing to say, only to show."[12] Synthia Sydnor's history of synchronised swimming, influenced by a Benjaminian approach, also adopts a similar form, eschewing explanatory narrative and linear argument in favour of an aphoristic montage and collection of key words, poetry and quotations – all rigorously footnoted – that perform a history of synchronised swimming in the manner of "seizing hold of memory" rather than representing the sport as it 'really was' and is.[13] Both 'histories' refuse to structure their materials or information as an answer to a historical problem; they instead require that the reader participates more consciously in the interpretative process and is explicitly responsible for establishing their own meanings.

Yet, not all historians are happy for history to become a performative, polyvocal montage in which multiple, contested meanings rupture any notion of a single, linear narrative and whose primary function is as an aesthetic experience. Piterberg is concerned that "the postmodernist threat to deny [history] any access to a real, experienced past existence" will result in history becoming "a vocation that forsakes moral and political responsibility".[14] *Pace* Piterberg, I believe recognising the situated and therefore ideological nature of historical discourse means foregrounding, not forsaking its political and ethical aspects.[15] As Pihlainen makes clear, the breakdown of epistemological history in fact opens the door to ethical considerations; it provides a space in which we can make historical discourses more socially and politically relevant, re-engage ethically with historical narratives and openly discuss the ideological and legitimising dimensions and functions of history.[16] Historians *could* stop structuring their materials, arguments and narratives as linear and authoritative solutions to historical problems and instead allow a cacophony of voices and contested interpretations to coexist in their work. They *could* produce consciously reflexive, interrogative, "morally coherent and politically effective" postmodern, present-centred narratives that would once again constitute "one of our primary forms of moral reflection".[17] Indeed for some scholars the separation of ethical reflection from forms of past talk is a complete impossibility. For example, for Harlan while there is little use in looking to the past for lessons or absolute truths, history can be "an essential and indispensable form of moral deliberation". However, its worth as a form of moral reflection comes not from "our ability to know the past but our ability to find the predecessors we need".[18] We use these predecessors as "moral exemplars from the past in order to govern our behavior in the present and guide our movement into the future", or as Arendt argued "our decision about right and wrong will depend on our choice of company [. . .] and this company is chosen through thinking in examples, examples of persons dead or alive, and in examples of incidences, past or present."[19] For others, though, the value of postmodern history lies in its capacity to surprise and startle, to empower or disempower, and the manner in which it produces an "ethically inspired cultural catharsis". Alternatively, for some the critical distance it provides for a re-evaluation of our values, the power it has to free the present from myth and its use as a political tool to challenge, undermine or rupture received ideologies, institutions and practices are of critical importance.[20]

For some theorists, though, history, even in a reflexive, socially inclusive, postmodern form, is so radioactive with toxic connotations that it is incapable of contributing to meaningful ethico-political discussions. Jenkins argues it is more interesting and less problematic to think about our present and future in ethical and emancipatory ways without having recourse to historical narratives.[21] He argues that "we really don't need the past any more" because we have other postmodern imaginaries to help us think in "future-orientated, emancipatory and democratising ways" and can therefore now 'forget history'.[22] Davies and Cohen agree with Jenkins that we should now 'forget history'. They argue that historical practices are generally the compliant instruments of socially dominant interests, governmental and cultural policies and neo-liberal ideologies in that they are used to give particular sociopolitical formations present credibility by providing them with the "illusion of noncontestable knowledge" and a sense of inevitability through an implied "trans-generational covenant with the present".[23] Davies contends that history, because of its tendency to interpret "the latest thing" as yet another instantiation of "the same old thing", is socially and politically conservative.[24] It works as a social anaesthetic, encouraging resignation towards the way things are and as such is an ideal instrument of dominant socio-economic and material interests.[25] It therefore renders insensible a critical ethical consciousness. Making a slightly related point, Simon also notes that remembering through histories or other forms of past talk can at times be problematic in that it can function as an "impetus to the reproduction of hatred and violence".[26]

As Mouffe has argued, though, there is nothing inherent in any articulatory practice that determines how it might be used politically, so is it necessary or desirable to abandon all forms of past-focused literary genres including history?[27] As the contributions to *Unarchived Histories* have shown, "insurgent practices of historical memory" can "contest the silences and legitimations structured into official sanctioned history"; they can recover lost or suppressed voices and can be deployed within counter-hegemonic discourses with the intention of affecting sociopolitical change, challenging unjust social relations and articulating alternative ethical visions.[28] Ilan Pappé, citing Said's call to Palestinians to extend their struggle into the realm of representation and historical narratives following the Israeli invasion of Lebanon in 1982, notes that academic Palestinian histories have, through the construction of an alternative narrative, successfully challenged the hegemonic Israeli discourse on events in 1948. He continues that the *absence* of a historical narrative and conversation on Palestine in general and the so-called peace process in particular, has in fact served the interests of the political elite and dominant powers.[29] In addition, Palestinian *liberation historiography* also serves an ontological or identitary function: reinforcing the idea of a Palestinian nation in the face of fragmentation and oppression.[30] For many historians and other writers, artists, activists and archivists, historical narratives can help us to articulate, discuss and contest the values we think are important; they can help us to imagine a better world and instigate social transformation; they dispossess us of our certainties and encourage us to "live as though the lives of others mattered".[31] Practices of remembrance that "sustain the prospect of democracy" can require us to *remember otherwise* and reject the hegemony of ontological narratives "tied to the consolidation of [. . .] corporate entities whether in the guise of state nationalism, ethnocultural hubris, or religious triumphalism".[32] *Remembering otherwise* entails the adjudication of responsibility and provision of just reparation; it requires us to critically examine or deconstruct the consoling identitary effects that historical narratives engender; it requires us to construct practices of remembering that alter the way the past is made present.[33] Such practices of remembrance encourage democratic forms of community and "the alterity of the historical experience of others – an alterity that disrupts the presumptions of the 'self-same' ".[34]

While writing this book, I found myself reflecting upon its relevance. Beyond a select group of academics interested in manuscript culture and Ottoman history, what interest or meaning could it have for twenty-first-century audiences? Is Davies correct? Is my history, despite its acknowledgement of the philosophical and disciplinary consequences arising from the postmodern challenge, in reality operating as another subtle means of justifying conservative interests and replicating the dominant political and social system? More worryingly, can my work on the Ottoman-Habsburg sieges of Nagykanizsa be read as simply another unthinking affirmation of the normality and thus, unavoidability, of violence and conflict, particularly in the context of Muslim-Christian interactions?[35] Janet Malcolm's *The Journalist and the Murderer* is a study of the thin line between fiction and non-fiction, the moral ambiguity inherent in narrating 'true' events, the ethical obligations of writers and the uneasy relationship between journalists and their subjects. She begins her work with the sentence: "Every journalist who is not too stupid or too full of himself to notice what is going on knows that what he does is morally indefensible."[36] Nearly fifty years after Hayden White claimed "that the task of the historian was less to remind men of their obligation to the past than to force upon them an awareness of how the past could be used to effect an ethically responsible transition from present to future", I too am concerned to make my work morally defensible – to *remember otherwise*.[37]

Making the sieges of Nagykanizsa morally defensible

The close textual readings of the various Nagykanizsa narratives undertaken in earlier chapters raise a number of points that could potentially make an interesting and relevant contribution to wider ethical and political conversations. Firstly, and in very general terms, the chapters through their discussion of the various accounts of the sieges demonstrate the positioned nature of *all* narratives. In particular, in Chapter 1 I argued that eyewitness accounts and state documents are not any more objective by virtue of their genre, nor as a result of the status, predisposition or location of the author, than other sources. All accounts are perspectival, and to argue that some are more neutral or do not embody a political or ideological agenda is futile and disingenuous – something that is worth remembering when reading or viewing not only histories but also other 'fact-based' genres including journalism, documentaries and news reports. Equipping a new generation of students with the tools of critical analysis is a fundamental priority if we want them to be informed, politically engaged, inquiring citizens. Not being explicit about how we, as interpretative communities, judge the reliability of texts does not help achieve this aim.

In Chapter 5 I explored how Katib Çelebi incorporated virtually verbatim an inscription of the Nagykanizsa *gazavatname* into his history of the Ottoman Empire. Although his account included no extra facts, and unlike the *gazavatname* narratives that have often been understood as rather unreliable examples of imaginative historical literature, his version has been read as fact. The ease with which fiction becomes fact, not through the addition of extra or more accurate facts but through the inclusion of a few culturally specific stylistic markers, is thus illustrated. An awareness of how we, as readers, actually make decisions as to the factual status and reliability of texts should encourage reflection upon and the interrogation of the cultural and epistemological authority that society unquestioningly bestows on certain types of historical praxis: practices that are accorded the status of truth arbiters because of their position in discursive and institutional matrices of power and not a correspondence with 'reality'. Academically authorised historical narratives, because of their privileged factual status, have the power to reify versions of the past, and they are therefore not only used to legitimise and authenticate particular socio-economic and identitary claims and practices but also to control and direct the expectations of subjects or citizens. Recognising this normalising potential of historical discourse facilitates a critical deconstruction of the foundational premises upon which our politico-cultural practices and institutions rest, ultimately demonstrating their contingency and historicised nature and thereby opening up the possibility of not only different pasts but alternative futures.[38]

My analysis also foregrounds how easily perspective shifts – how different implied audiences, genre conventions and sociopolitical cartographies all impact on a narrative and affect the nexus of meanings available to interpretative communities. In such a manner the notion of a singular truth owned by one community or audience is potentially problematised. If truth is not to be found in empiricist correspondence to reality as it is in-itself, but in the pragmatically informed conditions of warranted assertibility and adherence to communally determined norms and interpretative procedures, then such an analysis highlights the possibility and importance of understanding the plurality of opinions and truths in the past and today. Such an acknowledgement opens the way for more alethiologically nuanced histories, histories not used simply to reinforce dominant interests and exacerbate conflict but ones which challenge or undermine these interests and potentially open up discursive spaces in which better relations between peoples can be imagined, thereby moving communities beyond conflict and providing reparation for ongoing injustices.[39]

Histories of conflict perhaps more forcefully than other stories clearly demonstrate how narratives of the 'before now' contribute to the imagination of identities through a reification of dichotomies of us and them, self and other. The autonomy and coherence of the imagined self, whether it be of an individual or a community, is strengthened through negation. Agonistic others perpetuate the identity of those who locate them as oppositional, and this coalescing against outsiders is an effective way of establishing unity among communities of otherwise disparate people.[40] Encounters with an oppositional other and representations, or memories of such conflict, thus have an ontological role; they help construct, shape and perpetuate self-other definitions; they create space within which communities are imagined.[41] The various narratives of the sieges of Nagykanizsa illustrate how identities are differently constructed depending on the time, genre, function of the text or implied audience, thereby emphasising their inherently contingent and fluid character. Being aware of the provisional nature of identities means we can formulate the critical tools to deconstruct and challenge ontologies imposed upon us, ontologies that serve agendas with which we do not necessarily agree. It also frees us to construct identities which, to paraphrase Harlan, show who we want to be rather than who we are told to be.

One of the consequences of the teleological nature of history is the tendency of historians to retroactively imagine past communities in accordance

154 Conclusion

with contemporary, dominant geopolitical cartographies. For contemporary scholars, the hegemonic paradigm is that of the nation-state which is consequently reified, along with its concomitant emphasis on the concept of ethnolinguistic or religious homogeneity as a naturally occurring evolution rather than an imagined construct. Such a framing obscures different sites for the construction of allegiances and the imagination of identities. Therefore modern academics tend to accept the concept of ethnolinguistic homogeneity, ultimately given importance by the nation-state paradigm, as the only possible frame for articulating self and other identities. The late Ottoman and modern Turkish narratives of the Nagykanizsa sieges, read and inscribed against nation-state cartographies, indicate how easily the heterogeneity and plurality of the Ottoman borderlands are erased and forgotten and how quickly a new mono ethnocultural national identity can be inscribed and reified. Moreover, it exemplifies the ease with which current conflicts and antipathies can be projected backwards and therefore legitimised or normalised as something that has always been the case – "the *same old thing*".[42]

For me, ethically, the most important aspect of this research is its contribution to arguments that challenge *the clash of civilisations* metanarrative. The framing of Muslim-Christian interactions over the past fifteen hundred years as a clash of qualitatively distinct, antagonistic civilisations is prevalent not only in the popular media but also in academic discourse.[43] The substantiality and assumed veracity of this interpretative framework is enhanced by the teleological projection of anachronistic nationalist cartographies predicated on ethno-religious difference in some twentieth-century historians' imagining of the early modern Habsburg-Ottoman *militärgrenze* and through an over-reliance on official Ottoman and Habsburg sources which articulate the rhetoric of imperial ideologies with their concomitant emphasis on religious difference. Although acknowledgement is given in general to the theory that borders are areas of mediation, linkage and transfer, places where material and cultural exchanges occur, some scholars simultaneously argue that the Habsburg-Ottoman border was inimical in that very little, if any, interaction occurred between the communities living there.[44] The Habsburg-Ottoman marches are imagined as spaces in which the dichotomies of Muslim-Christian antipathy are preeminent.[45] However, as can be seen from the analysis of the *fethnames* in Chapter 2, one should be cautious of over-interpreting superficial rhetoric that emphasises the importance of jihad against the infidel. It is preferable and more coherent to read the *fethnames* as tools of diplomacy. The language used and events described in the *fethnames* suggest that the Ottomans used the opportunity presented by the capture of Nagykanizsa castle to reaffirm an informal Anglo-Ottoman political and military alliance, thus problematising interpretations of Ottoman foreign policy predicated on the *clash of civilisations* metanarrative.

Likewise, the study of *gazavatnames* in Chapter 4 highlights that for many audiences, the idea of a heterogenous, polylingual, multifaith inclusive border was an acknowledged reality as the narratives include Hungarians, non-Turkish speakers, Christians and Muslims in a construction of self. Indeed for the narrative to work and be coherent, the audience has to accept that Hungarians, both converts to Islam and those retaining their Christian faith, are fighting alongside their Muslim, Turkish-speaking comrades in the castle. The view that although local linguistic and religious identities endured in the liminal Habsburg-Ottoman borderlands relationships, connections and allegiances did not exclusively orient around loyalty to a particular religion, language or state but were instead based on geographical location, occupation, shared practices and customs, kinship or loyalty to a local lord or economic interest coheres with evidence in other texts. The border was, in the words of Stein, "a socially and economically dynamic zone of transition, where different people and states met and interacted" and formed "a joint community of sorts", a place of cultural synthesis where recent converts to Islam and local Christians were part of many of the Ottoman military garrisons.[46] The *gazavatnames* demonstrate that the Habsburg-Ottoman Long War is not reducible to a narrative predicated on Muslim-Christian hostility, and they also call into question the intellectually lazy and socially damaging reliance on the *clash of civilisations* interpretative frame when discussing Muslim-Christian interactions. Indeed Chapters 2, 3 and 4 foreground points of rupture in a genealogical history of the construction of self and other arising from the *clash of civilisation* metanarrative, demonstrating the contingency of such constructions and ontologies.[47]

I am not claiming that this study of how different people may have read and inscribed narratives about the 1600–1601 sieges of Nagykanizsa makes any great contribution to significant contemporary ethical or political discussions. Neither am I convinced that it really meets Munslow's criteria for a postmodern, multi-sceptical history that exhibits "a highly self-conscious ethical interventionism" by the historian.[48] However, in this conclusion I have made a preliminary attempt to show how a history of early modern Ottoman textualities and identities can contribute to contemporary, present-based ethical and political discussions.[49] In the final analysis, this book is simply a collection of stories that have evolved from a close study of a group of Ottoman and modern Turkish texts: stories with a political and moral agenda. I have read and interpreted the various sources and written my narrative in accordance with the main genre conventions of twenty-first-century academic history. However, I have also read the sources in such a way that they contribute to an argument that problematises *the clash of civilisations* metanarrative. I have done this because I do not think we need any more stories that stress difference based on religion, ethnicity or cultural background. Such stories, in my opinion, do not help transform our world into a more equitable place where everyone is valued. Instead, I would argue, we need stories that emphasise cooperation, toleration and coexistence as these are the stories which may actually help us address "the problems of the present", and in telling these stories we, as historians, may

156 *Conclusion*

be able to offer a practical contribution to contemporary political and ethical discussions and prevent academic history from its otherwise inexorable slide into cultural irrelevance and moral indefensibility.[50]

Notes

1 The main theoretical arguments in this chapter have evolved from numerous discussions with my colleague Mark Donnelly, undertaken in the context of co-teaching two historiographically focused undergraduate modules and co-writing a number of articles and books including *Doing History* and *Liberating Histories: Truths, Power, Ethics* (London: Routledge, forthcoming). The ideas I outline here owe a considerable debt to these discussions.
2 For example, the contributors to Elizabeth Fox-Genovese and Elizabeth Lasch-Quinn, eds., *Reconstructing History: The Emergence of a New Historical Society* (London: Routledge, 1999).
3 For example, Joyce Appleby, Lynn Hunt and Margaret Jacob, *Telling the Truth about History* (New York: W. W. Norton and Co., 1994); Richard Evans, *In Defence of History* (London: Granta, 1997).
4 Jonathan Walker, *Pistols! Treason! Murder! The Rise and Fall of a Master Spy* (Baltimore, MD: Johns Hopkins University Press, 2007); Paul Antick, "Bhopal to Bridgehampton: Schema for a Disaster Tourism Event," *Journal of Visual Culture* 26/1 (2013), and Antick, "Smith in Palestine (To Be Read Aloud, in Its Entirety)," *Journal of Visual Communication* 11/4 (2012). See also the various graphic histories by Joe Sacco including *Palestine* (London: Jonathan Cape, 2003); *Footnotes in Gaza* (London: Jonathan Cape, 2009); *Safe Area Goražde* (London: Jonathan Cape, 2007); Tony Klug, *How Peace Broke Out in the Middle East: A Short History of the Future* (Fabian Society, 2007) https://www.fabians.org.uk/wp-content/uploads/2012/04/HowPeaceBrokeOutInTheMiddleEast.pdf (accessed 8/5/15); and the various articles in Alun Munslow and Robert A. Rosenstone, eds, *Experiments in Rethinking History* (London: Routledge, 2004), which all experiment with form in different ways. For an extended discussion of the work of Sacco, Antick and Klug in the context of political, reflexive histories, see Claire Norton and Mark Donnelly, "Thinking the Past Politically: Palestine, Pedagogy, Power," *Rethinking History* 20/2 (2016).
5 For example, Bryant Simon, "Narrating a Southern Tragedy: Historical Facts and Historical Fictions," in *Experiments in Rethinking History*, ed. Alun Munslow and Robert A. Rosenstone (London: Routledge, 2004); Greg Dening, *Beach Crossings: Voyaging Across Times, Cultures and Self* (Philadelphia: University of Pennsylvania Press, 2004); Horacio N. Roque Ramirez, "A Living Archive of Desire: Teresita la Capesina and the Embodiment of Queer Latino Community History," in *Archive Stories: Facts, Fictions and the Writing of History*, ed. Antoinette Burton (Durham: Duke University Press, 2005).
6 Richard Price, *First-Time: The Historical Vision of an African American People*, 2nd ed. (Chicago: University of Chicago Press, 2002), and Price, *Alibi's World* (Baltimore, MD: Johns Hopkins University Press, 1990).
7 Gyanendra Pandey, ed., *Unarchived Histories: The 'Mad' and the 'Trifling' in the Colonial and Postcolonial World* (London: Routledge, 2014), 16.
8 Hans Ulrich Gumrecht, *In 1926: Living at the Edge of Time* (Cambridge, MA: Harvard University Press, 1997), ix, xii, xiv and 411.
9 Ibid., 425. Gumbrecht is, however, quite clear on the point that a representation of a past world is an impossibility and that while he is responding to a desire for immediacy with regard to past realities, this immediacy is only illusory, 436.
10 Kalle Pihlainen, "Towards a Postproblematic History," paper given at the Philosophy of History seminar at the Institute of Historical Research, University of London,

November 22nd 2012. I thank the author for generously providing me with a copy of his paper.
11 Gumrecht, *In 1926*, ix. Gumbrecht argues that if there is a question that his book addresses, it is to see "how far a text can go in providing the illusion of direct experience of the past", 425.
12 From Benjamin's filing system, *Konvolut V*, 574 [Nla, 8], as archived by Susan Buck-Morss, *The Dialectics of Seeing: Walter Benjamin and the Arcades Project* (Cambridge, MA: Harvard University Press, 1991), 222. Also cited in Synthia Sydnor, "A History of Synchronized Swimming," *Journal of Sport History* 25/2 (1998): 252 and n.6, available online: http://www.aafla.org/SportsLibrary/JSH/JSH1998/JSH2502/JSH2502e.pdf (accessed 6/12/12).
13 Sydnor, "Synchronized Swimming," 259. The quotation refers back to a quote by Walter Benjamin, *Illuminations*, trans. H. Zohn and ed. Hannah Arendt (New York: Schocken Books, 1968), 255.
14 Gabriel Piterberg, *An Ottoman Tragedy: History and Historiography at Play* (Berkeley: University of California Press, 2003), 4 and 6.
15 For a more detailed discussion of the cultural politics of historicisation and the role that historical narratives could have in broader emancipatory and political projects, see Norton and Donnelly, "Thinking the Past Politically," and Norton and Donnelly, *Liberating Histories*.
16 Kalle Pihlainen, "Escaping the Confines of History: Keith Jenkins," *Rethinking History* 17/2 (2013): 243.
17 Pihlainen, "Postproblematic history"; David Harlan, "Ken Burns and the Coming Crisis of Academic History," *Rethinking History* 7 (2003): 187; and Harlan, *The Degradation of American History* (Chicago: University of Chicago Press, 1997), 213.
18 Harlan, *Degradation*, 155 and 157.
19 Ibid., 92, and Hannah Arendt quoted in Ronald Beiner, "Hannah Arendt on Judging," in *Lectures on Kant's Political Philosophy*, ed. Hannah Arendt (Chicago: University of Chicago Press, 1992), 113, also cited in Roger I. Simon, *The Touch of the Past: Remembrance, Learning, and Ethics* (Basingstoke: Palgrave Macmillan, 2005), 2.
20 Robert A. Rosenstone, "Space for the Bird to Fly," in *Manifestos for History*, ed. Keith Jenkins, Sue Morgan and Alun Munslow (London: Routledge, 2007), 13; Alun Munslow, *The Future of History* (Basingstoke: Palgrave Macmillan, 2010), 203; Ann Rigney, "Being an Improper Historian," in *Manifestos*, ed. Keith Jenkins, Sue Morgan and Alun Munslow (London: Routledge, 2007), 153; Beverley Southgate, *What Is History For?* (London: Routledge, 2005), 159 and 176; Joan W. Scott, "History-Writing as Critique," in *Manifestos*, ed. Keith Jenkins, Sue Morgan and Alun Munslow (London: Routledge, 2007), 26–27; Ramirez, "A Living Archive," 119. For the power of a particular kind of history to "free the present from myth", see Benjamin's "Copernican revolution" as described by Buck-Morss, *The Dialectics of Seeing*, x.
21 Keith Jenkins, *Why History? Ethics and Postmodernity* (London: Routledge, 1999), 2, 9, 193 and 199–200.
22 Keith Jenkins, *At the Limits of History* (London: Routledge, 2009), 235. Jenkins qualifies the first quote by adding that he didn't think we ever really did need history. Jenkins, *Why History?*, 9 and 2.
23 Martin L. Davies, *Imprisoned by History* (London: Routledge, 2010), 57 and 61, and Davies, *Historics: Why History Dominates Contemporary Society* (London: Routledge, 2006), 133; Sande Cohen, *History Out of Joint: Essays on the Use and Abuse of History* (Baltimore: The John Hopkins University Press, 2006), 118; Simon, *The Touch of the Past*, 3.
24 Davies, *Historics*, 4.
25 Ibid., 5 and 8.

158 Conclusion

26 Simon, *The Touch of the Past*, 15; see also David Rieff, *In Praise of Forgetting* (New Haven: Yale University Press, 2016).
27 Chantal Mouffe, *Agonistics: Thinking the World Politically* (London: Verso, 2013), 2.
28 Simon, *The Touch of the Past*, 15.
29 Ilan Pappé, "The Old and New Conversations," in *On Palestine*, ed. Noam Chomsky and Ilan Pappé (London: Penguin, 2015), 14, citing Edward Said, "Permission to Narrate," *Journal of Palestine Studies* 13/3 (1984).
30 The phrase *liberation historiography* is from Herman Paul, *Hayden White: The Historical Imagination* (Cambridge: Polity, 2011). See Norton and Donnelly, "Thinking the Past Politically," for a discussion of other uses of histories of Palestine.
31 Simon, *The Touch of the Past*, 9. Harlan, "Ken Burns," 184 and 187; Southgate, *What Is History For?* 124–125 and 137–139. See also Donnelly and Norton, *Doing History*, 186–188.
32 Simon, *The Touch of the Past*, 9 – the phrase *remembering otherwise* is Simon's.
33 Ibid., 9–10.
34 Simon, *The Touch of the Past*, 4.
35 Davies, *Historics*, 7, argues that history results from symbolic and physical coercion and conflict and that it affirms violence as historically normal.
36 Janet Malcolm, *The Journalist and the Murderer* (London: Granta, 2012, first published in the US in 1990 by Alfred A. Knopf Inc. and published originally in a different form in the *New Yorker*), 3.
37 Hayden White, "The Burden of History," *History and Theory* 5 (1966): 132.
38 Scott, "History-Writing as Critique," 26–27; Beverley Southgate "'Humani Nil Alienum': The Quest for 'Human Nature'," in *Manifestos*, ed. Keith Jenkins, Sue Morgan and Alun Munslow (London: Routledge, 2007), 67–76, 71 and 73; and Southgate, *What Is History For?*, 159 and 176, argue that histories should be used as levers to challenge our institutions, practices and customs, to highlight their contingency and thus show us that things could be different in the future.
39 See Madeleine Fullard and Nicky Rousseau, "Truth-Telling, Identities and Power in South Africa and Guatemala," http://ictj.org/sites/default/files/ICTJ-Identities-TruthCommissions-ResearchBrief-2009-English.pdf (accessed 16/11/12); Simon, *The Touch of the Past*, especially Chapter 5, "The Touch of the Past: The Pedagogical Significance of a Transactional Sphere of Public Memory", and some of the examples given in Norton and Donnelly, "Thinking the Past Politically."
40 Shapiro, *Violent Cartographies*, 44.
41 Ibid., 42 and 138; see also B. Taithe and T. Thornton, "Identifying War: Conflict and Self-Definition in Western Europe," in *War: Identities in Conflict 1300–2000*, ed. B. Taithe and T. Thornton (Stroud: Sutton Publishing, 1998), 1 and 9.
42 Davies, *Historics*, 4.
43 The term *clash of civilizations* comes from an article by Samuel P. Huntington, "The Clash of Civilizations?" *Foreign Affairs* (Summer 1993); see here http://edvardas.home.mruni.eu/wp-content/uploads/2008/10/huntington.pdf (accessed 5/8/15) and later expanded into a book, *The Clash of Civilizations and the Remaking of World Order* (New York: Simon and Schuster, 1996). Huntington's *clash of civilization* thesis has been criticised by many scholars: see Bruce M. Russett, John R. Oneal and Michaelene Cox, "Clash of Civilizations, or Realism and Liberalism Déjà Vu? Some Evidence," *Journal of Peace Research* 37/5 (2000); Edward Said, "The Clash of Ignorance," *The Nation* (October 2001) available at http://thenation.com/article/clash-ignorance (accessed 5/8/15); and Amartya Sen, "Democracy as a Universal Value," *Journal of Democracy* 10/3 (1999). Chiara Bottici and Benoît Challand, *The Myth of the Clash of Civilizations* (London: Routledge, 2010), argue that Huntington simply provided a name for

Conclusion 159

a political myth and cognitive scheme that was already in the process of being made. For a number of examples, see Claire Norton, "Terror and Toleration, East and West, Despotic and Free: Dichotomous Narratives and Representations of Islam," *Holy Land Studies* 7/2 (2008), and also Norton, "East-West Dichotomy? Historiography as a 'Clash of Civilisations'," *Holy Land Studies* 10/1 (2011).

44 For example Géza Dávid and Pál Fodor, "Introduction," in *Ottomans, Hungarians, and Habsburgs in Central Europe: The Military Confines in the Era of Ottoman Conquest*, ed. Géza Dávid and Pál Fodor (Leiden, Boston, Köln: Brill, 2000), xii, xviii and xix–xx; Peter Sugar, *South Eastern Europe under Ottoman Rule, 1354–1804: A History of East Central Europe* (Seattle and London: University of Washington Press, 1977), 63; Lajos Fekete, *Buapest a törökkorban* (Budapest: 1944), 308, translation from Géza Dávid and Pál Fodor, "Hungarian Studies in Ottoman History," in *The Ottomans and the Balkans: A Discussion of Historiography*, ed. Fikret Adanir and Suraiya Faroqhi (Leiden, Boston and Köln: Brill, 2002), 318–9; Klara Hegyi, *Egy világbirodalom végvidékén* (Budapest: 1975), quoted in Dávid and Fodor "Hungarian Studies in Ottoman History," 319.

45 Norton, "Narrating the 'Yoke of Oppression'."

46 Mark L. Stein, *Guarding the Frontier: Ottoman Border Forts and Garrisons in Europe* (London: Tauris Academic Studies, 2007), 156; Mark Stein, "Seventeenth-Century Ottoman Forts and Garrisons on the Habsburg Frontier (Hungary)," (PhD diss., The University of Chicago, 2001), 145–149; Claire Norton, "'The Lutheran Is the Turks' Luck': Imagining Religious Identity, Alliance and Conflict on the Habsburg-Ottoman Marches in an Account of the Sieges of Nagykanizsa 1600 and 1601," in *Das Osmanische Reich und die Habsburgermonarchie in der Neuzeit. Akten des internationalen Kongresses zum 150-jährigen Bestehen des Instituts für Österreichische Geschichtsforschung, Wien, 22.-25. September 2004*, ed. Marlene Kurz, Martin Scheutz, Karl Vocelka, and Thomas Winkelbauer (Wien: Mitteilungen des Instituts für Österreichische Geschichtsforschung, 2005); Norton, "Nationalism."

47 Something similar is undertaken by Simon in Chapter 1 of *The Touch of the Past* in the context of counter-commemorative pedagogies arising from the five hundredth anniversary of the arrival of Columbus on the coast of what is now known as North America.

48 Munslow, *The Future of History*, 4.

49 Arguably, before the nineteenth century when the norms and practices of historical discourse were not only professionalised, but also reimagined in specifically empiricist epistemic terms and required to fulfill specific academic and state interests, history played a far more fundamental role in the ethico-political discussions in various cultures. For example, in Ottoman *nasihatname* literature Ottoman bureaucrat-historians frequently illustrated their moral points with historical examples. For examples see Howard, "Ottoman Advice". See also C. E. Bosworth, "Naṣīḥat al-Mulūk," in *Encyclopaedia of Islam*, ed. P. Bearman, Th. Bianquis, C. E. Bosworth, E. van Donzel and W. P. Heinrichs, 2nd ed., http://dx.doi.org/10.1163/1573-3912_islam_COM_0850; first published online: 2012, first print edition 1960–2007 (accessed 10/8/16). As discussed in Chapter 5, for the Ottoman historian Naima at least, the function of history was not solely about accurately representing the past or telling the truth about what really happened. An important function was to offer moral truths and didactic lessons.

50 White, "Burden," 125.

Bibliography

Note: Ottoman Turkish names are alphabetised in their conventional order and not divided into 'first' and 'last' names, for example, Ahmed Refik and not Refik, Ahmed. For works with a publication date given according to the *hicri* calendar, this has been given first followed by that according to the *common era* calendar.

Archival sources

Manuscripts in the *Gazavat-i Tiryaki Hasan Pasha* corpus (contemporaneous or later titles included where appropriate).

A.Oct.34, *Hatha Kitab-i Hikayet-i Hasan Paşa [ve] Kale-i Kanije*, fols.1b–64a (undated).
A.E.Tar.188, *Tiru Hasan Paşa Tarihi*, fols.1b–56a (1225/1810).
A.E.Tar.189, *Tarih-i Tiryaki Hasan Paşa*, fols.1b–19a (1127/1715).
Berlin: Preußische Nationalbibliothek, O.R.3442, *Hatha Kitab-i Tevarih-i Kanije*, fols .b–37b (1025/1616).
Bologna: Biblioteca Universitaria, Bub.3459, *Gazavat-i Kanije*, fols.79b–108b (1079/ 1668–1669).
Bratislava: Universitätsbibliothek, T.F.46, *untitled*, fols.1a–53b (1101/1689).
Budapest: Magyar Tudományos Akademia Konyvtara, O.216, *Hatha Risale-i Divan Efendisi ya Tiru Gazi Hasan Paşa*, fols.2b–71b (1128/1716).
Cairo: Dar al-Kutub, No.235, *Kanije Kalesi Muhasarasın[d]a Gazi Hasan Paşa Merhumun Vaki olan Gazve ve Cihadı Zikrindedir*, fols.1b–37a (undated).
Cambridge: University Library, O.R.700, *Tarihi-i Tiryaki Hasan Paşa*, fols 76b–107b (1187/1773–1774).
H.O.71a, *untitled*, fols.1a–25a (undated).
H.O.71b, *Hatha Kitab-i Gazavat-i Tiryaki Gazi Hasan Paşa*, fols.1b–149b (undated).
H.O.71c, *untitled*, fols.1b–43a (1082/1671).
H.O.71d, *Menakib-i Tiryaki Hasan Paşa (rahmetullahi aleyhi)*, fols.22a–67b (1168/1754).
Istanbul: Arkeoloji Müzesi, No.374, *Hatha Kitab-i Kanije [ve] Hikayet-i Devletlu Hasan Paşa Hazretleri*, fols.1a–57b (1218/1803).
Istanbul: Millet Kütüphanesi, A.E.Tar.187, *Tarih-i Tiriyaki Hasan Paşa*, fols 1b–61a (undated).
London: British Library, O.R.33, *Hatha Hikayet-i Feth-i Kanije ve Gaza-i Tiryaki Gazi Hasan Paşa*, fols 1b–59a (undated).

Manisa: İl Halk Kütüphanesi, No.5070, *Hatha Menakib-i Tiryaki Hasan Paşa*, fols 22a–68b (1170/1757).
Munich: Bayerische Staatsbibliothek, O.R.393, *Tarih-i Tiryaki Hasan Paşa*, fols 1a–64b (undated).
O.R.6442, *History of the Defence of Kanizsa*, fols.54b–95a (1230/1815).
O.R.12961, *Hikaye-i Tiryaki Gazi Hasan Paşa*, fols.1b-95a (1203/1789).
Paris: Bibliothèque Nationale, Nr.525, *Hikaye-i Tire Hasan Paşa*, fols.1b–61b (undated).
Sup.Turc.170, *Muharebe-i Tiryaki Hasan Paşa*, fols.1a–62a (1174/1760).
Sup.Turc.873, *untitled*, fols.1b–54a (1143/1731).
Vienna: National-Bibliothek, A.F.234, *untitled*, fols.2a–36b (1133/1720).
Vienna: Staatsarchiv, Nr.508, *Gazavat-i Tiryaki Gazi Ahmed Paşa*, fols.1a–8b (undated).

Other archival sources

Abdülkadir Topçularkatibi. *Tevarih-i âl-i Osman*. Vienna: National-Bibliothek, Mxt.130; Istanbul: Süleymaniye Kütüphanesi, Esat Efendi ktp, No.2151.
Ahmed Hasan Beyzade. *Telhis-i Tacü't-tevarih*. Istanbul: Arkeoloji Müzesi, No.234 and No.481; Istanbul: Nurosmaniye Kütüphanesi, No.3106.
Ahmed Hasan Beyzade. *Fethname-i Kanije*. London: National Archives, SP.102/4 and SP.102/61.
Câfer Iyânî. *Cihadname-i Tiryaki Hasan Paşa*. Istanbul: Millet Kütüphanesi, A.E.Tar.190.
Istanbul: Başbakanlık Osmanlı Arşivi: Hatt-i Hümayun, HAT.25303 (1226); Cevdet Maliye C.ML.3801 (1231); Cevdet Maliye, C.ML.6251 (1204).
Katib Çelebi. *Fezleke-i Tevarih*. Oxford: Bodleian Library, Rawl.or.20 (25 Receb 1100/15 May 1689) and Sale60 (undated).
Lam 'Ali Efendi. *Fethname-i Egri*. London: National Archives, SP. 102/4 11; and also in Berlin: Staatsbibliothek Preußischer Kulturbesitz, ms.or.fol.3332 fols 187b–189a.
London: National Archives, SP 97/4 Letters from the English Ambassador in Constantinople.
Mustafa Selaniki. *Tarih-i Selaniki*. Istanbul: Topakı Sarayı Müzesi, ms. Revan 1137.
Talikizade. *Şeyname-i Sultan-i Selatin-i Cihan*. Istanbul: Topkapı Sarayı Kütüphanesi, Hazine 1609.
———. *Şeyname-i Hümayun*. Istanbul: Türk ve İslam Eserleri Müzesi, no. 1965.
———. *Gürcistan Seferi*. Istanbul: Topkapı Sarayı Kütüphanesi, Revan 1300.
———. *Tebriziyye*. Istanbul: Topkapı Sarayı Kütüphanesi, Revan 1299.
Telhis-i Vezir-i Azam Yemişçi Hasan Paşa. Istanbul: Topkapı Sarayı Müzesi: Revan 1303.
Geschichte der Feldzüge Hasanpascha's. Vienna: National-bibliothek, Mxt 200.

Printed sources

Agnew, John, and Stuart Corbridge. *Mastering Space: Hegemony, Territory and International Political Economy*. London: Routledge, 1995.
Ágoston, Gábor. *Guns for the Sultan: Military Power and the Weapons Industry in the Ottoman Empire*. Cambridge: Cambridge University Press, 2005.
Ahmed Refik. *Meşhur Osmanlı Komandanları*. İstanbul: İbrahim Hilmi Matbaası, 1318/1900–1901.

Aksan, Virginia. "Military Reform and Its Limits in a Shrinking Ottoman World, 1800–1840." In *The Early Modern Ottomans: Remapping the Empire*, edited by Virginia Aksan and Daniel Goffman, 117–133. Cambridge: Cambridge University Press, 2007.

Akün, Ömer Faruk. "Namık Kemal." In *İslam Ansiklopedisi: Islam Alemi Tarih, Coğrafya, Etnografya ve Biyografya Lugatı*, vol. 9, edited by İstanbul Üniversitesi Edebiyat Fakültesi, 54–72. Istanbul: Milli Eğitim Basımevi, 1961–1979.

Alderson, A.D. *Structure of the Ottoman Dynasty*. Oxford: Clarendon Press, 1956.

Ali, A., trans. and commentary. *Al-Qur'an: A Contemporary Translation*. Princeton: Princeton University Press, 1984.

Anderson, Benedict. *Imagined Communities: Reflections on the Origin and Spread of Nationalism*. London: Verso Press, 1991.

Andrews, Walter G., and Mehmed Kalpaklı. *The Age of Beloveds: Love and the Beloved in Early-Modern Ottoman and European Culture and Society*. Durham: Duke University Press, 2005.

Ankersmit, Frank, and Hans Kellner, eds. *A New Philosophy of History*. London: Reaktion Books, 1995.

Anscombe, Frederick F., ed. *The Ottoman Balkans 1750–1830*. Princeton: Markus Wiener Publishers, 2006.

Antick, Paul. "Bhopal to Bridgehampton: Schema for a Disaster Tourism Event." *Journal of Visual Culture* 26/1 (2013): 165–185.

———. "Smith in Palestine (to Be Read Aloud, in Its Entirety)." *Journal of Visual Communication* 11/4 (2012): 443–460.

Appleby, Joyce, Lynn Hunt, and Margaret Jacob. *Telling the Truth about History*. New York: W.W. Norton and Company, 1994.

Armstrong, Paul. *Conflicting Readings: Variety and Validity in Interpretation*. London: North Carolina Press, 1990.

Atatürk, Mustafa. *Söylev (Nutuk)*. Ankara: Ankara Üniversitesi Basımevi, 1964.

Aumer, J. *Verzeichniss der orientalischen Handschriften . . . mit Ausschluss der hebræischen, arabischen und persischen. Nebst Anhang zum Verzeichniss der arabischen und persischen Handschriften*. Part 4 in the series *Catalogus codicum manscriptorum Bibliothecae Regiae Monacensis* by the Bayerische Staatsbibliothek. München, 1875.

Austin, Thomas. "'Desperate to See It': Straight Men Watching *Basic Instinct*." In *Identifying Hollywood's Audiences: Cultural Identity and the Movies*, edited by Melvyn Stokes and Richard Maltby, 147–161. London: BFI Publishing, 1999.

Aykut, Ş. Nezihi. "Hasan Beyzade Ahmed Paşa." In *Historians of the Ottoman Empire*, edited by Cemal Kafadar, Hakan Karateke, Cornell Fleischer. Turkish version 2005, English version 2008. https://ottomanhistorians.uchicago.edu/en/historian/hasan-beyzade-ahmed-pasa-hamdi (accessed 26/6/16).

Babinger, Franz. *Mehmed the Conqueror and His Time*. Princeton: Princeton University Press, 1978.

———. *Geschichtsschreiber der Osmanen und ihre Werke*. Leipzig: Otto Harrassowitz, 1927.

Babinger, Franz, and Christine Woodhead. "Peçewi." In *Encyclopaedia of Islam*, 2nd ed., edited by P.J. Bearman, Th. Bianquis, C.E. Bosworth, E. van Donzel, and W.P. Heinrichs, vol. 8, 291. Leiden: Brill, 1960–2000.

Baker, Patricia. "Islamic Honorific Garments." *Costume* 25 (1991): 25–35.

Başgöz, İlhan. "Digression in Oral Narrative: A Case Study of Individual Remarks by Turkish Romance Tellers." *Journal of American Folklore* 99/391 (1986): 5–23.

Bibliography

———. "The Epic Tradition among Turkic Peoples." In *Heroic Epic and Saga: An Introduction to the World's Great Folk Epics*, edited by F.J. Oinas, 310–335. Bloomington: Indiana University Press, 1978.

Bayerle, Gustav. "Hungarian Narrative Sources of Ottoman History." *Archivum Ottomanicum* 9 (1984): 5–26.

———. "One Hundred Fifty Years of Frontier Life in Hungary." In *From Hunyadi to Rákóczi: War and Society in Late Medieval and Early Modern Hungary*, edited by Janos M. Bak and Béla K. Király, 227–242. New York: Brooklyn Press: Distributed by Columbia University Press, 1982.

———. *Ottoman Tributes in Hungary: According to Sixteenth Century Tapu Registers*. The Hague and Paris: Mouton, 1973.

———. "Ottoman Records in the Hungarian Archives." *Archivum Ottomanicum* 4 (1972): 5–22.

———. *Ottoman Diplomacy in Hungary*. Bloomington: Indiana University Press, 1972.

Baysun, Cavid. *Tiryaki Hasan Paşa ve Kanije Savaşı*. Istanbul: Milli Eğitim Bakanlığı Köy Kitaplığı no.15, Milli Eğitim Basımevi, 1950.

Beiner, Ronald. "Hannah Arendt on Judging." In *Lectures on Kant's Political Philosophy*, edited by Hannah Arendt, 89–156. Chicago: University of Chicago Press, 1992.

Benjamin, Walter. *Illuminations*, edited by Hannah Arendt, translated by H. Zohn. New York: Schocken Books, 1968.

Benson, C. David. "Another Fine Manuscript Mess: Authors, Editors, and Readers of *Piers Plowman*." In *New Directions in Later Medieval Manuscript Studies*, edited by Derek Pearsall, 15–28. York: York Medieval Press, 2000.

Bérenger, Jean. *A History of the Habsburg Empire 1273–1700*. London and New York: Longman, 1994.

Berger, Thomas L. "'Opening Titles Miscreate': Some Observations on the Titling of Shakespeare's Works." In *The Margins of the Text*, edited by D.C. Greetham, 155–172. Ann Arbor: The University of Michigan Press, 1997.

Berkenkotter, Carol, and Thomas N. Huckin. *Genre Knowledge in Disciplinary Communication: Cognition/Culture/Power*. Hove, UK: Lawrence Erlbaum Associates, 1995.

Berkhofer, Robert F. *Beyond the Great Story: History as Text and Discourse*. Cambridge, MA: The Belknap Press of Harvard University Press, 1995.

Berktay, Halil. "The 'Other' Feudalism: A Critique of Twentieth Century Turkish Historiography." PhD diss., Birmingham: University of Birmingham, 1990.

Biber, D. "Spoken and Written Textual Dimensions in English: Resolving the Contradictory Findings." *Language* 62/2 (1986): 384–414.

Binark, İsmet. *Türk Sefer ve Zaferleri Bibliyografyası (Izahli)*. Ankara: Millî Kütüphaneye Yardım Derneği, 1969.

Birge, John K. *The Bektashi Order of Dervishes*. London: Luzac and Co., 1937.

Birnbaum, Eleazar. "The Transliteration of Ottoman Turkish for Library and General Purposes." *Journal of the American Oriental Society* 87/2 (April 1967): 122–156.

Blake, Norman F. *The Textual Tradition of the Canterbury Tales*. London: Arnold, 1985.

Blaškovič, Josef, Karel Petráček, and Rudolph Veselý, eds. *Arabische, türkische und persische Handschriften der Universitätsbibliothek in Bratislava*. Bratislave: Univerzitní Kniznica, 1961.

Blochet, Edgar. *Catalogue des manuscrits turcs par E. Blochet*. 2 vols. Paris: Bibliothèque Nationale, 1932–1933.

Boffey, Julia. "Short Texts in Manuscript Anthologies: The Minor Poems of John Lydgate in Two Fifteenth-Century Collections." In *The Whole Book: Cultural Perspectives on the Medieval Miscellany*, edited by S. Nichols and S. Wenzel, 69–82. Ann Arbor: The University of Michigan Press, 1996.

———. "The Manuscripts of English Courtly Love Lyrics in the Fifteenth Century." In *Manuscripts and Readers in Fifteenth Century England*, edited by D. Pearsall, 3–14. Woodbridge: D. Brewer, 1981.

Boratav, P. N. "Hikaye." In *Encyclopaedia of Islam*, 2nd ed., edited by P.J. Bearman, Th. Bianquis, C.E. Bosworth, E. van Donzel, and W.P. Heinrichs, vol. 3, 373–375. Leiden: Brill, 1960–2000.

Bosworth, C.E. "Naṣīḥat al-Mulūk." In *Encyclopaedia of Islam*, 2nd ed., edited by P.J. Bearman, Th. Bianquis, C.E. Bosworth, E. van Donzel, and W.P. Heinrichs. http://dx.doi.org/10.1163/1573-3912_islam_COM_0850 (accessed 10/8/16). First published online 2012. First print edition 1960–2007.

Bottici, Chiara, and Benoît Challand. *The Myth of the Clash of Civilizations*. London: Routledge, 2010.

Brandom, Robert. "Truth and Assertibility." *Journal of Philosophy* 73 (1976): 137–149.

Bransford, John D., and Jeffery J. Franks. "The Abstraction of Linguistic Ideas." *Cognitive Psychology* 2 (1971): 331–350.

Bransford, John. D., and Marcia Johnson. "Consideration of Some Problems in Comprehension." In *Visual Information Processing*, edited by William G. Chase, 383–438. New York: Academic Press, 1973.

Browne, Edward G. *A Supplementary Hand-List of the Muhammadan Manuscripts Preserved in the Libraries of the University and Colleges of Cambridge*. Cambridge: Cambridge University Press, 1922.

Brummett, Palmira. *Image and Imperialism in the Ottoman Revolutionary Press 1908–1911*. Albany: State University of New York Press, 2000.

Bruns, Gerald L. "The Originality of Texts in a Manuscript Culture." *Comparative Literature* 32 (1980): 113–129.

Buck-Morss, Susan. *The Dialectics of Seeing: Walter Benjamin and the Arcades Project*. Cambridge, MA: MIT Press, 1991.

Bursalı, Mehmed Tahir. *Osmanlı Müellifleri*. 2 vols. Istanbul: Matbaa-ı Amise, 1333/ 1914–1915.

Çabuk, Vahit. *Tiryaki Hasan Paşa'nın Gazaları ve Kanije Savunması*. Istanbul: Tercüman 1001 Temel Eser No.129, 1978.

Carrard, Philippe. "Theory of a Practice: Historical Enunication and the Annales School." In *A New Philosophy of History*, edited by Frank Ankersmit and Hans Kellner, 108–126. London: Reaktion Books, 1995.

Carruthers, Mary. *The Book of Memory: A Study of Memory in Medieval Culture*. Cambridge: Cambridge University Press, 1990.

Cerwinka, G. "Die Eroberung der Festung Kanizsa durch die Türken im Jahre 1600." In *Innerösterreich 1564–1619*, edited by Alexander Novotny and Berthold Sutter, 409–511. Graz: Steiermärkische Landesregierung, 1968.

Chadwick, Nora K., and Victor Zhirmunsky. *Oral Epics of Central Asia*. Cambridge: Cambridge University Press, 1969.

Chafe, Wallace L. "Integration and Involvement in Speaking, Writing and Oral Literature." In *Spoken and Written Language: Exploring Orality and Literacy*, edited by Deborah Tannen, 35–53. Norwood, NJ: Ablex, 1982.

Chafe, Wallace L., and J. Danielewicz. *Properties of Written and Spoken Language.* Berkeley and Los Angeles: University of California, 1987. Also published as chapter 3 in *Comprehending Oral and Written Language*, edited by R. Horowitz and S. J. Samuels, 82–113. London: Academic Press, 1987.

Charles, Robert Henry, trans. *The Apocrypha and Pseudepigrapha of the Old Testament.* Oxford: Clarendon Press, 1913.

Chartier, Roger. *Forms and Meanings: Texts, Performances, and Audiences from Codex to Computer.* Philadelphia: University of Pennsylvania Press, 1995.

Chisholm, Roderick. "Why the Theory of Knowledge Has to Be Realistic." In *Realism/Antirealism and Epistemology*, edited by C. Kulp, 95–108. Lanham and New York: Rowman and Littlefield Publishers, Inc., 1997.

Çipa, H. Erdem, and Emine Fetvacı, eds. *Writing History at the Ottoman Court: Editing the Past, Fashioning the Future.* Bloomington: Indiana University Press, 2013.

Claus, Peter, and John Marriott. *History: An Introduction to Theory, Method and Practice.* Harlow: Pearson, 2012.

Cohen, Sande. *History Out of Joint: Essays on the Use and Abuse of History.* Baltimore: John Hopkins University Press, 2006.

Coote, Mary. "Serbo-Croatian Heroic Songs." In *Heroic Epic and Sages: An Introduction to the World's Great Folk Epics*, edited by Felix Oinas, 257–285. Bloomington: Indiana University Press, 1978.

Crosman, Robert. "Do Readers Make Meanings?" In *The Reader in the Text: Essays on Audience and Interpretation*, edited by Susan Suleiman and Inge Crosman, 149–164. Princeton: Princeton University Press, 1980.

Culler, Jonathan. *Framing the Sign: Criticism and Its Institutions.* Oxford: Basil Blackwell, 1988.

———. "Prolegomena to a Theory of Reading." In *The Reader in the Text: Essays on Audience and Interpretation*, edited by Susan Suleiman and Inge Crosman, 46–66. Princeton: Princeton University Press, 1980.

Cuttica, Cesare. "Anti-Jesuit Patriotic Absolutism: Robert Filmer and French Ideas (c. 1580–1630)." *Renaissance Studies* 25/4 (2012): 559–579.

Dagenais, John. *The Ethics of Reading in Manuscript Culture: Glossing the Libro de Buen Amor.* Princeton: Princeton University Press, 1994.

———. "That Bothersome Residue: Toward a Theory of the Physical Text." In *Vox Intexta: Orality and Textuality in the Middle Ages*, edited by A.N. Doane and C. Braun Pasternack, 246–262. Madison: University of Wisconsin Press, 1991.

Danişmend, İ. H. *Izahlı Osmanlı Tarihi Kronolojisi.* 4 vols. Istanbul: Türkiye Yayınevi, 1947–1955.

Dávid, Géza. "Administration in Ottoman Europe." In *Süleyman the Magnificent and His Age: The Ottoman Empire in the Early Modern World*, edited by Metin Kunt and Christine Woodhead, 71–90. London and New York: Longman, 1995.

———. "Ottoman Administrative Strategies in Western Hungary." In *Studies in Ottoman History in Honour of Professor V.L. Ménage*, edited by Colin Heywood and Colin Imber, 31–44. Istanbul: Isis Press, 1994.

Dávid, Géza, and Pál Fodor. "Hungarian Studies in Ottoman History." In *The Ottomans and the Balkans: A Discussion of Historiography*, edited by Fikret Adanir and Suraiya Faroqhi, 305–350. Leiden, Boston and Köln: Brill, 2002.

———. "Introduction." In *Ottomans, Hungarians, and Habsburgs in Central Europe: The Military Confines in the Era of Ottoman Conquest*, edited by Géza Dávid and Pál Fodor, xi–xxvii. Leiden, Boston and Köln: Brill, 2000.

Davies, Martin L. *Imprisoned by History*. London: Routledge, 2010.
———. *Historics: Why History Dominates Contemporary Society*. London: Routledge, 2006.
Dawson, Graham. *Soldier Heroes: British Adventure, Empire and the Imagining of Masculinities*. London and New York: Routledge, 1994.
De Looze, Laurence. "Signing Off in the Middle Ages: Medieval Textuality and Strategies of Authorial Self-Naming." In *Vox Intexta: Orality and Textuality in the Middle Ages*, edited by A.N. Doane and C. Braun Pasternack, 162–178. Madison: University of Wisconsin Press, 1991.
Demirel, B. *Türk Silahlı Kuvvetleri Tarihi: Osmanlı Devri III. Cilt 3. Kısım Kanuni'nin ölümünden sonra ikinci Viyana kuşatmasına kadar olan devre (1566–1683)*. Ankara Gnkur. Basımevi, T.C. Genelkurmay askeri Tarih ve Stratejik etüt Baþkanlığı Askeri Tarih Yayınları Seri No. 2, 1981.
Dening, Greg. *Beach Crossings: Voyaging Across Times, Cultures and Self*. Philadelphia: University of Pennsylvania Press, 2004.
———. *Mr Bligh's Bad Language: Passion, Power and Theatre on the Bounty*. Cambridge: Cambridge University Press, 1992.
Denny, J.P. "Rational Thought in Oral Culture and Literate Decontextualization." In *Literacy and Orality*, edited by David Olson and Nancy Torrance, 66–89. Cambridge: Cambridge University Press, 1991.
Deringil, Selim. *The Well-Protected Domains: Ideology and the Legitimation of Power in the Ottoman Empire 1876–1909*. London: I.B.Tauris, 1998.
———. "The Ottoman Origins of Kemalist Nationalism: Namık Kemal to Mustafa Kemal." *European History Quarterly* 23/2 (1993): 165–192.
———. "Legitimacy Structures in the Ottoman State: The Reign of Abdülhamid II (1876–1909)." *International Journal of Middle East Studies* 23 (1991): 345–359.
Derrida, Jacques. *Of Grammatology*, translated by Gayatri Chakravorty Spivak. Baltimore: Johns Hopkins University Press, 1976.
Doane, Alger N., and Carol Braun Pasternack, eds. *Vox Intexta: Orality and Textuality in the Middle Ages*. Madison: University of Wisconsin Press, 1991.
Donnelly, Mark, and Claire Norton. *Doing History*. London: Routledge, 2011.
Dumézil, Georges. *The Stakes of the Warrior*, translated by Alf Hiltebeitel. Berkeley: University of California Press, 1992.
———. *The Destiny of the Warrior*. Chicago and London: University of Chicago Press, 1970.
Eberhard, Wolfram. *Minstrel Tales from South-Eastern Turkey*. Berkeley: University of California Press, 1955.
Edwards, A.S.G. "Representing the Middle English Manuscript." In *New Direction in Later Medieval Manuscript Studies*, edited by Derek Pearsall, 65–79. Woodbridge: York Medieval Press, 2000.
Eichborn, R. von. *Cambridge-Eichborn German Dictionary: Economics, Administration, Law, Business*, vol. 2 German-English. Cambridge: Cambridge University Press, 1983.
Eken, Ahmet. *Kartpostallarda İstanbul*. Istanbul: Büyükşehir Belediyesi, 1992.
Embree, Dan, and Elizabeth Urquhart. "*The Simonie*: The Case for a Parallel Text Edition." In *Manuscripts and Texts: Editorial Problems in Later Middle English Literature*, edited by Derek Pearsall, 49–59. Woodbridge: D.S. Brewer, 1987.
Enginün, İnci. "Turkish Literature and Self-Identity: From Ottoman to Modern Turkish." In *Ottoman Past and Today's Turkey*, edited by Kemal Karpat, 212–235. Leiden, Boston and Köln: Brill, 2000.

Erendil, Muzaffer. *Topçuluk Tarihi*. Ankara: Genelkurmay Basımevi, 1988.
Erkan, M. "Gazavatname." In *Türkiye Diyanet Vakfı İslam Ansiklopedisi*, vol. 13. Türkiye Diyanet Vakfı, İslâm Ansiklopedisi Genel Müdürlüğü, 439–440. Istanbul: Türkiye Diyanet Vakfı yayınları, 1998.
Ersanlı, Büşra. "The Ottoman Empire in the Historiography of the Kemalist Era: A Theory of Fatal Decline." In *The Ottomans and the Balkans: A Discussion of Historiography*, edited by Fikret Adanir and Suraiya Faroqhi, 115–154. Leiden, Boston and Köln: Brill, 2002.
Ersever, H.Z. *Kanije Savunması ve Tiryaki Hasan Paşa*. Ankara: Türk Asker Büyükleri ve Türk Zaferleri Seri No. 12, Genelkurmay Askeri Tarih ve Stratejik Etüt Baskanlığı Yayınları Gnkur. Basımevi, 1986.
Ethé, Herman. *Catalogue of the Persian Mss. in the Bodleian Library Part II Turkish, Hindustani, Pushtu and Additional Persian MSS*. Oxford: Clarendon Press, 1930.
Evans, Richard. *In Defence of History*. London: Granta, 1997.
Farah, Caesar. E. "Announcing an Ottoman Victory in Hungary to a Yemeni Amir." In *A Miscellany of Middle Eastern Articles: In Memoriam T.M. Johnstone 1924–83*, edited by A.K. Irvine, R.B. Sergeant, and G.R. Smith, 28–37. Harlow: Longman, 1988.
Faroqhi, Suraiya. "Ottoman Views on Corsairs and Piracy in the Adriatic." In *The Kapudan Pasha, His Office and His Domain*, edited by E. Zachariadou, 357–371. Rethymnon: Crete University Press, 2002.
———. *Approaching Ottoman History: An Introduction to the Sources*. Cambridge: Cambridge University Press, 1999.
Fekete, Lajos. *Die Siyaqat-Schrift in der Türkischen Finanzverwaltung*. Budapest: Akadémiai kiadó, 1955.
———. "Osmanlı Türkleri ve Macarlar 1366–1699." *Belleten* 13/52 (1949): 663–743.
———. *Budapest a törökkorban*. Budapest: Egyetemi Nyomda, 1944.
———. *Türkische Schriften aus dem Archive des Palatins Nikolaus Esterhazy 1606–1645*. Budapest: Im Auftrage des Fürsten Paul Esterházy, 1932.
———. "A velencei állami levéltár magyar vonatkozású fethnāméi." *Levéltari közlemények* 4 (1926): 139–157.
Feldman, Carol. "Oral Metalanguage." In *Literacy and Orality*, edited by David Olson and Nancy Torrance, 47–65. Cambridge: Cambridge University Press, 1991.
Fentress, James, and Chris Wickham. *Social Memory*. Oxford: Blackwell, 1992.
Ferenc, Szakaly. "The Early Ottoman Period, Including Royal Hungary, 1526–1606." In *A History of Hungary*, edited by Peter Sugar, 83–99. London and New York: I.B. Tauris and Co. Ltd., 1990.
Feridun Bey. *Mejmu'a-i munşe'at al-selatin*. Istanbul: Takvimhane-yi Amire, 1265–1274/1848–1858.
Fetvacı, Emine. *Picturing History at the Ottoman Court*. Bloomington: Indiana University Press, 2013.
Fine, John V. A. *When Ethnicity Did Not Matter in the Balkans: A Study of Identity in Pre-Nationalist Croatia, Dalmatia, and Slavonia in the Medieval and Early-Modern Periods*. Ann Arbor: The University of Michigan Press, 2006.
Finkel, Caroline. "French Mercenaries in the Habsburg-Ottoman War of 1583–1606: The Desertion of the Papa Garrison to the Ottomans in 1600." *Bulletin of the School of Oriental and African Studies* 55/3 (1992): 451–471.
———. *The Administration of Warfare: The Ottoman Military Campaigns in Hungary, 1593–1606*. Wien: VWGO, 1988.

Finnegan, Ruth. "What Is Oral Literature Anyway? Comments in the Light of Some African and Other Comparative Material." In *Oral Formulaic Theory: A Folklore Casebook*, edited by J. M. Foley, 243–82. CT: Taylor and Francis Inc., 1990. Also in *Oral literature and the Formula*, edited by Stolz and Shannon, 127–166. Ann Arbor: Centre for Coordination of Ancient and Modern Studies, University of Michigan, 1976.

———. "Literacy versus Non-Literacy: The Great Divide?" In *Modes of Thought: Essays on Thinking in Western and Non-Western Societies*, edited by Robin Horton and Ruth Finnegan, 112–144. London: Faber and Faber, 1973.

Fish, Stanley. "Introduction, or How I Stopped Worrying and Learned to Love Interpretation." In *Is There a Text in This Class? The Authority of Interpretive Communities*, edited by Stanley Fish, 1–17. Cambridge, MA: Harvard University Press, 1980.

———. "*Interpreting the* Variorum." In *Is There a Text in This Class? The Authority of Interpretive Communities*, edited by Stanley Fish, 147–173. Cambridge, MA: Harvard University Press, 1980.

———. "How to Do Things with Austin and Searle: Speech-Act Theory and Literary Criticism." In *Is There a Text in This Class? The Authority of Interpretive Communities*, edited by Stanley Fish, 197–245. Cambridge, MA and London: Harvard University Press, 1980.

———. "Demonstration vs. Persuasion: Two Models of Critical Activity." In *Is There a Text in This Class? The Authority of Interpretive Communities*, edited by Stanley Fish, 356–371. Cambridge, MA and London: Harvard University Press, 1980.

———. "Normal Circumstances, Literal Languages, Direct Speech Acts, the Ordinary, the Everyday, the Obvious, What Goes without Saying and Other Special Cases." *Critical Inquiry* 4 (1978): 625–644.

Fisher, D.F. "Spatial Factors in Reading and Search: The Case for Space." In *Eye Movements and Psychological Processes*, edited by Richard A. Monty and John W. Senders, 417–428. Hillsdale, NJ: Erlbaum, 1976.

Fleischer, Cornell. "From Sehzade Korkud to Mustafa Ali: Cultural Origins of the Ottoman *Nasihatname*." In *Proceedings of the Third Congress on the Social and Economic History of Turkey Princeton 1983*, edited by H. Lowry and S. Hatto, 67–77. Istanbul: Isis Press, 1990.

———. *Bureaucrat and Intellectual in the Ottoman Empire: The Historian Mustafa Ali* Princeton and Guildford: Princeton University Press, 1986.

Flemming, Barbara. "Public Opinion under Sultan Süleyman." In *Süleyman the Second and His Time*, edited by H. İnalcık and C. Kafadar, 49–58. Istanbul: İsis Press, 1993.

Flemming, Barbara, Manfred Götz, and Hanna Sohrweide. *Türkische Handschriften*. Wiesbaden: Steiner, 1968.

Flügel, Gustav. *Concordantiae Corani Arabicae: ad literarum ordinem et verborum radices diligenter disposuit Gustavus Flügel*. Lipsiae: Sumptibus Ernesti Bredtii, 1898.

———. *Die arabischen, persischen und türkischen Handschriften der kaiserlich-königlichen Hofbibliothek zu Wien*. 2 vols. Wien: K. K. Hof- und Staatsdruckerei, 1865–1867.

Foley, John Miles. "Orality, Textuality, and Interpretation." In *Vox Intexta: Orality and Textuality in the Middle Ages*, edited by Alger N. Doane and Carol Braun Pasternack, 34–45. Madison: University of Wisconsin Press, 1991.

———. *Oral-Formulaic Theory and Research: An Introduction and Annotated Bibliography*. New York: Garland, 1985.

170 Bibliography

———. "The Oral Theory in Context." In *Oral Traditional Literature: A Festschrift for Albert Bates Lord*, edited by J.M. Foley, 27–122. Columbus: Slavica, 1980.
Foucault, Michel. "Questions on Geography." In *Michel Foucault: Power/Knowledge*, edited by Colin Gordon, 63–77. New York: Patneon, 1980.
Fox-Genovese, Elizabeth, and Elisabeth Lasch-Quinn, eds. *Reconstructing History: The Emergence of a New Historical Society*. London: Routledge, 1999.
Frank, Armin Paul. "*Schattenkultur* and Other Well-Kept Secrets: From Historical Translation Studies to Literary Historiography." In *Translating Literatures, Translating Cultures: New Vistas and Approaches in Literary Studies*, edited by K. Mueller-Vollmer and M. Irmscher, 15–30. Berlin: Erich Schmidt Verlag, 1998.
Friend, Stacie. "Fiction as a Genre." *Proceedings of the Aristotelian Society* 12/2 (2012): 179–209.
———. "Fictive Utterance and Imagining II." *Aristotelian Society Supplementary Volume* 85/1 (2011): 163–180.
Fullard, Madeleine and Nicky Rousseau. "Truth-Telling, Identities and Power in South Africa and Guatemala." http://ictj.org/sites/default/files/ICTJ-Identities-Truth Commissions-ResearchBrief-2009-English.pdf accessed 16/11/12.
Gelb, Ignace Jay. *A Study of Writing*, 2nd ed. Chicago: University of Chicago Press, 1963.
Gellner, Ernest. *Thought and Change*. London: Weidenfeld and Nicolson, 1964.
Gervers, Veronika. *The Influence of Ottoman Turkish Textiles and Costume in Eastern Europe*. Toronto, Canada: Royal Ontario Museum, 1982.
Gévay, Anton von. *A' budai pasák*. Bécsben: Strauss Antal' Özvegye Betűivel, 1841.
Gontaut-Biron, Théodore de. *Ambassade en Turquie de Jean de Gontaut Biron, Baron de Salignac 1605 a 1610 correspondance diplomatique & documents inédits*. Paris: Honorè Champion, 1888.
Gönültaş, Güler. *Manisa İl Halk Kütüphanesi Türkçe El Yazmaları Kataloğu*. Manisa: Türk Kütüphaneciler Derneği Manisa Şubesi Yayınları, 1986.
Goody, Jack, and Ian Watt. "The Consequences of Literacy." In *Literacy in Traditional Societies*, edited by J. Goody, 27–68. Cambridge: Cambridge University Press, 1968.
Götz, Manfred. *Türkische Handschriften*, vol. 13 part 4 of the series *Verzeichniss der orientalischen Handschriften in Deutschland*. Wiesbaden: Steiner, 1979.
Gövsa, I. A. *Turk Meşhurları Ansiklopedisi: Edebiyatta, Sanatta, ilimde, Harpte, Politikada ve her sahada şöhret kazanmış olan Türklerin Hayatları Eserleri*. Istanbul: Yedigün Neşriyatı, 1946.
Grazia, Margreta de. *Shakespeare Verbatim: The Reproduction of Authenticity and the 1790 Apparatus*. Oxford: Clarendon Press, 1991.
Griswold, William J. *The Great Anatolian Rebellion 1000–1020 / 1591–1611*. Berlin: Klaus Schwarz Verlag, 1983.
Gumrecht, Hans Ulrich. *In 1926: Living at the Edge of Time*. Cambridge, MA: Harvard University Press, 1997.
Hagen, Gottfried. "Katib Çelebi." In *Historians of the Ottoman Empire*, edited by Cemal Kafadar, Hakan Karateke, and Cornell Fleischer, 2007. https://ottomanhistorians.uchicago.edu/en/historian/katib-celebi (accessed 25/8/16)
Hajda, Lubomyr Andrij. "Two Ottoman Gazanames Concerning the Chyhyryn Campaign of 1678." PhD diss., Cambridge, MA: Harvard University, 1984.
Hammer-Purgstall, J. von. *Geschichte des osmanischen Reiches*. Pest: In C.A. Hartleben's Verlag, 1829.

Hanna, Ralph. "Producing Manuscripts and Editions." In *Crux and Controversy in Middle English Textual Criticism*, edited by A. J. Minnis and Charlotte Brewer, 109–130. Cambridge: D.S. Brewer, 1992.
Harlan, David. "Ken Burns and the Coming Crisis of Academic History." *Rethinking History* 7 (2003): 169–192.
———. *The Degradation of American History*. Chicago: University of Chicago Press, 1997.
Harris, K. "John Gower's *Confessio Amantis*: The Virtues of Bad Texts." In *Manuscripts and Readers in Fifteenth Century England: The Literary Implications of Manuscript Study*, edited by Derek Pearsall, 27–40. Cambridge: Brewer, 1983.
Havelock, Eric Alfred. *The Literate Revolution in Greece and Its Cultural Consequences*. Princeton and Guildford: Princeton University Press, 1982.
Heath, S.B. *Ways with Words: Language, Life, and Work in Communities and Classrooms*. Cambridge: Cambridge University Press, 1983.
Hegyi, Klara. "The Ottoman Network of Fortresses in Hungary." In *Ottomans, Hungarians, and Habsburgs in Central Europe: The Military Confines in the Era of Ottoman Conquest*, edited by Géza Dávid and Pál Fodor, 163–193. Leiden, Boston and Köln: Brill, 2000.
———. *Török Berendezkedés Magyarországon*. Budapest: Histöriá Könyvtár, Monográfiák, 7. 1995.
———. *Egy Világbirodalom végvidékén*. Budapest: Gondolat, 1975.
Hickok, Michael Robert. *Ottoman Military Administration in Eighteenth Century Bosnia*. Leiden: Brill, 1997.
Hilmi, A. *Fihrist al-kutub al-Turkiyah al-mawjudah fi al-Kutubkhanah al-Khidiwiyah*. al-Qahirah: al-Matba'ah al-'Uthmaniyah. 1306/1888–1889.
Himmelfarb, Gertrude. "Postmodern History." In *Reconstructing History: The Emergence of a New Historical Society*, edited by Elizabeth Fox-Genovese and Elisabeth Lasch-Quinn, 71–93. London: Routledge, 1999.
———. "Telling It as You Like It: Postmodernist History and the Flight from Fact." In *The Postmodern History Reader*, edited by K. Jenkins, 158–174. London and New York: Routledge, 1997.
Hobsbawm, Eric. *On History*. London: Abacus, 1998.
———. *Nations and Nationalism since 1780: Programme, Myth and Reality*. Cambridge: Cambridge University Press, 1990.
Hodgson, Phyllis, ed. *The Cloud of Unknowing and the Book of Privy Counselling*. London: Early English Text Society, 1944.
Holland, Norman. "Re-Covering 'The Purloined Letter': Reading as a Personal Transaction." In *The Reader in the Text: Essays on Audience and Interpretation*, edited by Susan Suleiman and Inge Crosman, 350–370. Princeton: Princeton University Press, 1980.
Holt, P.M. "Al-Jabarti's Introduction to the History of Ottoman Egypt." *Bulletin of the School of Oriental and African Studies* 25 (1962): 38–51.
Holton, Milne, and Vasa Mihailovich, eds. *Songs of the Serbian People*. Pittsburgh: University of Pittsburgh Press, 1997.
Howard, Douglas A. "The Ottoman Advice for Kings Literature." In *The Early Modern Ottomans: Remapping the Empire*, edited by Virginia H. Aksan and Daniel Goffman, 137–166. Cambridge: Cambridge University Press, 2007.
Huntington, Samuel P. *The Clash of Civilizations and the Remaking of World Order*. New York: Simon and Schuster, 1996.

172 Bibliography

———. "The Clash of Civilizations?" *Foreign Affairs* (Summer 1993). http://edvardas.home.mruni.eu/wp-content/uploads/2008/10/huntington.pdf (accessed 5/8/15)

Huot, Sylvia. "A Book Made for a Queen: The Shaping of a Late Medieval Anthology Manuscript (B.N. fr. 24429)." In *The Whole Book: Cultural Perspectives on the Medieval Miscellany*, edited by Stephen G. Nichols and Siegfried Wenzel, 123–143. Ann Arbor: University of Michigan Press, 1996.

Ibrahim Peçevi. *Tarih-i Peçevi*. Istanbul, 1283/1866–1867.

İnalcık, Halil. "How to Read Aşıkpaşazade's History." In *Studies in Ottoman History in Honour of Professor V.L. Ménage*, edited by Colin Heywood and Colin Imber, 139–156. Istanbul: Isis Press, 1994.

İnalcık, Halil, and Mevlüd Oğuz, edited and transcribed. *Gazavat-i Sultan Murad b. Mehemmed Han: İzladi be Varna Savaşları (1443–1444) Üzerinde Anonim Gazavatname*. Ankara: Türk Tarih Kurumu Basımevi, 1978.

———. "Yeni Bulunmuş bir 'Gazavat-i Sultan Murad.'" *Ankara Üniversitesi Dil ve Tarih-Coğrafya Fakültesi Dergisi* 7/2 (1949): 481–495.

Irvine, Martin. "Medieval Textuality and the Archaeology of Textual Culture." In *Speaking Two Languages: Traditional Disciplines and Contemporary Theory in Medieval Studies*, edited by A.J. Frantzen, 181–210. Albany: State University of New York Press, 1991.

Isom-Verhaaren, Christine. "An Ottoman Report about Martin Luther and the Emperor: New Evidence of the Ottoman Interest in the Protestant Challenge to the Power of Charles V." *Turcica* 28 (1996): 299–318.

İstanbul Kütüphaneleri Tarih – Coğrafya Yazmaları Katalogları. İstanbul: Maarif Matbaası, 1943-1962.

Istvánffy, N. *Historiarum de rebus vngaricis*. Köln: Hierat, Anton, 1622.

Jacob, Georg. "Turkisches aus Ungarn." *Der Islam* 8 (1918): 237–245.

Jarrett, Dennis. "Pragmatic Coherence in an Oral Formulaic Tradition." In *Coherence in Spoken and Written Discourse*, edited by Deborah Tannen, 155–171. Norwood, NJ: Ablex, 1984.

Jauss, Hans Robert. *Literaturgeschichte als Provokation*. Frankfurt: Suhrkamp, 1970.

Jaworski, A., and N. Coupland. "Introduction: Perspectives on Discourse Analysis." In *The Discourse Reader*, edited by A. Jaworski and N. Coupland, 1–44. London and New York: Routledge, 1999.

Jenkins, Brian, and Spyros Sofos. "Nation and Nationalism in Contemporary Europe: A Theoretical Perspective." In *Nation and Identity in Contemporary Europe*, edited by Brian Jenkins and Spyros Sofos, 9–32. London and New York: Routledge, 1996.

Jenkins, Keith. *At the Limits of History*. London: Routledge, 2009.

———. *Rethinking History*, 3rd ed. London: Routledge, 2003.

———. *Why History? Ethics and Postmodernity*. London: Routledge, 1999.

———. "Introduction: On Being Open about Our Closures." In *The Postmodern History Reader*, edited by Keith Jenkins, 1–30. London and New York: Routledge, 1997.

———, ed. *The Postmodern History Reader*. London: Routledge, 1997.

———. *On "What Is History?": From Carr and Elton to Rorty and White*. London: Routledge, 1995.

Jenkins, Keith, and Alun Munslow, eds. *The Nature of History Reader*. London: Routledge, 2004.

Jones, Ann Rosalind, and Peter Stallybrass. *Renaissance Clothing and the Materials of Memory.* Cambridge: Cambridge University Press, 2000.
Jones, Trevor, ed. *Harrap's Standard German and English Dictionary.* London: Harrap and Co. Ltd., 1967.
Kafadar, Cemal. *Between Two Worlds: The Construction of the Ottoman State.* Berkeley: University of California Press, 1995.
Kane, G. "The Text." In *A Companion to Piers Plowman*, edited by J.A. Alford, 175–200. Berkeley: University of California Press, 1988.
Kanije Kalesi (35mm) directed by Yılmaz Atadeniz, screenplay by Turgut Ozakman, produced by Dadas Film (Kadir Kesemen). Turkey, 1982.
Kant, Immanuel. *The Metaphysics of Morals*, translated by Mary Gregor. Cambridge: Cambridge University Press, 1991.
Karahan, A. "Nabi." In *İslam Ansiklopedisi: Islam Alemi Tarih, Coğrafya, Etnografya ve Biyografya Lugatı*, vol. 9, 3–7, edited by İstanbul Üniversitesi Edebiyat Fakültesi. Istanbul: Milli Eğitim Basımevi, 1961–1979.
Karatay, F. E. *Topkapı Sarayı Müzesi Kütüphanesi: Türkçe Yazmalar Kataloğu.* Istanbul: Topkapı Sarayı Müzesi, 1961.
Kassis, Hanna. *A Concordance of the Qur'an.* Berkeley, Los Angeles and London: University of California Press, 1983.
Kastritsis, Dimitris. *The Sons of Bayezid: Empire Building and Representation in the Ottoman Civil War of 1402–1413.* Leiden: Brill, 2007.
Katib Çelebi. *Fezleke-i Katib Çelebi.* Istanbul: Ceride-i Havadis Matbaası, 1286–1287/ 1869–1870.
Kelenik, József. "The Military Revolution in Hungary." In *Ottomans, Hungarians, and Habsburgs in Central Europe: The Military Confines in the Era of Ottoman Conquest*, edited by Géza Dávid and Pál Fodor, 117–159. Leiden, Boston and Köln: Brill, 2000.
Kinross, Patrick B. *Ataturk: A Biography of Mustafa Kemal, Father of Modern Turkey.* New York: Quill, William Morrow, 1964.
Kiparsky, Paul. "Oral Poetry: Some Linguistic and Typological Considerations." In *Oral Literature and the Formula*, edited by Benjamin Stolz and Richard Shannon, 73–106. Ann Arbor: University of Michigan Press, 1976.
Klinger, Barbara. "Digressions at the Cinema: Reception and Mass Culture." *Cinema Journal* 28/4 (1989): 3–19.
Klug, Tony. *How Peace Broke Out in the Middle East: A Short History of the Future.* Fabian Society, 2007. https://www.fabians.org.uk/wpcontent/uploads/2012/04/How PeaceBrokeOutInTheMiddleEast.pdf accessed 8/5/15.
Knolles, Richard. *The Generall Historie of the Turks*, 3rd ed. London: Adam Islip, 1621.
Kocatürk, V. M. *Türk Edebiyat Antolojisi.* Ankara: Edebiyat Yayınevi, 1967.
Köhbach, Markus. "Der osmanische Historiker Topçılar Katibi 'Abdü'l-qadir Efendi. Leben und Werk." *Osmanlı Araştırmaları* 2 (1981): 75–96.
Kortepeter, Carl Max. *Ottoman Imperialism during the Reformation: Europe and the Caucasus.* London: University of London Press Ltd., 1972.
Krafft, A. *Die arabischen, persischen und türkischen Handschriften der K. K. Orientalischen Akademie zu Wien.* Wien: Gedruckt bei den PP. Mechitaristen, 1842.
Kroll, Barbara. "Combining Ideas in Written and Spoken English." In *Discourse across Time and Space*, edited by Elinor Ochs Keenan and Tina Bennett Kastor, 69–108. Los Angeles: Department of Linguistics, University of Southern California, 1977.

Bibliography

Krstić, Tijana. *Contested Conversions to Islam: Narratives of Religious Change in the Early Modern Ottoman Empire*. Stanford: University of Stanford Press, 2011.

Kushner, David. *The Rise of Turkish Nationalism 1876–1908*. London: Frank Cass, 1977.

Kutlu, Mustafa. "Namık Kemal," in *Türk Dili ve Edebiyatı Ansiklopedisi*. Istanbul: Dergah Yayımları, 1985–1986.

Labov, William. *Language in the Inner City*. Philadelphia: University of Pennsylvania Press, 1972.

Lefaivre, Albert. *Les Magyars pendant la domination ottomane en Hongrie: 1526–1722*. Paris: Perrin Et Cie, 1902.

Levend, A.S. *Gazavat-nameler ve Mihaloğlu Ali Bey'in Gazavat-namesi*. Ankara: Türk Tarih Kurumu Yayınlarından / XI. Seri No. 8, Türk Tarih Kurumu Basımevi, 1956.

Lewis, Bernard. *Istanbul and the Civilisation of the Ottoman Empire*. Norman, OK: University of Oklahoma Press, 1963.

———. "The Use by Muslim Historians of Non-Muslim Sources." In *Historians of the Middle East*, edited by Bernard Lewis and P.M. Holt, 180–191. London: Oxford University Press, 1962.

Lewis, Geoffrey L. "The Utility of Ottoman Fethnames." In *Historians of the Middle East*, edited by Bernard Lewis and Peter Malcolm Holt, 192–196. London: Oxford University Press, 1962.

———. "Fathname." In *Encyclopaedia of Islam*, 2nd ed., edited by P.J. Bearman, Th. Bianquis, C.E. Bosworth, E. van Donzel, and W.P. Heinrichs, vol. 2, 839–840. Leiden: Brill, 1960–2000.

Little, Donald P. *History and Historiography of the Mamluks*. London: Variorum Reprints, 1986.

———. *An Introduction to Mamluk Historiography: An Analysis of Arabic Annalistic and Biographical Sources for the Reign of al-Malik an-Nasir Muhammad ibn Qala'un*. Wiesbaden: Franz Steiner Verlag GMBH, 1970.

Löbl, A. H. *Zur Geschichte des Türkenkrieges von 1593–1606*. Prague: Rohlíček und Sievers, 1899–1904.

Locke, John. *Two Treatises of Government*, edited by Peter Laslett. Cambridge: Cambridge University Press, 1988.

Lord, Albert Bates. "Oral Poetry." In *Encyclopaedia of Poetry and Poetics*, edited by A. Preminger, 591–593. Princeton: Princeton University Press, 1965.

———. *The Singer of Tales*. Cambridge, MA: Harvard University Press, 1960.

MacCaffrey, Wallace T. *Elizabeth I: War and Politics 1588–1603*. Princeton: Princeton University Press, 1992.

Machan, Tim. W. "Middle English Text Production and Modern Textual Criticism." In *Crux and Controversy in Middle English Textual Criticism*, edited by A.J. Minnis and C. Brewer, 1–18. Woodbridge: D.S. Brewer, 1992.

———. "Editing, Orality, and Late Middle English Texts." In *Vox Intexta: Orality and Textuality in the Middle Ages*, edited by Alger N. Doane and Carol Braun Pasternack, 229–245. Madison: University of Wisconsin Press, 1991.

Malcolm, Janet. *The Journalist and the Murderer*. London: Granta, 2012. First published in a different form in the *New Yorker*.

Mardin, Şerif. *The Genesis of Young Ottoman Thought: A Study in the Modernization of Turkey*. New York: Syracuse University Press, 2000.

———. "A Note on the Transformation of Religious Symbols in Turkey." *Turcica* 16 (1984): 115–127.

Marsigli, L.F. *Stato militare dell'Imperio Ottomano*. Amsterdam: Gosse et al, 1732.

Marwick, Arthur. *The Nature of History*, 3rd ed. London: Macmillan, 1989.
McCullagh, C. Behan. *The Truth of History*. London: Routledge, 1997.
McLaverty, Jim. "Questions of Entitlement: Some Eighteenth-Century Title Pages." In *The Margins of the Text*, edited by David Greetham, 173–198. Ann Arbor: University of Michigan Press, 1997.
Mehmed, Süreyya. *Sicill-i Osmani*. 4 vols. Istanbul: Matbaa-i Amire, 1308–16?/1891–9?.
Ménage, V.L. "Bashir Celebi." In *Encyclopaedia of Islam*, 2nd ed., edited by P.J. Bearman, Th. Bianquis, C.E. Bosworth, E. van Donzel, and W.P. Heinrichs, vol. 1, 1078. Leiden: Brill, 1960–2000.
Mengüç, Murat Cem. "A Study of 15th Century Ottoman Historiography." PhD diss., Cambridge: Cambridge University, 2007.
Messick, Brinkley. *The Calligraphic State: Textual Domination and History in a Muslim Society*. Berkeley: University of California Press, 1993.
Mordtmann, I.H., and V.L. Ménage. "Hasan Bey-Zade." In *Encyclopaedia of Islam*, 2nd ed., edited by P.J. Bearman, Th. Bianquis, C.E. Bosworth, E. van Donzel, and W.P. Heinrichs, vol. 3, 248–249. Leiden: Brill, 1960–2000.
Moser, Paul. *Philosophy after Objectivity*. Oxford: Oxford University Press, 1993.
Mouffe, Chantal. *Agonistics: Thinking the World Politically*. London: Verso, 2013.
Mufassal Osmanlı Tarihi, edited by an Anonymous Commission. Istanbul: Tan Matbaası, 1959.
Munslow, Alun. *The Future of History*. Basingstoke: Palgrave Macmillan, 2010.
———. *Deconstructing History*. London: Routledge, 1997.
Munslow, Alun and Robert A. Rosenstone, eds, *Experiments in Rethinking History*. London: Routledge, 2004.
Murphey, Rhoads. *Essays on Ottoman Historians and Historiography*. Istanbul: Eren, 2009.
———. *Ottoman Warfare, 1500–1700*. London: UCL Press, 1999.
———. "Ottoman Historical Writing in the Seventeenth-Century: A Survey of the General Development of the Genre after the Reign of Sultan Ahmed I (1603–1617)." *Archivum Ottomanicum* 13 (1993–1994): 277–312. Also published in Murphey, *Essays on Ottoman Historians and Historiography*, 89–119. Istanbul: Eren, 2009.
———. "The City of Belgrade in the Early Years of Serbian Self-Rule and Dual Administration with the Ottomans: Vignettes from Rashid's History Illuminating the Transformation of a Muslim Metropolis of the Balkans." In *Habsburgisch-osmanische Beziehungen Relations Habsburg-ottomanes Wien, 26–30. September 1983 Colloque sous le patronage du Comité international des études pré-ottomanes et ottomans*, edited by A. Tietze, 281–292. Wien: Verlag des Verbundes der wissenschaftlichen Gesellschaften Österreichs, 1985.
Mustafa Selaniki. *Tarih-i Selâniki*, edited by Mehmed İpşirli. Istanbul: Edebiyat Fakültesi Basımevi, 1989.
Nagel, Thomas. *View from Nowhere*. New York: Oxford University Press, 1986.
Naima. *Tarih-i Naima*. [also known as *Ravzatü'l-Hüseyn fî hulâsati ahbâri'l-hâfikayn*] Istanbul: Matbaa-i âmire, 1281–1283/1864–1866.
Nall, Cath. *Reading and War in Fifteenth Century England: From Lydgate to Malory*. Woodbridge: D.S. Brewer, 2012.
Namık Kemal. *Osmanlı Tarihi*. Istanbul: Mahmud Bey Matbaası, 1326/1908.
———. *Kanije*. Istanbul: Matbaa-i Ebüzziya, 1311/1893–1894.
———. *Silistre Muhasarası*. Istanbul: Teodor Kasap Matbaası, 1290/1873–1874.

Necipoğlu, Gülrü. "Süleyman the Magnificent and the Representation of Power in the Context of Ottoman-Habsburg-Papal Rivalry." In *Süleyman the Second and His Time*, edited by Halil İnalcık and Cemal Kafadar, 163–194. Istanbul: Isis Press, 1993.

Neumann, Christoph. "Bad Times and Better Self: Definitions of Identity and Strategies for Development in Late Ottoman Historiography, 1850–1900." In *The Ottomans and the Balkans: A Discussion of Historiography*, edited by Fikret Adanir and Suraiya Faroqhi, 57–78. Leiden, Boston and Köln: Brill, 2002.

Nicholson, P. "Poet and Scribe in the Manuscripts of Gower's *Confession Amantis*." In *Manuscripts and Texts: Editorial Problems in Later Middle English Literature*, edited by Derek Pearsall, 130–142. Woodbridge: D.S. Brewer, 1987.

Norton, Claire. "Iconographs of Power or Tools of Diplomacy? Ottoman *Fethnames*." *Journal of Early Modern History* 20 (2016): 331–350.

———. "Liminal Space in the Early Modern Ottoman-Habsburg Borderlands: Historiography, Ontology, and Politics." In *The Uses of Space in Early Modern History 1500–1850*, edited by Paul Stock, 75–96. New York: Palgrave Macmillan, 2015.

———. "Sacred Sites, Severed Heads and Prophetic Visions." *Journal of the Anthropology of the Contemporary Middle East and Central Eurasia* 2/1 (2014): 81–96.

———. "'Lords of Lewdness': Imagining the Infidel 'Other' in Ottoman *Fethnames*." In *Osmanischer Orient und Ostmitteleuropa*, edited by Robert Born and Andreas Puth, 281–299. Stuttgart: Steiner Verlag, 2014.

———. "Being Tiryaki Hasan Pasha: The Politico-Textual Appropriations of an Ottoman Hero." In *Frontiers of the Ottoman Imagination: Essays in Honour of Rhoads Murphey*, edited by Marios Hadjianastasis, 86–110. Leiden: Brill, 2014.

———. "East-West Dichotomy? Historiography as a 'Clash of Civilisations'." *Holy Land Studies* 10/1 (2011): 121–129.

———. "Terror and Toleration, East and West, Despotic and Free: Dichotomous Narratives and Representations of Islam." *Holy Land Studies* 7/2 (2008): 221–228.

———. "Nationalism and the Re-Invention of Early-Modern Identities in the Ottoman-Habsburg Borderlands." *Ethnologia Balkanica* 11 (2008): 79–101.

———. "Erasing Oral Residue and Correcting Scribal Error: Re-Interpreting the Presence of Mnemo-Technical Practices in Ottoman Manuscripts in the Early Modern Period." In *Culture of Memory in East Central and in the Late Middle Ages and Early Modern Period*, edited by Rafal Wojcik, 27–42. Poznan: Biblioteka Uniwersytecka, 2008.

———. "Smack-Head Hasan: Why Are All Turkic Superheroes Intemperate, Treacherous, or Stupid?" In *Super/Heroes: From Hercules to Superman*, edited by Angela Ndalianis, Chris Mackie, and Wendy Haslem, 263–274. Washington: New Academia Press, 2007.

———. "Narrating the 'Yoke of Oppression': Twentieth-Century Hungarian Scholarship of the Ottoman-Hungarian Borderlands." In *Nationalism, Historiography and the (Re)Construction of the Past*, edited by Claire Norton, 185–198. Washington: New Academia Press, 2007.

———. "'The Lutheran Is the Turks' Luck': Imagining Religious Identity, Alliance and Conflict on the Habsburg-Ottoman Marches in an Account of the Sieges of Nagykanizsa 1600 and 1601." In *Das Osmanische Reich und die Habsburgermonarchie in der Neuzeit. Akten des internationalen Kongress zum 150-jährigen Bestehen des Instituts für Österreichische Geschichtsforschung, Wien, 22.-25. September 2004*, edited by Marlene Kurz, Martin Scheutz, Karl Vocelka, and Thomas Winkelbauer, 65–79. Wien: Mitteilungen des Instituts für Österreichische Geschichtsforschung, 2005.

Norton, Claire, and Mark Donnelly. "Thinking the Past Politically: Palestine, Pedagogy, Power." *Rethinking History* 20/2 (2016): 192–216.

———. "The Siege, the Book and the Film: *Welcome to Sarajevo* (1997)." In *The Fiction of History*, edited by. A.L. MacFie, 85–105. London: Routledge, 2014.

Novick, Peter. *That Noble Dream: The "Objectivity Question" and the American Historical Profession*. Cambridge: Cambridge University Press, 1988.

Ocak, Ahmet Yaşar. *Kültür Tarihi Kaynaşı Olarak Menâkıbnâmeler (Metodolojik Bir Yaklaşım)*. Ankara: Türk Tarih Kurumu Basımevi, 1992.

———. *Türk Folklorunda Kesik Baş*. Ankara: Türk Kültürünü Araştırma Enstitüsü, 1989.

———. *Bektaşî Menâkıbnâmelerinde İslam Öncesi İnanç Motifleri*. Istanbul: Enderun Kitabevi, 1983.

Ochs, Eva. "Planned and Unplanned Discourse." In *Discourse and Syntax*, edited by T. Givon, 51–80. New York: New York Academic Press, 1979.

Oja, Matt F. "Fictional History and Historical Fiction: Solzhenitsyn and Kis as Exemplars." *History and Theory* 27/2 (1988): 111–124.

Olson, David. *The World on Paper: The Conceptual and Cognitive Implications of Writing and Reading*. Cambridge: Cambridge University Press, 1994.

———. "Literacy and Objectivity: The Rise of Modern Science." In *Literacy and Orality*, edited by David Olson and Nancy Torrance, 149–165. Cambridge: Cambridge University Press, 1991.

———. "Literacy as Metalinguistic Activity." In *Literacy and Orality*, edited by David Olson and Nancy Torrance, 251–270. Cambridge: Cambridge University Press, 1991.

———. "From Utterance to Text: The Bias of Language in Speech and Writing." *Harvard Educational Review* 47/3 (1977): 257–281.

Olson, David, and Nancy Torrance, eds. *Literacy and Orality*. Cambridge: Cambridge University Press, 1991.

Omurtak, Salih, Hasan Ali Yücel, İhsan Süngü, Enver Ziya Karal, Faik Reşat Unat, Enver Sökmen and Uluğ İğdemir, "Atatürk," in *İslam Ansiklopedisi: İslam Alemi Tarih, Coğrafya, Etnografya ve Biyografya Lugatı*, edited by İstanbul Üniversitesi Edebiyat Fakültesi, vol. 1, Istanbul: Milli Eğitim Basımevi, 1965.

Ong, Walter. *Orality and Literacy: The Technologizing of the Word*. London and New York: Methuen, 1982.

Orhonlu, Cengiz. *Osmanlı Tarihine âid Belgeler: Telhisler (1597–1607)*. İstanbul: Edebiyat Fakültesi Basımevi, 1970.

Orr, Linda. "Intimate Images: Subjectivity and History – Staël, Michelet and Tocqueville." In *A New Philosophy of History*, edited by Frank Ankersmit and Hans Kellner, 89–107. London: Reaktion Books, 1995.

Özcan, A. "Gazi." In *Türkiye Diyanet Vakfı İslam Ansiklopedisi*, vol. 13. Türkiye Diyanet Vakfı, İslâm Ansiklopedisi Genel Müdürlüğü, 443–445. Istanbul: Türkiye Diyanet Vakfı yayınları, 1998.

Özege, M. Seyfettin. *Eski Harflerle Basılmış Türkçe Eserler Kataloğu*. Istanbul: Fatih Yayınevi Matbaası, 1975.

Özel, A. "Cihad." In *Türkiye Diyanet Vakfı İslam Ansiklopedisi*, vol. 7. Türkiye Diyanet Vakfı, İslâm Ansiklopedisi Genel Müdürlüğü, 528–529. Istanbul: Türkiye Diyanet Vakfı yayınları, 1993.

Özgüç, Agah. *Türk Filmleri Sözlüğü:1980–1983*. Istanbul: Sıralar Matbaası, n.d.

Özkırımlı, Umit. *Theories of Nationalism: A Critical Introduction*. Basingstoke: Palgrave, 2000.

Pakalın, M.Z. *Osmanlı Tarih Deyimleri ve Terimleri Sözlüğü*. Istanbul: Milli Eğitim Bakanlığı Yayınları, 1993.

Bibliography

Pálffy, Géza. "The Origins and Developments of the Border Defence System against the Ottoman Empire in Hungary (Up to the Early Eighteenth Century)." In *Ottomans, Hungarians, and Habsburgs in Central Europe: The Military Confines in the Era of Ottoman Conquest*, edited by Géza Dávid and Pál Fodor, 3–69. Leiden, Boston and Köln: Brill, 2000.

Panaite, Viorel. "The *Re'ayas* of the Tributary-Protected Principalities: The Sixteenth through the Eighteenth Centuries." *International Journal of Turkish Studies* 9 (2003): 79–104.

Pandey, Gyanendra, ed. *Unarchived Histories: The "Mad" and the "Trifling" in the Colonial and Postcolonial World*. London: Routledge, 2014.

Pappé, Ilan. "The Old and New Conversations." In *On Palestine*, edited by Noam Chomsky and Ilan Pappé. London: Penguin, 2015.

Parks, Ward. "The Textualisation of Orality in Literary Criticism." In *Vox Intexta: Orality and Textuality in the Middle Ages*, edited by Alger N. Doane and Carol Braun Pasternack, 46–66. Madison: University of Wisconsin Press, 1991.

Parry, V.J. "Kanizsa." In *Encyclopaedia of Islam*, 2nd ed., edited by P.J. Bearman, Th. Bianquis, C.E. Bosworth, E. van Donzel, and W.P. Heinrichs, vol. 4, 546. Leiden: Brill, 1960–2000.

Partner, Nancy. "Historicity in an Age of Reality-Fictions." In *A New Philosophy of History*, edited by Frank Ankersmit and Hans Kellner, 21–39. London: Reaktion Books, 1995.

Paul, Herman. *Hayden White: The Historical Imagination*. Cambridge: Polity, 2011.

Pearsall, Derek, ed. *New Directions in Later Medieval Manuscript Studies*. York: York Medieval Press, 2000.

———, ed. *Manuscripts and Texts: Editorial Problems in Later Middle English Literature*. Woodbridge: D.S. Brewer, 1987.

———. "Texts, Textual Criticism, and Fifteenth-Century Manuscript Production." In *Fifteenth-Century Studies*, edited by R. Yeager, 121–136. Hamden: Archon, 1984.

———, ed. *Manuscripts and Readers in Fifteenth Century England*. Woodbridge: D. Brewer, 1981.

Pedani, Maria Pia. "Ottoman *Fetihnames*: The Imperial Letters Announcing a Victory." *Tarih incelemeleri dergisi* 13 (1998): 181–192.

———, ed. *I "Documenti turchi" dell'Archivio di Stato di Venezia*. Roma: Instituto Poligrafico e Zecca dello Stato, 1994.

Peirce, Leslie. *The Imperial Harem: Women and Sovereignty in the Ottoman Empire*. New York and Oxford: Oxford University Press, 1993.

Penzi, Marco. "From 'Frenchman' to Crusader: The Political and Military Itinerary of Philippe Emmanuel Duke of Mercoeur (1558–1602)." In *Türkenkriege und Adelskultur in Ostmitteleuropa vom 16. bis zum 18. Jahrundert*, edited by Robert Born and Sabine Jagodzinski, 155–163. Ostfildern: Thorbecke Jan Verlag, 2014.

Pertsch, W. *Verzeichniss der türkischen Handschriften der Königlichen Bibliothek zu Berlin*. Berlin: A. Asher & Co., 1889.

Pichler, Franz. "Captain John Smith in the Light of the Styrian Sources." *The Virginia Magazine of History and Biography* 65 (1957): 332–354.

Pihlainen, Kalle. "Escaping the Confines of History: Keith Jenkins." *Rethinking History* 17/2 (2013): 235–252.

———. "Towards a Post-Problematic History." Paper given at the Philosophy of History Seminar at the Institute of Historical Research, London: University of London, November 22nd 2012.

———. "Narrative Objectivity versus Fiction: On the Ontology of Historical Narratives." *Rethinking History: The Journal of Theory and Practice* 2/1 (1998): 7–22.
Piterberg, Gabriel. *An Ottoman Tragedy: History and Historiography at Play*. Berkeley: University of California Press, 2003.
———. "Speech Acts and Written Texts: A Reading of a Seventeenth-Century Ottoman Historiographic Episode." *Poetics Today* 14/2 (1993): 387–418.
———. "A Study of Ottoman Historiography in the Seventeenth Century." PhD diss., Oxford: Oxford University, 1992.
Pollock, Sheldon, ed. *Literary Cultures in History: Reconstructions from South Asia*. Berkeley: University of California Press, 2003.
Price, Richard. *First-Time: The Historical Vision of an African American People*, 2nd ed. Chicago: University of Chicago Press, 2002.
———. *Alibi's World*. Baltimore: Johns Hopkins University Press, 1990.
Rader, Margaret. "Context in Written Language: The Case of Imaginative Fiction." In *Spoken and Written Language: Exploring Orality and Literacy*, edited by Deborah Tannen, 185–198. Norwood, NJ: Ablex, 1982.
Radlov, Vasiliĭ V., ed. *Proben der Volkslitteratur der türkischen Stämme Südsibiriens und der Dsungarischen Steppe*. St Petersburg: Kaiserl. Akad. d. Wiss, 1866–1904.
Ramberg, Bjørn. "Richard Rorty." In *The Stanford Encyclopaedia of Philosophy*, Spring 2009 ed., edited by Edward N. Zalta. http://plato.stanford.edu/archives/spr2009/entries/rorty/ (accessed on 24/08/16)
Ramirez, Horacio N. Roque. "A Living Archive of Desire: Teresita la Capesina and the Embodiment of Queer Latino Community History." In *Archive Stories: Facts, Fictions and the Writing of History*, edited by Antoinette Burton, 111–135. Durham: Duke University Press, 2005.
Rasim, A. *Şehir Mektupları*. İstanbul: Milli Eğitim Basımevi, 1971.
Redhouse, James W. *Redhouse Turkish-English Dictionary*, 18th ed. Istanbul: Redhouse Yayınevi, 1991.
———. *A Turkish and English Lexicon*. Beirut: Librairie de Liban, 1974.
Rieff, David. *In Praise of Forgetting*. New Haven: Yale University Press, 2016.
Rieu, Charles. *Catalogue of the Turkish Manuscripts in the British Museum*. London: British Library, 1888.
Rigney, Ann. "Being an Improper Historian." In *Manifestos for History*, edited by Keith Jenkins, Sue Morgan, and Alun Munslow, 149–159. London: Routledge, 2007.
Rohlf, Michael. "Immanuel Kant." In *The Stanford Encyclopedia of Philosophy*, Spring 2016 ed., edited by Edward N. Zalta. http://plato.stanford.edu/archives/spr2016/entries/kant/ (accessed 24/8/16)
Rorty, Richard. *Truth and Progress: Philosophical Papers*, vol. 3. Cambridge: Cambridge University Press, 1998.
———. "Representation, Social Practise, and Truth." In *Objectivity, Relativism and Truth: Philosophical Papers*, edited by Richard Rorty, vol. 1, 151–161. Cambridge: Cambridge University Press, 1991.
———. *Objectivity, Relativism and Truth: Philosophical Papers*, vol. 1. Cambridge: Cambridge University Press, 1991.
Rosen, V. *Remarques sur les manuscrits orientaux de la collection Marsigli à Bologne suivies de la liste complète des manuscrits arabes de la même collection*. Roma: Imprimerie de l'Académie royale des Lyncei, 1885.
Rosenstone, Robert A. "Space for the Bird to Fly." In *Manifestos for History*, edited by Keith Jenkins, Sue Morgan, and Alun Munslow, 11–18. London: Routledge, 2007.

―――. *Visions of the Past: The Challenge of Film to our Idea of History*. Cambridge, MA and London: Harvard University Press, 1995.

Rosenthal, Franz, trans. *The History of al-Tabari (Ta'rikh al-rusul wa'l-muluk)*, vol. 1 *General Introduction and from the Creation to the Flood*. Albany: State University of New York Press, 1989.

Rothman, Natalie. "Afterword: Intermediaries, Mediation, and Cross-Confessional Diplomacy in the Early Modern Mediterranean." *Journal of Early Modern History* 19 (2015): 245–259.

Russett, Bruce M., John R. Oneal, and Michaelene Cox. "Clash of Civilizations, or Realism and Liberalism Déjà Vu? Some Evidence." *Journal of Peace Research* 37/5 (2000): 583–608.

Ryan, Marie-Laure. "Truth without Scare Quotes: Post-Sokalian Genre Theory." *New Literary History* 29/4 (1998): 811–830.

Sacco, Joe. *Footnotes in Gaza*. London: Jonathan Cape, 2009.

―――. *Safe Area Goražde*. London: Jonathan Cape, 2007.

―――. *Palestine*. London: Jonathan Cape, 2003.

Saenger, Paul. "The Separation of Words and the Physiology of Reading." In *Literacy and Orality*, edited by David Olson and Nancy Torrance, 198–214. Cambridge: Cambridge University Press, 1991.

Said, Edward. "The Clash of Ignorance." *The Nation* (October 2001). http://thenation.com/article/clash-ignorance (accessed 5/8/15)

―――. "Permission to Narrate." *Journal of Palestine Studies* 13/3 (1984): 27–48.

Sautman, Francesca, Diana Conchado, and Giuseppe Carlo Di Scipio, "Texts and Shadows: Traces, Narratives, and Folklore." In *Telling Tales: Medieval Narratives and the Folk Tradition*, edited by Francesca Sautman, Diana Conchado, and Giuseppe Carlo Di Scipio, 1–17. Basingstoke: Macmillan, 1998.

Savaşkurt, Avni. *Kanije Müdafaası*. İstanbul: Askeri Mecmua 138 sayılı Askeri Matbaası, 1945.

Schaefer, Ursula. "Hearing from Books: The Rise of Fictionality in Old English Poetry." In *Vox Intexta: Orality and Textuality in the Middle Ages*, edited by Alger N. Doane and Carol Braun Pasternack, 117–136. Madison: University of Wisconsin Press, 1991.

Schemann, Hans, and Paul Knight. *German-English Dictionary of Idioms*. London and New York: Routledge, 1995.

Schmidt, Jan. "The Egri-Campaign of 1596: Military History and the Problem of Sources." In *Habsburgisch-osmanische Beziehungen – Relations habsbourg-ottomanes Wien, 26.-30. September 1983: Colloque sous le patronage du Comité international des études pre-ottomanes et ottomans*, edited by Andreas Tietze, 125–144. Wien: Verlag des Verbandes der wissenschaftlichen Gesellschaften Österreichs, 1985.

Scott, Joan W. "History-Writing as Critique." In *Manifestos for History*, edited by Keith Jenkins, Sue Morgan, and Alun Munslow, 19–38. London: Routledge, 2007.

Sebastian, Peter. "Ottoman Government Officials and Their Relations with the Republic of Venice in the Early Sixteenth Century." In *Studies in Ottoman History in Honour of Professor V.L. Ménage*, edited by Colin Heywood and Colin Imber, 319–338. Istanbul: Isis Press, 1994.

Sen, Amartya. "Democracy as a Universal Value." *Journal of Democracy* 10/3 (1999): 3–17.

Shapiro, Michael J. *Violent Cartographies: Mapping Cultures of War*. Minneapolis: University of Minnesota Press, 1997.

Sharp, Tony. *Pleasure and Ambition: The Life, Loves and Wars of Augustus the Strong 1670–1707*. London: I.B. Tauris, 2001.

Silay, Kemal, "The Usage and Function of Digression in Ahmedi's History of the Ottoman Dynasty." *Turcica* 25 (1993): 143–151.
Simon, Bryant. "Narrating a Southern Tragedy: Historical Facts and Historical Fictions." In *Experiments in Rethinking History*, edited by Alun Munslow and Robert A. Rosenstone, 156–182. London: Routledge, 2004.
Simon, Roger I. *The Touch of the Past: Remembrance, Learning, and Ethics*. Basingstoke: Palgrave Macmillan, 2005.
Smith, John. *The True Travels, Adventures and Observations of Captain John Smith, In Europe, Asia, Affrica, and America, from Anno Domini 1593 to 1629 [. . .]*. London: printed by J. H. for Thomas Slater, and are to be sold at the Blew Bible in Greene Arbour, 1630.
Southgate, Beverley. "'Humani nil alienum': The Quest for 'Human Nature'." In *Manifestos for History*, edited by Keith Jenkins, Sue Morgan, and Alun Munslow, 67–76. London: Routledge, 2007.
———. *What Is History For?* London: Routledge, 2005.
Spiegel, Gabriel. "History and Postmodernism." In *The Postmodern History Reader*, edited by Keith Jenkins, 260–273. London and New York: Routledge, 1997.
———. "History, Historicism and the Social Logic of the Text in the Middle Ages." In *The Postmodern History Reader*, edited by K. Jenkins, 180–203. London and New York: Routledge, 1997.
Stavrides, Théoharis. *The Sultan of Vezirs: The Life and Times of the Ottoman Grand Vezir Mahmud Pasha Angelović (1453–1474)*. Leiden: Brill, 2001.
Stein, J.M. "A Letter to Queen Elizabeth I from the Grand Vezir as a Source for the Study of Ottoman Diplomacy." *Archivum Ottomanicum* 11 (1986): 231–247.
Stein, Mark. *Guarding the Frontier: Ottoman Border Forts and Garrisons in Europe*. London and New York: Tauris Academic Studies, 2007.
———. "Seventeenth-Century Ottoman Forts and Garrisons on the Habsburg Frontier (Hungary)." PhD diss., Chicago: The University of Chicago, 2001.
Steingass, Francis Joseph. *A Comprehensive Persian-English Dictionary: Including the Arabic Words and Phrases to be Met with in Persian Literature*, 9th ed. London and New York: Routledge, 1995.
Stich, Stephen. *The Fragmentation of Reason*. Cambridge, MA: MIT Press, 1990.
Stitt, Michael J. "Ambiguity in the Battle of Þórr and Hrungnir." In *Telling Tales: Medieval Narratives and the Folk Tradition*, edited by Francesca Canadé Sautman, Diana Conchado, and Giuseppe C. Di Scipio, 121–136. Basingstoke: Macmillan, 1998.
Stoljar, D. "The Deflationary Theory of Truth." In *The Stanford Encyclopaedia of Philosophy*, Summer 1997 ed., edited by E. Zalta. http://plato.stanford.edu/archives/summer1997/entries/Deflationary theory of truth/ (accessed on 24/8/16)
Strauss, Johann. "Ottoman Rule Experienced and Remembered: Remarks on Some Local Greek Chronicles of the Tourkokratia." In *The Ottomans and the Balkans: A Discussion of Historiography*, edited by Fikret Adanir and Suraiya Faroqhi, 193–221. Leiden, Boston and Köln: Brill, 2002.
Street, Brian. *Literacy in Theory and Practice*. Cambridge: Cambridge University Press, 1984.
Strohm, Paul. "Chaucer's Audiences: Fictional, Implied, Intended, Actual." *The Chaucer Review* 18/2 (1983): 137–145.
Subrahmanyam, Sanjay. *Courtly Encounters: Translating Courtliness and Violence in Early Modern Eurasia*. Cambridge: Cambridge University Press, 2012.
Sugar, Peter. *A History of Hungary*. London: I.B. Tauris, 1990.

———. *South Eastern Europe under Ottoman Rule, 1354–1804: A History of East Central Europe*. Seattle and London: University of Washington Press, 1977.

———. "The Ottoman 'Professional Prisoner' on the Western Borders of the Empire in the Sixteenth and Seventeenth Centuries." *Études Balkaniques* 7 (1971): 82–91.

Suleiman, Susan. *Authoritarian Fictions: The Ideological Novel as a Literary Genre*. New York: Columbia University Press, 1983.

Suleiman, Susan, and Inge Crosman, "Introduction." In *The Reader in the Text: Essays on Audience and Interpretation*, edited by Susan Suleiman and Inge Crosman, 3–45. Princeton: Princeton University Press, 1980.

Süreyya, Mehmed. *Sicill-i Osmani*, 4 vols. Istanbul: Matbaa-i Amire, 1308–1316?/1891–1899?.

Sydnor, Synthia. "A History of Synchronized Swimming." *Journal of Sport History* 25/2 (1998): 252–267. http://www.aafla.org/SportsLibrary/JSH/JSH1998/JSH2502/JSH2502e.pdf (accessed 6/12/12)

Szakály, Ferenc. "The Early Ottoman Period, Including Royal Hungary, 1526–1606." In *A History of Hungary*, edited by Peter Sugar, 83–99. Bloomingdale: Indiana University Press, 1990.

Taithe, Bertrand, and Tim Thornton. "Identifying War: Conflict and Self-Definition in Western Europe." In *War: Identities in Conflict 1300–2000*, edited by Bertrand Taithe and Tim Thornton, 1–20. Stroud: Sutton Publishing, 1998.

Talikizade. *Şeyname-i Hümayun*. Istanbul: Türk ve İslam Eserleri Müzesi, no. 1965.

Tannen, Deborah. "What's in a Frame? Surface Evidence for Underlying Expectations." In *Framing in Discourse*, edited by Deborah Tannen, 14–56. Oxford: Oxford University Press, 1993. Also in *New Directions in Discourse Processing*, edited by R. Freedle, 137–181. Norwood, NJ: Ablex, 1979.

———. "Introduction." In *Framing in Discourse*, edited by Deborah Tannen, 3–13. Oxford: Oxford University Press, 1993.

———. "The Orality of Literature and the Literacy of Conversation." In *Language, Literacy and Culture: Issues of Society and Schooling*, edited by J. Langer, 67–88. Norwood, NJ: Ablex, 1987.

———. "Relative Focus on Involvement in Oral and Written Discourse." In *Literacy, Language and Learning: The Nature and Consequences of Reading and Writing*, edited by David Olson, Nancy Torrance, and Angela Hildyard, 124–147. Cambridge: Cambridge University Press, 1985.

———. "Spoken and Written Narrative in English and Greek." In *Coherence in Spoken and Written Discourse*, edited by Deborah Tannen, 21–41. Norwood, NJ: Ablex, 1984.

———. "Oral and Literate Strategies in Spoken and Written Discourse." In *Literacy for Life: The Demand for Reading and Writing*, edited by R.W. Bailey and R.M. Fosheim, 79–96. New York: Modern Language Association, 1983.

———. "Oral and Literate Strategies in Spoken and Written Narratives." *Language* 58 (1982): 1–21.

———. "The Oral/Literate Continuum in Discourse." In *Spoken and Written Language: Exploring Orality and Literacy*, edited by Deborah Tannen, 1–16. Norwood, NJ: Ablex, 1982.

Tannus, ibn Yusuf Shidyaq, and Butrus Bustānī. *Kitab-i akhbar al-aʿyan fi Djabal Lubnan*. Beirut, 1859.

Tarama Sözlüğü II C-D XIII. Yüzyıldan Beri Türkiye Türkçesiyle Yazılmış Kitaplardan Toplanan Tanıklarıyla. Türk Dil Kurumu Yayınları sayı: 212. Ankara: Türk Tarih Kurumu Basımevi, 1965.

Tedlock, Dennis. "The Speaker of Tales Has More Than One String to Play On." In *Vox Intexta: Orality and Textuality in the Middle Ages*, edited by Alger N. Doane and Carol Braun Pasternack, 5–33. Madison: University of Wisconsin Press, 1991.
Tezcan, Baki. "The Politics of Early Modern Ottoman Historiography." In *The Early Modern Ottomans: Remapping the Empire*, edited by Virginia H. Aksan and Daniel Goffman, 167–198. Cambridge: Cambridge University Press, 2007.
Thomas, Lewis Victor. *A Study of Naima*, edited by Norman Itzkowitz. New York: New York University Press, 1972.
Toews, John E. "Intellectual History after the Linguistic Turn: The Autonomy of Meaning and the Irreducibility of Experience." *American Historical Review* 92 (1987): 879–907.
Troyan, Scott David. *Textual Decorum: A Rhetoric of Attitudes in Medieval Literature*. New York and London: Garland Publishing, Inc., 1994.
Türk Ansiklopedisi. Ankara: Milli Eğitim Basmevi, 1971.
Unat, Faik R. *Hicrî Tarihleri Milâdî Tarihe Çevirme Kilavuzu*. Ankara: Türk Tarih Kurumu Basımevi, 1959.
Ursinus, Michael. "Gazette and Independent: Early Disputes between Ottoman Newspapers, Metropolitan versus Provincial." In *Querelles privées et contestations publiques. Le rôle de la presse dans la formation de l'opinion publique au Proche Orient*, edited by Christoph Herzog, Raoul Motika, and Michael Ursinus, 99–114. Istanbul: Isis Press, 2002.
———. "Midhat Efendi at TUNA." In *Amtsblatt, vilayet gazetesi und unabhängiges Journal: Die Anfänge der Presse im Nahen Osten*, edited by Anja Pistor-Hatam, 47–54. Frankfurt: Peter Lang, 2001.
Vardarli, Emel, Ayla Bayaz, Ömer Asım Aksoy, Cem Dilçin, Perihan Kutlar, Meral Tolluoğlu, Günay Atabey, Ayla Çıngı, Güneş Bayraktaroğlu, Aysel Barlas, Aysel Dikmen, Olcay Sarıbaş, Aycan Ünver, and Şakir Ülkütaşır. *Türkiye'de Halk Ağzından Derleme Sözlüğü*. vol. 10. S-T Türk Dil Kurumu Yayınları – Sayı: 211/10. Ankara: Türk Tarih Kurumu Basmevi, 1978.
Walker, Jonathan. *Pistols! Treason! Murder!: The Rise and Fall of a Master Spy*. Baltimore: Johns Hopkins University Press, 2007.
Wearden, Jennifer. "Siegmund von Herberstein: An Italian Velvet in the Ottoman Court." *Costume* 19 (1985): 22–29.
Weeks, Linton. "The No-Book Report: Skim It and Weep." *Washington Post* (May 14, 2001): CO1.
Wehr, Hans. *A Dictionary of Modern Written Arabic*, 3rd ed., edited by J. Milton Cowan. New York: Spoken Language Services, Inc., 1976.
Wessely, Kurt. "The Development of the Hungarian Military Frontier until the Middle of the Eighteenth Century." *The Austrian History Yearbook* 9–10 (1973–1974): 55–110.
White, Hayden. *The Practical Past*. Evanstone: Northwestern University Press, 2014.
———. "Historical Emplotment and the Problem of Truth." In *The Postmodern History Reader*, edited by K. Jenkins, 392–396. London and New York: Routledge, 1997.
———. *The Content of the Form: Narrative Discourse and Historical Representation*. Baltimore and London: John Hopkins University Press, 1987.
———. "The Historical Text as Literary Artifact." In *The Writing of History: Literary Form and Historical Understanding*, edited by R.H. Canary and H. Kozicki, 41–62. Madison: University of Wisconsin Press, 1978.

———. "The Fictions of Factual Representation." In *Tropics of Discourse: Essays in Cultural Criticism*, edited by Hayden White, 121–134. Baltimore: John Hopkins University Press, 1978.

———. "History, Historicism and the Figurative Imagination." *History and Theory* 14 (1975): 48–67.

———. "The Burden of History." *History and Theory* 5 (1966): 111–134.

Will, Frederick. *Pragmatism and Realism*. Lanham and New York: Rowman and Littlefield Publishers, Inc., 1997.

Wittgenstein, Ludwig. *Philosophical Investigations*, edited by G.E.M. Anscombe, R. Rhees, and G.H. von Wright, translated by G.E.M. Anscombe. Oxford: Basil Blackwell, 1958.

Woodhead, Christine M. "Fetihnāme." In *Encyclopedia of Islam, THREE*, edited by Kate Fleet, Gudrun Krämer, Denis Matringe, John Nawas, and Everett Rowson. Leiden: Brill, 2014. http://dx.doi.org/10.1163/1573-3912_ei3_COM_27035 (accessed 22/7/16)

———. "Taliqizade Mehmed." In *Historians of the Ottoman Empire*, edited by Cemal Kafadar, Hakan Karateke, and Cornell Fleischer, 2005. https://ottomanhistorians.uchicago.edu/en/historian/taliqizade-mehmed (accessed 26/6/16)

———. "The Ottoman Gazaname: Stylistic Influences on the Writing of Campaign Narratives." In *The Great Ottoman-Turkish Civilization*, vol. 3 *Philosophy, Science and Institutions*, edited by Kemal Çiçek, Ercüment Kuran, Nejat Göyünç, Halil İnalcık, İlber Ortaylı, and Güler Eren, 55–60. Ankara: Yeni Türkiye, 2000.

———. "Ottoman Historiography on the Hungarian Campaigns: 1596 the Eger Fethnamesi." In *VII. CIÉPO Sempozyumu [Proceedings of the VIIth Conference of the Comité des Études Ottomanes et Pré-Ottomanes (CIÉPO), at Pécs, Hungary, 1986]*, edited by J.L. Bacqué-Grammont, İ. Ortaylı, and E. van Donzel, 469–477. Ankara: Türk Tarih Kurumu Basımevi, 1994.

———, ed. *Talikizade's Şehname-i Hümayun: A History of the Ottoman Campaign into Hungary, 1593–94*. Berlin: Klaus Schwarz Verlag, 1983.

———. "Tarikh." In *Encyclopaedia of Islam*, 2nd ed., edited by P.J. Bearman, Th. Bianquis, C.E. Bosworth, E. van Donzel, and W.P. Heinrichs, vol. 10, 290–295. Leiden: Brill, 1960–2000.

Zellermayer, Michal. "An Analysis of Oral and Literate Texts: Two Types of Reader-Writer Relationship in Hebrew and English." In *The Social Construction of Written Communication*, edited by Bennett A. Raforth and Donald L. Rubin, 287–303. Norwood, NJ: Ablex, 1988.

Zimmermann, W.P. *Eikonographia aller deren ungarischer Statt Vostunge Castellen und Hauser welche von Anfang der Regierung Rudolphi des anderen Romischen Keyser biss auffdas 1603 [. . .]*. Augsburg, 1603.

Zumthor, Paul. *La Lettre et la Voix: De la "littérature" medieval*. Paris: Seuil, 1987.

Zürcher, Erik. "The Vocabulary of Muslim Nationalism." *International Journal of the Sociology of Science* 137 (1999): 81–92.

———. *Turkey: A Modern History*. London and New York: I.B. Tauris and Co. Ltd., 1997.

Zwaan, R.A. "Effect of Genre Expectations on Text Comprehension." *Journal of Experimental Psychology: Learning, Memory, and Cognition* 20/4 (1994): 920–933.

Index

academic praxis and scholarship 9, 22, 25–6, 30, 31n21, 34, 56, 112, 113, 116, 117, 120, 125n27, 126–7n41, 134, 142n34, 155
Ahmed Refik 131, 132, 140n10, 141n18, 142–3n34
annotation *see* marginalia
anthology 101n32–3, 104n81
Arabic 13n7, 24, 36, 48n4, 57, 58, 61, 69n10, 78, 81, 84, 103n63, 112, 113
audience 6, 7, 8, 11, 15n17, 16n26, 17n27, 26, 34, 35–6, 44, 46n1, 49n10, 56, 58, 74n58, 74n55, 76, 79, 82, 96–8, 99n9, 104n91, 105nn102–3, 108, 109, 111, 114, 115, 116, 119, 133, 139, 140n10, 147, 154, 155; academic 112–3; actual 17n29, 65, 83, 84; English 37–9; expectations 11, 36, 98; implied 9, 10, 12, 17n29, 20, 23, 36, 43, 60, 62, 65, 66, 77, 78, 83–4, 87, 88, 90, 91, 94, 95, 97, 107, 153; intended 17n29, 24, 25, 37, 45, 55, 97, 107; listening 57, 66–7, 68n7, 69n10, 96, 101n35, 113; reading 67, 81–2, 83–4
author 7, 8, 17n29, 43, 55, 57, 60–1, 84–5, 107, 108, 110, 111, 113, 126n41, 132–3, 139; authorial meaning 7; authorial scribes 7, 84–5, 101n38, 108; authorial work 17n30, 56, 59–60; copying authors 7; implied 96; intentions 7, 98; original 7, 9, 17n30, 59–61, 97; *see also* scribe; citation practices
authority 59–60, 63, 64, 73n46, 85–6, 112
Azazel 109–10, 121, 125n13, 125n15

Babócsa (Bubofca) castle 37, 93
Barthélemy de Cœur 37, 40, 50n23, 52n38

Baysun, Cavid 32n24, 47n2, 130, 134, 136, 137, 138, 139, 143n37, 143n48, 143n49, 144n51, 144n54, 144n61, 145n66
Book of the Other Campaign Narratives 83–4
borders *see* Ottoman-Habsburg marches
Budapest Magyar Tudományos Akademia Konyvtara O.216 (BMTAK) 61, 67, 72n33, 82–4, 91, 98n2, 99n3

Câfer Iyânî 61, 107, 137
Cambridge: University Library, O.R.700 (CUL: O.R.700) 84–8, 91, 94, 96, 98n2, 100n16, 101n38, 104n81
Christianity 36, 38–41, 44, 53n44, 87, 88, 89, 97, 104nn90–2, 109, 143n46, 144n57, 155; Ottoman Christians 38–9, 93, 94, 136, 144n53, 144n57
Christian-Muslim: alliances 39–40, 45–6, 87; antipathy 12, 39, 97, 136, 154; co-existence and co-operation 46, 87, 93–4, 151, 154–5
citation practices 22, 31n21, 107–11, 117–18, 120, 121–4, 132–4, 142n31, 142n34; *see also* Fa'izi
clash of civilisations 12, 154, 155, 158n43
contextualised discourse 22, 58, 133; *see also* decontextualised discourse
copyist 57, 60–1, 62, 66, 77, 80, 84; *see also* scribe
correspondence 19, 20, 147; ambassadorial 12; between Ottoman and Habsburg border commanders 145n64; between Zirinoğlu and Tiryaki Hasan Pasha 86, 102n53; grand vizierial *see telhis*; inter-state (diplomatic) 8, 33–46, 53n44; letter from Tiryaki Hasan Pasha to grand vizier 28, 29

186 Index

Dagenais, John 17n27, 59–60, 62; see also ethical reading
David and Goliath 78, 80, 99n12, 99–100n12
Davies, Martin 2, 150–1
decontextualised discourse 24, 32n28, 36, 58, 112, 125n27, 126n27, 127n41; see also contextualised discourse
digression 9, 10, 65, 66, 68n7, 69n10, 80, 81, 82, 88, 89, 100n16, 105n103
diplomacy 35, 36, 42–4, 46, 49n10, 154
discourse of authority 59–62, 67, 78, 99n9; see also performative model

Eger castle 35, 40, 41, 47n4, 53n39, 68n3
Eger *fethname* see *fethnames*
elites 23–4, 26, 35, 57, 77, 90–1, 95, 97, 101n43, 102n49, 110, 131, 136, 144n57, 151
Elizabeth I 8, 9, 17n29, 21, 33, 36, 37, 40, 43, 45, 47n4, 49n10, 50n18, 50n23, 51n33, 81
episodic narrative see narrative
epistemology 4–6, 14–15n13, 34, 114–17, 152; correspondence between histories and a past reality 4, 5, 11, 26, 30, 34, 111, 114–16, 117, 123, 133, 152, 153; correspondence theory of knowledge 14–15n13, 115; correspondence theory of truth 4, 15n15; non-representationalim 5, 11, 15n15, 126n35, 147; representationalism 5, 15n15, 19, 30n1, 113, 115–6, 123
Ersever, H.Z. 132, 134, 136, 141–2n25, 144n61
Esztergom 41
ethically-engaged scholarship 149–52, 155
ethical reading 8, 10, 17n27, 56, 62–5, 67, 73n40, 73n44, 80, 97, 110, 121, 122, 128n57
ethical viewing 73n43
experimental histories 148
eyewitness accounts 1, 8, 19–26, 30, 120, 152

facts: blurring the facts 33–4; factual status 147; see also fiction
Fa'izi 11, 132–4, 139, 141n23
fethnames 1, 8, 9, 17n29, 21, 33–46, 46nn1–2, 47n4, 49n10, 50n15, 50n23, 67n2, 81, 114, 120, 123, 128n67, 154; Eger *fethname* 34–5, 37, 39, 40, 41, 47n3, 49n10, 49n14; grand vizierial Nagykanizsa *fethname* 36, 39, 41, 42–6, 47n2, 49n10, 50n18; literary *fethname* 49–50n1, 49n11; sultanic Nagykanizsa *fethname* 36–42, 47n2, 49n10, 50n18
fiction 6, 34, 76; categorisation 10; fact-fiction distinction 4, 6, 34, 48n9, 108, 111–17, 151; fictional historians see Fa'izi; fictionalisation 9, 27; fictive events 26, 114; making fiction fact 11, 111–17, 123, 132–4, 152
framing 6, 10, 19, 27, 28, 36, 43, 74n48, 77–82, 83, 92, 107, 110–17, 123, 127n41, 133, 139, 154
Frenk soldiers 26, 45–6, 52n34–5

gaza (campaign) 39, 61, 67, 79, 80, 98n2, 120
gazavatnames 1, 7, 25, 26, 28, 41, 55–6, 76; endings 80–2; ethical reading 62–5; framings 77–8; *Gazavat-i Sultan Murad b. Mehemmed Han* 71n26; *Gazavat-i Tiryaki Hasan Paşa* corpus 7, 9, 23, 55–7, 60, 66, 97, 107, 122; introductions 78–80; models for interpretation 55–67; rubrication 76–7; scribal re-inscription 59–62; see also Budapest Magyar Tudományos Akademia Konyvtara, O.216; Cambridge: University Library, O.R.700; London: British Library, O.R.12961; oral characteristics; typographic model
gazi (warrior) 61, 67, 70n13, 82, 83, 85, 91, 96–7, 100n29, 101n35, 110, 119, 127, 137
genre: boundaries 67–8n2, 139; classification 58, 77, 108, 123–4, 147; conventions 11, 111, 116, 133, 155; fluidity 98, 148
gift-giving 85–6, 91, 96, 102n48–51
glossing 59, 60, 78, 84, 100n13, 110, 121
Goliath see David and Goliath
Görösgál 92, 99n11, 118
grammar 141; corrections 61; 1 fluid 9, 24, 57, 60, 68n6; incorrect (unusual) 69n10, 71n25; stable 6, 61

Habsburgs 37–9, 52n36, 63; alliances with Hungarians 86–7; alliances with other Christian countries 39–40, 45–6, 51n33; as the enemy other 37–8, 81; relief army 37

Haile-i Osmaniye 2, 13n7, 118, 120, 128n67
Hasan Beyzade 8, 19, 20–1, 22, 23, 24, 26, 42, 107, 111, 114, 117, 120, 123, 128n67, 124n3, 144n61; Nagykanizsa *fethname* 31–46, 47n2
hatt-i hümayun (imperial rescript) 110, 111
hikaye (story) 76, 98n2, 176
historical method 5, 116
horizon of expectation 8, 10, 16n26, 43, 76, 79, 111, 112
Hungarian 1, 86–7, 93, 105n102, 131–2, 137; forces 86; historians 22, 50n18; Hungarian-Habsburg alliance 87, 93, 138; infidels (enemy) 26, 93, 132, 136, 137; king 86–7, 102n56; Ottomans 26, 93, 97, 105n102, 155; sources 25; *see also* Ibrahim Peçevi
Hungarian borderlands *see* Ottoman-Habsburg marches

Ibrahim Pasha (grand vizier) 9, 24, 27, 32n38, 32n38, 42, 95, 118, 138, 142n28, 142n33
Ibrahim Peçevi 8, 20, 21–2, 23, 25–6, 42, 92, 104n80, 107, 111, 113, 114, 120, 122, 124n3, 127n55, 134, 142n31, 142n34, 144n61
identity: alternate 89; imagination (performance) of 3, 35, 37, 58, 77, 130, 139, 153; late Ottoman 130–1; national 11, 129–30; self and other 9, 12, 26, 35, 38, 39, 44, 49n10, 89, 93–5, 94, 97, 131–2, 134, 136–8, 139, 153, 154, 155; shared identities 35, 37, 89; Turkish 134–9
illiteracy 10, 57–8
implied audience *see* audience
infidels 26, 36, 37, 94, 131–2, 137
inşa collections 8, 33, 47n3, 48n4, 49n14, 50n15
interpretative communities 3, 7, 8, 10, 16n23, 56, 77, 82, 84, 98, 108, 117, 147, 152, 153
interpretative frameworks 4, 5, 10, 12, 16n26, 19, 74n48, 81, 82, 83, 110, 115, 147, 154, 155; *see also* framing
interpretative naming 37, 92, 94, 100n29, 108, 131, 141n18
interpretative practices 7, 80, 108, 115, 149, 153
intertextuality 10, 22–3, 27, 31n21, 92, 97, 107, 108, 109, 111, 112, 133, 137, 142n31

jihad 37, 39, 137, 154
justice 80–2, 87–8, 89, 100n21

Katib Çelebi 7, 10–11, 17n29, 17n31, 20, 26, 53nn45–6, 60–1, 64, 104n90, 105n104, 107–14, 117–19, 120, 121–4, 124n1, 124n3, 125n13, 125nn16–17, 125n21, 126n30, 126n34, 128n58, 128n62, 131, 133, 137, 139, 145n69, 152
kesik baş (severed head) literature 74n47, 79, 89, 92

Lala Mehmed Pasha 26, 121, 141n23
liberation historiography 151, 158n30
literacy 97; interiorised literacy 10, 56, 57, 58, 65, 97; linear model of literacy 58; literacy practices 2, 3, 7, 8, 9, 10, 20, 24, 56–8, 62, 73n43, 77, 83, 97, 124; stalled (not fully interiorised) literacy 22, 58, 59, 62, 65, 98; *see also* orality-literacy debate
London: British Library, O.R. 12961 (LBL: O.R.12961) 72n39, 88–98, 103n63, 103n72, 105n103
Long War 2, 12n1, 20, 21, 22, 68n3, 155
lords of lewdness 38
Lutherans (king of) 87, 103n59

Machan, Tim W. 59, 66
manuscript: correction 61–2; culture 3, 9, 58, 59; reception 2, 10, 59, 66–7; re-inscription 56, 59–62, 82; scholarship 3, 7, 56–7, 59, 113–14; variation 35–6, 56, 57, 58, 59–60, 69n11; *see also* performative model (discourse); typographic model
marches *see* Ottoman-Habsburg marches
marginalia 3, 7, 59, 61–2, 66, 80, 84, 97, 105n104, 110, 113, 121–4
meaning as use *see* reader-response (reception theory); *see also* theories of language
menakibname 64, 72n30, 73n47, 74n48, 77, 79, 89, 92, 97, 98, 98n2, 104nn78–9, 104n81, 108, 137; *Menakib-i Başir Çelebi Tabib* 104n81; *Menakib-i Mahmud Paşa-i Veli* 71n26; *Menakib-i Şamsu'd-Din* 104n81; *menakibname* warrior saints *see* warrior saints; *Risale fi Menakib al-Şeyh Mehmed Ak Şamsu'd-Din* 104n81
militärgrenze 1, 145n64, 154; *see also* Ottoman-Habsburg marches

miracles 64, 90, 92
montage 149
Moses 109
Muslim-Christian *see* Christian-Muslim
Mustafa Ali 22, 134, 142n31

Nagykanizsa (Kanije) castle: Habsburg capture (1690) 1; *Kanije Kalesi* (film) 145–6n73; mentioned in ambassadorial correspondence 12n1; Ottoman capture (1600) 1, 8–9, 20, 23–4, 36–46, 47n4, 50n18, 50n23; Ottoman defence (1601) 1, 8–9, 20, 23, 26, 27–9, 32n24, 55, 56, 107, 109–10, 114, 118–20; Ottoman tricks and stratagems used in 1601 defence 9, 28, 63–5; partial reconstruction 1; *see also* Budapest Magyar Tudományos Akademia Konyvtara, O.216 (BMTAK); Cambridge: University Library, O.R.700 (CUL: O.R.700); *fethnames*; *Gazavat-i Tiryaki Hasan Paşa* corpus; London: British Library, O.R. 12961 (LBL: O.R.12961); Ottoman historians; *telhis*
Naima 10–11, 7n29, 20, 21, 26, 32n24, 38, 53n45, 99n6, 105n104, 107, 117–24, 127n43, 127n55, 128n61–2, 128n66–7, 134, 142nn33–4, 159n49
Namık Kemal 38, 130–3, 137, 140n10, 141n11, 141n25; *Kanije* 32n24, 130, 131, 132, 133–4, 136, 140n6, 142n28, 142n30, 142nn33–4
naming *see* interpretative naming
narrative: episodic 9, 68n7, 96; function 3, 12; incoherency 9, 56, 62, 64, 73n43, 97; linear 62, 64, 65, 110, 121, 149; repetition 9, 10, 65–6, 68n7, 96, 105n102; stability 56, 59, 60, 61, 62, 124n5; transmission 2, 13n7, 57–8, 88
nationalism: constructionist theories of 129–30, 154; essentialist theories of 129; historical forgetfulness 138–9; Ottoman 130–2; Turkish 134–6
nation-state cartographies 11, 129–31, 134–5, 137–9, 154; *see also* Turkey
Nieuwpoort (Nieuport) 44, 45
Nüşirevan (king) 81–2, 87–8, 89

obedience to authority 64, 80–2, 89, 100n21, 121
ocularity 10, 74n56, 113, 126n30; vocality-ocularity continuum 65–7, 97

oral: composition 58; narrative 69n10; narrator 84; performance 57, 58, 66, 69n10, 70n13; reception 65; sources 84; story-telling frame 84–5, 96; transmission 57, 84; *see also* vocality
oral characteristics 56–8, 66, 68nn6–7, 69n10–11; *see also* digressions; episodic narrative; narrative incoherency
orality 9, 70n13; orality-literacy debate 13n7, 70n12; residual orality 22, 56, 62, 65, 66
orthography 9, 24, 36, 57, 58, 59, 60, 61, 62, 68n7
Ottoman-Habsburg marches 2, 22, 23, 27, 97, 139, 145n64, 154–5
Ottoman historians 3, 8, 133; *see also* Hasan Beyzade; Ibrahim Peçevi; Katib Çelebi; Mustafa Ali; Naima; Selaniki; Topçularkatibi

pagination 103n63, 113
Pápa 40, 45–6, 52n34, 52n35, 53n39
performative model (discourse) 10, 13n7, 56, 59–62, 67, 71n26, 72n28, 82, 97; *see also* discourse of authority; typographic model
Persian language 24, 25, 36, 61, 69n10, 112, 119, 141n18
Persians 21
Piers Plowman 73n40
Piterberg, Gabriel 2, 3, 13n7, 19, 31n21, 69n10, 70n13, 120, 124n2, 149
plagiarism *see* intertextuality
plural pasts 3, 148
polysemic 82
polytheism 94, 97, 104n91
polyvocal 149
polyvocality 25, 149
pope 40, 89, 95, 97
postmodernism 147–8, 149, 155
power 63, 64, 73n46, 85–6, 91, 131
prophetic visions 92, 99n11, 104n78, 118, 134
Protestant 37, 39

Qur'an 66, 71n25, 74n58, 78, 79, 80–1, 84, 85, 89, 99–100n12, 109, 137

reader-response (reception theory) 8, 16n23, 59; *see also* theories of language
reading: ethical *see* ethical reading; heterodox readings 84–98; linear 110, 113; meditative 73n41;

orthodox readings 79–80; plural readings 77, 82, 118–19; reading strategies 9, 64, 73n40, 97, 110, 147
re'aya and beraya 37, 38, 51n31
reception of texts 2–3, 8, 10, 11, 36, 50n20, 56, 65–7, 74n52, 74n56, 76, 79, 96, 97, 101n35, 107, 112, 123, 133
remembering otherwise 151
robes of honour 86, 91, 102nn48–50
Rorty, Richard 5, 15n15, 30n1, 115
rubrication 10, 25, 56–7, 59, 66, 76–7, 83, 98n2, 99n3, 108, 111, 118; Persian rubrics 25

Savaşkurt, A. 134, 135, 136
scribe 60, 66–7, 77; authorial scribes 7; scribal error 9, 59, 60, 97; scribal illiteracy 10, 57; scribal reinscription 97, 100n29, 107
scripta 10, 60–2, 66–7, 72n28, 72n39, 76–98
scriptum see scripta
Selaniki 35, 47n3, 68n5
semiotic system 79
short vowels 61; short-vowelling 66, 74n53, 74n59, 81–2, 100n24
Smith, John (Captain) 12n1, 53n40
Szekesfehérvár (Istolni Belgrad/ Stuhlweissenburg) castle 21, 24, 25, 27–8, 29, 53n40
Szigetvár castle 27, 28, 29, 87, 93

Tannen, Deborah 58
tarih (history) 31n8, 76–7, 98n2
Tarih-i Al-i Osman genre 20, 117
teleology 129, 149, 153
telhis (report) 1, 23, 27–30, 32n46, 43
textual framing see framing
textualities 2, 6, 59; Arabic 13n7
theories of knowledge see epistemology
theories of language (meaning) 6–8, 16n23; correspondence (theory of meaning) 7, 14–15n13, 15n15, 115
Thury, György 1

Tiryaki Hasan Pasha 26, 28, 29, 63–5, 66, 67, 77–83, 85–9, 95–6, 101n32, 102nn49–51, 102n53, 103n71, 105n96, 105n102, 109–11, 118–21, 124n3, 132, 135, 136, 137, 138, 141n23, 142n28, 142n30; communing with god 91–3; contested hero 89–93, 108–9; heterodox warrior-saint 85–6, 89–90; ideal Ottoman commander 77, 82–4, 100–1n29, 108, 110; marriage to sultan's daughter 23; opium addict 83, 90, 103n66, 103n68; outside of the military-administrative hierarchy 85–6, 90–1; physical infirmities 90, 103n70; see also Gazavat-i Tiryaki Hasan Paşa corpus
titles see rubrication
Topçularkatibi 8, 20, 21, 23, 24–5, 26, 32n30, 42, 107, 111, 113, 114, 120, 122, 124n3, 127n55, 144n61
Turkey 134–7, 139
Turkish war of Independence 139, 145n71, 145n73
typographic model 9, 10, 17n30, 56–8, 59, 76, 82, 97
tyranny 38, 39, 79, 80–2, 87, 137, 100n21

vernacular 59, 141n18
vocality 10, 65, 74n52, 74n56, 84–5; performance in vocality 65–7, 74n52, 84–5, 96; vocality-ocularity continuum 10, 56, 65–7, 96–7; see also ocularity; oral performance

warrior 35, 108, 136; warrior-saint 64, 77, 89, 92, 104n78, 108, 137; see also gazi
weathermonger 92–3, 109

Yemişçi Hasan Pasha (grand vizier) 27–9

Zirinoğlu 52n36, 86–7, 95, 102n53, 105n96; György Zrínyi 102n57
Zrínyi, Miklós 87